The Crocodile Prize
2012 Anthology

The Crocodile Prize Anthology 2012

Copyright © 2012 Pacifica Sene
ISBN: 978-0-9871321-1-6

Cover design by Joe Bilbu

Sir Vincent Serei Eri (1936-1993)

The Crocodile, by Vincent Eri, was the first novel to be written by a Papua New Guinean, and was published by Jacaranda Press in 1970.

Vincent Eri was born in Moveave in Gulf Province and later became Director of Education, Papua New Guinea's first Consul General in Australia, a Member of Parliament and Governor General.

His novel is set in Papua New Guinea before and during World War II and is a coming of age story about Hoiri, whose life poses a continuing contradiction between traditional life and the modern world.

OUR SPONSORS

The Crocodile Prize is an initiative of *PNG Attitude* & the PNG *Post-Courier*

The national literary contest for Papua New Guinean writers could not continue to grow and expand were it not for the sponsors and donors who have shown such great commitment to this important cultural activity.

MAJOR SPONSORS

AustAsia Pacific Health Services Writers Forums
British American Tobacco (PNG) Prize for Lifetime Contribution to Literature (Sir Paulias Matane Award)
Cleland Family Prize for Heritage Literature
Ex PNG Chalkies' Yokomo Prize for Student Writing
Ok Tedi Mining Prize for Women's Literature (Dame Carol Kidu Award)
PNG Chamber of Mines and Petroleum Prize for Essays & Journalism (Sean Dorney Award)
PNG Society of Writers, Editors and Publishers Prize for Poetry (John Kasaipwalova Award)
Steamships Prize for Short Stories (Russell Soaba Award)

SPONSORS & DONORS

Australian High Commission
Bob & Julie Ellis
Corney K Alone & Tanya Zeriga-Alone
David Wall
Don Hook
Dr Lance Hill
Ed Brumby
Eric Johns
Firewall Logistics

Philip Fitzpatrick
Frank Hiob
Graham King
Henry Bodman
John Groenewegen
Keith Jackson AM
Michael Ahrens
MRSM Group of Companies
Murray & Joan Bladwell
Norma McCall
Paige West
Paul A Povey
Paul Dennett
Paul Oates
Sean Dorney AM MBE
South Pacific Strategic Solutions
Star Mountains Institute of Technology
Stuart Hoare
Sue and Kev Ellison
Taipei Economic and Cultural Office, Brisbane

CONTENTS

Foreword	1
The Winners	4
Short Stories	8
Adults *Jimmy Apiu*	9
Binge with Mary Jane *Jimmy Apiu*	14
False Tears *Dominica Are*	17
The Finger *Dominica Are*	20
He Broke the Egg *Kela Kapkora Sil Bolkin*	25
Now I Can Die *Kela Kapkora Sil Bolkin*	29
Fire Truck *Biango Buia*	34
Angel *Regina Dorum*	39
Oh, It's the Songs They Sing *Jeffrey Mane Febi*	48
Love When Bought *Eric Gabriel*	51
The K50 House *Ian Dabasori Hetri*	54
Diary of Phoenix *Peter Jokise*	58
Nightmare *Ruth Kamasungua*	62
An Adventure with Potholes *Hogande Kiafuli*	66
Missed by the Wielding Axes *Peter Maime*	69
Father of the Man *Grace Maribu*	73
Third from the Fourth Marriage *Dilu D Okuk*	78
Burnt *Gelab Piak*	82
Dancing in a Redskin's Arawa *Leonard Fong Roka*	85
Dominoes of Love *Peter Severa*	88
The Bamboo Master *Bernard Sinai*	94
The Dilemma *Bernard Sinai*	96
The Fan *C. V. Vada*	99
Norah Jones *Nou Vada*	105
Happily Ever After *Alma Warokra*	109

#Second *Alma Warokra*	113
The Knocks *Brigette Wase*	115
The Mountain *Brigette Wase*	119
God's Blessing in Every Step of the Way *Elizabeth Wawaga*	123
My Name is Sandy *Imelda Yabara*	127
Poetry	**130**
Circle of Tears *Agnes Are*	131
Sonnet 3: I met a pig farmer the other day *Michael Dom*	132
Beauty is in da water *Michael Dom*	133
Ples we mitupela I bin stap wantaim *Michael Dom*	134
So near, so far – a sonnet to transience *Michael Dom*	135
As I bask in her afterglow *Michael Dom*	136
A candlelight mark in Port Moresby Michael Dom	137
Johnny got wan nu muruk insait his banis *Michael Dom*	138
This is My Place *Michael Dom*	139
Haiku written about night time at a village along the Papua coast *Michael Dom*	142
Today another good man passed *Michael Dom*	144
Hearing rain approach while reading in bed at night: Morobe Province *Michael Dom*	147
i got sex on my mind – in the club! *Michael Dom*	147
State of the Public Service *Michael Dom*	149
Sonnet 3: Parallel Lanes to Nowhere *Michael Dom*	150
Lucky Little Lizard *Michael Dom*	150
A pendulum plays a well-known rhythm *Michael Dom*	151
Return to Mambon Nil *Michael Dom*	152
Mama *Jimmy Drekore*	155
Seasonal Seducers *Jimmy Drekore*	156
A Poet's Quest *Jeffrey Mane Febi*	157
Dreams of a Place *Jeffrey Mane Febi*	158
The Bougainville Crisis *Sophie Garana*	160
Legal Joke *David Gonol*	162
A Dog's Philosophy *Anthony Kippel*	163
I am sorry it has been so frustrating *Mary Koisen*	164
This Part of the World *Anita M Konga*	165
Mama's Bilum *Erick Kowa*	167
Trials of the Yellow Man *Erick Kowa*	168
The Great Speech – A Bush Poet's Commentary *Erick Kowa*	171
She's a Mother – That's How! *Lapieh Landu*	174
For You I Will … *Lapieh Landu*	175
Misconception *Lapieh Landu*	176

What Happened Back Then! *Lapieh Landu*	178
Struggling between two cultures *Patricia Martin*	179
Road to Seclusion *Hinuvi Onafimo*	181
Nervous Poet *Hinuvi Onafimo*	182
A Poet's Chant *Hinuvi Onafimo*	182
Old Sibuta *Hinuvi Onafimo*	183
A Journey to My Womb *Hinuvi Onafimo*	184
Paddle Me Back *Gelab Piak*	185
Christianity *Leonard Fong Roka*	186
Dance to the Beautiful Sea *Leonard Fong Roka*	187
The Magic of Kunu'nava *Leonard Fong Roka*	188
A Journey Far Away *Marie-Rose Sau*	193
Timeless Attitudes *Peter Severa*	195
Trupla Man *Bernard Sinai*	196
Twenty Two Women *Loujaya Toni*	197
Once Upon a Prime Time *Loujaya Toni*	198
She Lied *Loujaya Toni*	199
To Whom it May Concern *Loujaya Toni*	201
The Making of Me *Emma Wakpi*	202
In Bed With Me #2 *Imelda Yabara*	205
Way out of reach *Imelda Yabara*	206
Essays	**208**
Untighten Your Fist *Lorraine Basse*	209
Is Sex Education Compatible in Primary Schools in PNG? *Werner Cohill*	213
Robust Force or Rogue Cops: The Future of the Royal Papua New Guinea Constabulary *Werner Cohill*	218
Let's Not Mince Words About Buai Bisnis *Michael Dom*	222
What's Buai Got To Do With It? *Michael Dom*	225
Sir Koitaga Mano OBE and the House of Assembly *David Gonol*	229
Get the balance right between social and economic realities that underlie the development of professional sport in PNG *David Kitchnoge*	233
Are we ready 30 years on …? *Lapieh Landu*	237
Nakan in Madang Town *Stanley Mark*	240
Does PNG really have an attitude problem? *Martyn Namorong*	243
What is Development? *Martyn Namorong*	246
How to Break Free from the Vicious Cycle of dinau *Francis Nii*	250

Wake Up PNG! *Francis Nii*	254
My Atoll, My Home *Raroteone Tefuarani*	256
Delusion, Disillusionment and the Devil's advocate: A bedtime story for Papua New Guineans who believe in change *Nou Vada*	260
A Tribute to My Fathers *Emma Wakpi*	263
The Haunting *Emma Wakpi*	267
Heritage	**271**
Barasi – The Manam Way of Celebrating a New Year *Lorraine Basse*	272
Traditions of the Bena Bena People of the Eastern Highlands *Anthony Kippel*	275
The Story of Totoga Wai from Babaka Village *Beauty Rupa Loi*	284
The Migration of Wanigela People of Central Province to Tufi in Oro Province *Golova Mari*	287
Modernisation of Tribal War: A Threat to Civilisation *Francis Nii*	289
Migration and Mythology: The Way from Shortland to Kieta *Leonard Fong Roka*	292
The Complex Rituals of Death in Kieta Society *Leonard Fong Roka*	297
The Last of the Segera Tutubes *Miriam Roko*	301
How Yari Siwi Got Their Body Decoration *Henry Sape*	304
Malah's Initiation to Womanhood *Hilda Fromai Yerive*	307
Students	**310**
Pink and Round *Brenda Anduwan*	311
Man's Best Friend *Macquin Anduwan*	312
Sporty: A Dog's Life *Clara Philomena Are*	313
Great Man's Tale *Jovie Hriehwazi*	316
Where Have All The Children Gone? *Hannah Ilave*	318
Wonderful Sphere *Vanessa Kavanamur*	319
Going Through the Unimaginable *Angeline Low*	320
Sweet Sophie *Angeline Low*	327
First Day at a New School *Sharina Paliou*	328
Baia Village Kayla Reimann	330
Peace on Earth *Kayla Reimann*	333
The Fight *Joshua Rere*	335
What Have We Come To? *Axel Rice*	337
We are Children of God *Pusateryanna Tandak*	338
In the Memory *Jeremiah Toni*	339
The Contributors	**340**

The Crocodile Prize Anthology 2012

FOREWORD

2012 will be remembered as a tumultuous year in Papua New Guinea. It was a year of political upheaval and uncertainty where the very fabric of parliament, the courts and even the constitution were tested. This was followed by a frustrating election dogged by disorganisation, faulty electoral rolls, corruption and vote buying.

Many Papua New Guineans were hoping that at election end a new batch of younger, better educated and ethically sound politicians would emerge to haul Papua New Guinea out of the political, social and economic morass in which it seemed to be mired.

The year since the last anthology was published was also a time characterised by tragic events, both in the airline and shipping industries. There was unrest in several towns with riots and demonstrations related to migration and the relentless pressures of development. There were also individual and horrific tragedies like the beheading of a woman in broad daylight at Koki Market.

If you read this anthology you will see how many of these events have coloured the stories, poems and articles written in 2012. What also differentiated many of these events was the growing impact and immediacy of social media. In many cases news was broadcast on Twitter, Facebook and a plethora of blogs well before it appeared in the traditional media.

Not only that but it was raw news without the spin added by vested interests. 2012 may well be remembered as the year when social media came into its own in Papua New Guinea. In so doing it has cast a whole new light over politics and life in general. Where it is going is anyone's guess.

The Crocodile Prize, now in its second year, has been a beneficiary of this digital revolution. This is demonstrated both in the fourfold leap in the number of entrants and entries and also in the subject matter. The competition now seems to be inexplicably linked to digital media in Papua New Guinea.

Keith Jackson and Friends' *PNG Attitude* blog is a co-founder of the Crocodile Prize and a significant number of stories and articles published on the blog during 2012 were derived from the contest.

Many new writers, seeing their work published for the first time, were motivated to continue submitting material to the blog to the extent where Keith could happily claim that well over 50% of its content originated in Papua New Guinea - truly reflecting *PNG Attitude's* aim of being a forum for the exchange of ideas between Australians and Papua New Guineans.

One of the other spin-offs of the combined success of the competition and the blog has been the exponential growth of readership to include not only the general public but also relevant movers and shakers in both countries.

Many of the entries published on the blog and appearing in this anthology have been read and sometimes commented upon by politicians and people of influence in Papua New Guinea, Australia and beyond.

There are three important matters worth mentioning which make *PNG Attitude* and the Crocodile Prize significant.

The first is the willingness of the writers to attach their own names to their work; a small thing you might imagine but in a place like Papua New Guinea, where vendettas can be a way of life, it is something that is particularly brave.

Too often a wise and erudite observation on a blog or in a Papua New Guinea newspaper loses its impact because writers are too wary to identify themselves. It is well known that the power of conviction fizzles quickly to nothing without the courage of identified authorship.

The second matter has been the willingness of writers to think outside the square. Sometimes this has become provocative. I won't mention names but when you read this collection you will see what I mean. This is refreshing and challenging writing, which provides great food for thought.

The third matter worth mentioning is the quality of the work submitted. There has been a marked improvement from 2011. Not only have the writers from that year improved their skills but we can witness a new crop of talented writers. This augurs well for literature in Papua New Guinea.

When you read the stories, essays and poems in this anthology you will also notice a distinctive Papua New Guinean flavour coming through, much more so than last year, and most significantly in the poetry. The poetry contest attracted the most number of entries by far.

You will also notice the balance between male and female writers; in

2012 it is running around the 50/50 mark. This must surely be an indication of the importance and potential of the female voice in Papua New Guinea. Perhaps one day it will be reflected in national politics.

We hope you enjoy this year's writing and are looking forward, as much as we are, to what 2013 might bring.

For those entrants who didn't win a prize or haven't appeared in the anthology don't despair. There was an abundance of brilliant material that we just couldn't fit into the space available.

Keep writing. One day your name will be here.

Philip Fitzpatrick
September 2012

THE WINNERS

This year there were nearly six hundred entries in the competition, all vying for ten prizes on offer. Among those entries there were a considerable number of accomplished and well written pieces. This made the judges' task most difficult but they put their minds to it and came up with the following prize winners.

The winner of the **Steamships** Prize for Short Stories (Russell Soaba Award) was C. V. (**Charlotte**) **Vada for** her story *The Fan*. Commenting on this story one of the judges said "It's assured, with a strong narrative arc, a good build-up of tension, well resolved and surprisingly so, with the return to the fan. Very neat indeed. I also liked the balance of points of view between the two boys, and I found both of them very believable. Good dialogue, I liked her confidence in using *tok pisin* without feeling the need to translate. Her prose style is confident, economical and relaxed. A very accomplished piece of work by a writer in control of her craft."

The winner of the **PNG Society of Writers, Editors and Publishers** Prize for Poetry (John Kasaipwalova Award) was **Michael Dom** for his poem *Sonnet 3: I met a pig farmer the other day*. This poem has a number of outstanding aspects. Firstly, it successfully conveys both the traditional and contemporary in Papua New Guinea. Secondly it is technically accomplished; the sonnet is an old but not easily mastered poetic form but Michael has not only achieved mastery but has given it a distinctly Papua New Guinean flavour. Lastly, the poem comes from a body of submitted work which is singularly outstanding, particularly for its mix of innovative, quirky and traditional styles.

The winner of the **PNG Chamber of Mines and Petroleum** Prize for Essays & Journalism (Sean Dorney Award) was **Emma Wakpi** for her essay *The Haunting*. Emma has demonstrated an easy-to-read but incisive style in this essay and in her other entries in the competition as well as a positive and encouraging outlook, something that Papua New Guinea really needs at the moment. Her work stands in stark contrast to those entries which dwell so much on the negative aspects of Papua New Guinea society or are written in a deliberately provocative manner. Provocation, as distinct from sensationalism, has a place in journalism but it does not work so well when it overwhelms its subject matter. Emma's essay is also refreshingly free of any pseudo-academic obfuscation.

The winner of the **Cleland Family** Prize for Heritage Literature was **Lorraine Basse** for her story *Barasi - The Manam Way*. The judges had a difficult time with this category because so many entries were an ad hoc mix of heritage, history and modern themes. In contrast, Lorraine's entry is a very well researched and readable account of an age-old tradition which has survived the perilous journey into modern times largely intact. As opposed to many of the other entries it resonates with factual authority, not least because of its rendering of traditional song. The piece also highlights the place of women in tradition, something that is often overlooked in favour of men.

The winner of the **Ex PNG Chalkies'** Yokomo Prize for Student Writing was **Angeline Low** for her short story *Going Through the Unimaginable*. The story is outstanding for several reasons. Firstly, the subject matter is extremely sensitive and one which would test the talents of someone much older than Angeline's sixteen years. It also has a ring of authenticity which is helped tremendously by Angeline's confident control of dialogue and narrative as the tension builds up to its shocking culmination. Lastly it is a bold attempt to expose an element of society that is often shamefully hidden. One of the judges said the story, "is a reflection of the social conscience, not only of what happens in PNG but all around the world".

One of the major sponsors and a judge of the Yokomo Prize made the following observation, "Given the breast beating about the decline of educational standards, the quality of the English language expression was rather good, better than I'd expected ... and comforting."

With this in mind and a desire to encourage young writers in Papua New Guinea a last-minute decision was made to extend the award to three other runners-up in the student category. The three winners in the

AustAsia Pacific Health Services Encouragement Awards for Student Writers are **Axel Rice, Jeremiah Toni and Kayla Reimann.** Axel impressed the judges with his choice of 'adventure' genre and journalistic flavour, Jeremiah with his surprising poetic imagery and Kayla for her maturity and breadth of subject matter.

As readers will note, this year's winners are dominated by women writers. This made the choice in the **Ok Tedi Mining Prize for Women's Literature (Dame Carol Kidu Award)** extra difficult but the judges agreed that the winner should be **Imelda Yabara** for her short story, *My Name is Sandy* and her poems *In Bed with Me* and *Way Out of Reach*. In making this judgement particular attention was made to the relevance of the subject matter to women and, of course, excellence in writing. Imelda impressed the judges in 2011 and they were further impressed by how her work maintained a consistently high standard into 2012.

The final award in the competition and the easiest to judge was the **British American Tobacco (PNG) Prize for Lifetime Contribution to Literature (Sir Paulias Matane Award).** The judges had no hesitation in agreeing that the award should go to **Russell Soaba.**

Russell was there at the beginning with Vincent Eri and all those other founders and he is still advancing the cause of Papua New Guinea literature. Along the way he has produced an impressive list of publications, including the novels *Wanpis* (1977) and *Maiba* (1985), the poetry collections *Naked Thoughts: Poems and Illustrations* (1978), *Ondobondo Poster Poems* (1979) and *Kwamra, A Season of Harvest: Poems* (2000). His newspaper column *Soaba's Storyboard* has given many new Papua New Guinean writers their first taste of published success. His courses at UPNG are legendary and people line up to get into them.

Steven Winduo, himself a great writer, says of Russell, "He is the portrait of the odd man out, an individual, and a great thinker. Russell Soaba is also one of the greatest, if not the greatest, writer in Papua New Guinea. His works, particularly novels *Maiba* and *Wanpis*, are studied in universities around the world by students of literature and philosophy. Followers of the existentialism philosophy around the world dote on the writings of Russell Soaba.

Russell was born in Tototo, Milne Bay in 1950. He was educated in

Papua New Guinea, Australia and at Brown University, Providence, Rhode Island. He currently teaches at the University of Papua New Guinea and works as an editor for a local publisher. He has been a strong supporter of the *Crocodile Prize* since its inception.

SHORT STORIES

Adults
Jimmy Apiu

The south easterly wind left Markham's vast savannah expanse in its wake as it sped a few kilometres and detoured west, sweeping over the roof of a lone night club before heading north.

Under the roof, Et-Kalsa, a contemporary music band was finishing final touches to its rehearsals for the upcoming music festival at Eriku. Standing at the far end of the bar where the light was dim, John, after 15 beers was comatose. His speech was slurred and his eyes saw two of everything.

He was escorted first to the gents to throw up and later dragged outside and bundled into an old Toyota dump truck and left there to recuperate. The band kept fine tuning.

Monpi, with her belly protruding her third was clad in a silk night gown, stitching a meri blouse, looking at her watch every four minutes. The ash tray beside her was slowly filling with cigarette butts and the room was thick with its stench. She decided to call him, again, and punched in the 8 digits but the lady in the mobile phone told her the number she called was switched off.

She cursed the lady under her breath and absent-mindedly took the last of the 25 Winfield filtered cigarettes and lit it, inhaling till her lungs were full before exhaling, crumpling the empty cigarette packet before throwing it at her husband's picture frame. She puffed some more and smothered the cigarette in the ash tray and took out the 'Jeffrey Archer' paper back from her vast collection of the same author near the bedside drawer and continued reading where she had left off.

She completed a chapter and was up to four pages and decided to call it a night, when she heard the knock on the door.

She looked at her Seiko wrist watch. The long hand was sniffing 3 am. Gathering herself she walked to the door and slowly opened it and stared at John, who met her gaze and bowed his head, looking very sorry.

She pointed her finger at him after letting him in, while the other arm caressed her belly as she paced the floor in the small lounge room and glared at John, who reeked of sweat, vomit and alcohol, with both hands in his trousers pocket.

He tried to string a few words together for his lateness but nothing came out, as he swayed unsteadily. The atmosphere was tense.

"Who were you with!?" she demanded, her voice was amplified and full of hatred as it cut the silent night.

"Oh for Christ shakes Monpi, not again." he moaned. "Just because I am late you assume I was out with someone!? Oh Paleez!" he continued, his voice incoherent.

"Who were you with John Yobukwa'u!?" she repeated, this time louder as she advanced toward him with a clenched fist.

It meant one of two things; either he would get a hiding or a barrage of the filthiest foul language you could ever imagine was about to be launched. Addressing him by his full name was even worse. It meant two lonely months on the bare mat in the lounge room.

John cowered till his back was against the wall and he shut his eyes in despair and slowly bent his knees, lowering his small frame to the floor. He stole a glance at Monpi's menacing, advancing figure and covered his head with his palms.

A few neighbours flicked their lights on while others silently opened their windows to eavesdrop.

Her anger was something between a mad dog and a child throwing a tantrum because she was not satisfied, except this was an adult with considerable height and 105 kilograms of fat, muscle, and bones she had inherited from her ancestors in the Western Highlands.

John chewed his tongue as if to extort some plan of exit from his head but to no avail as the volley of disgusting and tainted language continued.

"You have not answered me!" she shouted, looking down at him.

"No one, I told you." He pleaded and sunk lower.

"Don't give me that crap, John Yobukwa'u, I married you and practically pampered you long enough to know a lie when I hear one, you useless drunk, how dare you lie to me?!" She screamed.

"But that's the Gospel truth, paleez" he moaned, still trying to look innocent.

"John Yobukwa'u! I have yet to see you drag your hopeless, pathetic carcass to a church, any church, and don't give me that gospel truth nonsense, you idiot!" she screamed.

"It's the truth; it's the truth!" he pleaded.

"Then who was that bitch riding shotgun!?"

"Who?!" he was buying time, thinking.

"That thing riding with you!"

A long pause.

"Well!?" she demanded.

"That thing was Amanda, our new company secretary. I took her out in the company car, in the company hour to buy company stationary because the company driver decided to go down with malaria at the companies' expense, and I thought you were supposed to be at home tending your stomach!" He emphasized 'company' to rid her suspicion but regretted the minute he mentioned her stomach.

Her face was now centimetres from his and he could smell her garlic and cigarette odour and spittle when she screamed his name and pointed at her stomach.

"Tell me who did this, go on tell me?!" She snarled and back handed a slap to his left ear, flooring him.

Funny, the detailed part did not creep in.

"Marrying a Trobriand Islander seemed like a good idea six years ago and I am already regretting it and doubting this marriage, you bastard!" she yelled and took a step back.

Loading all her anger and frustrations to her trunk-like right leg, she gritted her teeth and moved in, planting a mule kick between his legs.

John's whole body lifted a good four centimetres from the floor and landed.

He lay still, then convulsed and recoiled like a trapped animal holding his crotch, sucking air as tears gushed from his eyes. The pain was excruciating and he struggled to breath.

He twisted and turned and twisted again before moaning, uttering incoherent sounds first in Motu, then in his mother's Kitava dialect, crossing over to English and Pidgin, back to Motu and finally Kitava.

Sensing Monpi was about to kick again, he gritted his teeth and shut his eyes and feigned unconsciousness.

Monpi admired her handy work and put her hands on her hips breathing heavily, monitoring him and contemplating what other pain she could mete out.

A few minutes passed and he did not move.

Something is wrong, she thought as she studied his still figure.

"Oh my God!" she gasped, both her hands flying to her mouth.

"Oh my God!" she repeated and knelt beside him, shaking him and pinching him. There was no sign of movement. Even his breathing seemed to have stopped and she went into panic mode.

She did not plant her ear on his chest to hear the heart beat which was revving like a formula one engine.

"Someone help!" she screamed.

"Help, someone help!"

The children's door partly opened.

She got up and half ran, half walked to the main door and opened it and yelled outside, begging and pleading for help. She looked frantically at her watch, then back where she had left John and sped back knocking some furniture and cursing, after closing the door. She thought of waking the children up but decided not to. She did not see their door close.

She knelt beside John and took his hands in hers and craned her neck to see if anyone followed.

"I have a man dying here and need help," she screamed.

"What happened?" someone called in the dark.

"He got kicked!" she replied.

"Who kicked him?"

"Me!"

"Where?"

"Why do you ask?" she spat back.

"Because we want to help," They replied.

"Between his legs!"

Someone found it humorous and replied with a hoarse laugh.

"Why?"

"None of your business, bastard!" she screamed back.

"Then it's none of our business to help as well, bastard!" they replied.

"No, it's your business as well, don't you understand! Paleez!" she cried and held up her hands in despair.

"The door is locked!" the same voice.

"No it isn't, just turn the knob and pull it!" she cried.

The neighbours congregated at the doorway amazed to see an adult bunched up like a small child, with Monpi beside him with her face on his, crying and planting small kisses on it, apologizing and begging forgiveness, whispering sweet nothings until she reached his lips when all of a sudden his tongue snaked into her mouth and she flinched in horror and embarrassment and pulled away. She was so stunned she could not think what to do.

The neighbours had witnessed it and were dumbfounded.

John got up, very slowly, and adjusted his trousers and grinned at the neighbour and limped to the bed room; with Monpi looking totally humiliated and shell shocked.

At least I got one back, in front of the neighbours too, he thought as he locked the door and collapsed on the bed to complete his agony.

"Please die in bed!" Monpi screamed.

Somewhere in the dark the hoarse laugh began again, this time louder.

"Shut up!" she yelled in its direction.

The hoarse laugh increased in volume.

The neighbours looked at each other and snickered and bowed their heads and walked out as Monpi glared at them.

Two little pairs of eyes and ears had observed and heard enough.

"Adults!" They mumbled and shot off to bed.

Binge with Mary Jane
Jimmy Apiu

Young and Blissful
Oh so playful
Someone's brother
Son, dear lover
Only this once
Then I renounce
Fly the height
High as a kite
Serenade to Mary Jane
Marry me oh Mary Jane
Ride the sane with Mary Jane
Oh what madness
Into Darkness

Akin to his backdrop which looked dull and gloomy, the lone figure reminded me of Bingmalu, a clerk come beggar I met some months back in Lae.

His face was contorted, perhaps from the hardship the city dished out to him; no one could tell, as his feeble hand stretched forth its open palm over the pathway which the town populace used each day.

Someone found it irresistible to parody the placard behind him with 'Sick man, Seek mani'.

His faded 'T' Shirt, displaying Australian Rock Band, 'Cold Chisel', was placed neatly before him, as he bent his knees together, with the soles of his feet cushioning his bottom.

A few passers-by felt it their duty to donate so they tossed coins with occasional notes onto the 'T' shirt, while others were dispelled by his coughing and wheezing.

My observations were disturbed by the sound of voices, which pitched at every opportunity. I directed my gaze to its source and, lo and behold, five young girls, dressed in smart school attire were gesticulating in their own version of a 'Lady Gaga' number with vigour.

As they passed the beggar a petite one among them made remarks which were immediately punctuated by various exclamations of 'True?!', 'Oh my God!', 'Oh no!' and 'Oh please!'

I never considered myself a sensitive person, but after eavesdropping on their shocking expletives I scurried across the bitumen road to a snitchy little buai reseller from Tari, who was at the peak of his sales. I bought two and as I attacked the buai offered him one so as to notch up friendship. Spitting a load of crimson red, I threw in a shaggy dog story, immediately transforming his ill-humoured expression.

I felt I was accepted in his little environment and sat myself close by, engaging in friendly banter with him, he reminded me of an information kiosk.

The conversation led to Money, Politics, and Women until I touched on Drugs, then he nudged my side to follow his glance to the beggar.

"See Tumun over there?" he asked.

I nodded.

"That's your classic example of a smart kid gone insane" he said.

"How?" I asked.

"Marijuana." he answered casually, pulling his stool closer to me. "I didn't know marijuana could make one insane and look so bewildered."

"You mean?" I was perplexed.

"Yeah," he replied.

"We went to the same school together till I dropped out and he continued to year 12 and University, where he never let up and flunked semester 2." He paused to serve a customer.

"It never ceased to amaze me to see the glint in his eyes when he was up to something big and to say he was a small time pusher would be an understatement. He practically ruled the streets."

"What?" I was confused.

"At Uni he had a long queue of sorts and not a day went by without one of them asking for more. In other words the small doses they took did not affect their cravings and he increased the intake. He added tolerance to its effect, so to speak." He smiled sheepishly.

"Tumun was, if you may, a chronic heavy distributer, he practically merged them with Mary Jane. The young bloke had a string of girlfriends too, who could not cope with the hefty fees he charged and had to succumb to his demand." He paused as I offered him a cigarette and he lit it and drew in a lung full. I wondered if the petite one was one of his girlfriends.

"Who's Mary Jane?" I enquired.

He exhaled the used nicotine and discarded a mouth load of buai spittle smack on the pavement.

"Marijuana, weed, joint, nail, Mary Jane, the same thing" He replied.

This was getting interesting. I was surprised he could come up with all the street names.

"He had a canny way of spotting the cops too and was two steps behind - rather ahead." He corrected himself.

I shook my head.

"One morning, they found him covered in his own blood, concussed, his face beyond recognition. He had a stint in hospital on life support. No one knew who, how or why they did it, but the rumour is; he was hospitalised by one of his clients."

I kept shaking my head.

"Tumun does not know his own name these days and his speech is slurred. His movements are sluggish you'd think he was doped and nobody knows where he kept the thousands as well," he continued and let out a yawn.

I knew my time was up and said thanks and strolled across to Tumun.

I placed a K2 note on the 'T' shirt and in doing so had a good look at his face and was intrigued by his eyes.

The glint was definitely there.

False Tears
Dominica Are

The whole village was filled with sorrow when their chief suddenly passed away after a long illness. Men and women were forbidden to go out gardening or hunting for a whole day. The family had to gather enough food, children were told to keep quiet and not to play around. There were no arguments, fights or unnecessary noises as this was their custom whenever a chief dies. The whole village went into great silence as a sign of respect to their great chief and warrior, Chief Baulin.

Two weeks of mourning was resolutely observed and the body was finally buried. There was a big feast to end the 'hauskrai' with many pigs and cows slaughtered. Garden foods came in multitudes. When the feasting was over, the chief's immediate family thanked everyone for their cooperation at the time of mourning. Everyone went home satisfied with their portion of the food but sympathized at the passing of their chief.

'Oh, what a tiresome day,' said Lucy as she sulkily put down her bilum filled with food from the feast. Her eyes were swollen from crying, her hair was scrappy and her body needed a thorough washing and scrubbing. She made certain that the food was properly stored before going off to a nearby stream to take a shower. She was later joined by her two cousin sisters and they all began to talk about the late chief.

'He was a great leader indeed,' said Heli.

'He always brought about peace whenever there was a problem,' added Giba.

'That's true,' agreed Lucy. 'I wonder who's going to take his place.'

The three are married to three cousin brothers from the same clan and live close to each other. A week after the chief's burial, an uncle of Lucy's husband whom she was very close to died. He died in a faraway village which is an eight hours walk right through rough mountains and terrains.

'Mama, mama,' Beka cried running home one afternoon. 'Uncle Mau has died.'

'Who told you that?' asked Lucy angrily, thinking her nine year old daughter might be lying.

When Beka said that one of their relatives came and told her at the market, Lucy without holding her breath started crying. Later in the night, their relatives met in Lucy and Ken's house to plan for their trip the next day. Early the next morning, Lucy with some of the deceased's immediate family and relatives began the long, tiring trip. Everyone was soaked in mud all over their bodies. The men armed with bows and arrows went as well to claim compensation for the loss of Mau. This was a practice as when a man dies in the village of the wife the relatives will forcefully claim compensation despite what has actually caused the death.

After the long and hectic journey, they managed to arrive. Everyone joined in the mourning but the armed men kept their distance and shouted angrily at the deceased's in-laws. They threatened to burn their houses and destroy food gardens if no one came forward to ascertain why Mau had died and compensate them. Eventually, a village leader came forward and explained.

'Mau died of sickness,' he said. 'We tried different herbal medicines and witch doctors, but all was to no avail.'

'Then why couldn't you bring him to us?' asked a relative.

'It's because of the distance and rainy weather,' he replied.

A consensus was reached when everything was clearly explained. The in-laws gave K200 and 2 pigs as a form of conciliatory compensation. Reflecting back on the long distances they walked Lucy sighed painfully.

"It's so sad when someone so close dies," Lucy said later while doing her laundry with Heli and Bagi. The three were always seen together, either to gossip, share their problems or simply to be together as often as possible.

'That's true and the sorrow may last,' Heli added.

'I hope there won't be any more deaths soon,' added Bagi, who hated being in the state of mourning.

'Who knows,' Lucy absentmindedly replied.

To their surprise just after three days had passed since Uncle Mau's' death, one of their tribesman died in the city.

'I don't really know him,' argued Lucy 'how can I go to the mourning place?'

'You just have to go,' said Ken calmly.

Never known or seen him. But as this was a custom she still had to go. Only three days after mourning and now this, thought Lucy unsympathetically. While the body was in the city, there was a 'hauskrai' at the village. Everyone was expected to go to the 'hauskrai.'

'I really don't feel like crying,' complained Bagi sarcastically.

'Me too,' said Heli.

'Don't ask me,' Lucy told them 'I think I don't have any more tears to shed.'

'If you cry, we'll cry, if not, we won't cry,' reiterated Bagi.

To be more respectful to their elder, Bagi and Heli often follow Lucy in what she does and say. Lucy just laughed and continued, 'I cry easily when someone I know dies but not strangers.'

While they were busy discussing their crying issue, they heard people wailing loudly down the road. Quickly they dashed out of the mourning place. The arrival was abrupt and they were just confused. They tried to shed tears but they wouldn't fall easily. They covered their faces pretending to cry in order not to be embarrassed and be scolded.

As they approach the mourning house, they put their heads down. Lucy realized how difficult it was to have tears forming in her eyes. She briskly got her saliva and rubbed it on her eyes when nobody was watching. She did that a couple of times surreptitiously and continued pretending to cry.

'Stop it,' whispered Lucy annoyingly when Bagi pinched her back to see if she really cried.

'What do you think you were doing?' asked Lucy when they were back at home after the 'hauskrai.'

'I was checking to see if you really cried,' replied Bagi, 'because we didn't cry.'

'You know what we did?' Heli jokingly said. 'When our tears didn't fall easily, we were frightened and ashamed so we secretly got our saliva and rubbed it on our eyes to make it look like tears.'

'What?' Lucy was stunned. 'I also did that. I hope you're not following me.'

'No, we didn't,' they screamed.

And they all burst out laughing not too loud as they didn't want to get attention. ... not at this time of sorrow.

The Finger
Dominica Are

Her heart pounded loudly against her chest like the bass of a stereo as she dashed down the hill towards Obil. There was no sign of them and it was slowly growing dark. With tears running down her cheeks, legs aching, sweat pouring profusely from her face and her heart doubled its beating pace she continued to run as fast as her two bony feet could carry her.

"Hurry up with your bamboo containers, it's getting late!" Alebia screamed at her children. Quickly but tiredly they stuffed their leftover pork meat into their string bilums, grabbed their *'male muguhs'* (bamboo container) and were off like the wind towards "*Noge-habe nule*' to fetch water.

When they were gone, Alebia and her husband, Sinegare, quickly packed their few belongings along with Dagi's. They left Korai's beside their hut and waited impatiently for Dagi to come home first, hoping that their plan might work out well.

Talking, laughing and imitating their mother's facial expression when she loses her temper, they at last reached the cool mountain spring. They were excited too that they would be leaving for Omkolai to settle there permanently with some relatives as a tribal fight was about to erupt in Urmil. Unfortunately, they hadn't noticed that Korai's bamboo container which was big had a hole at the bottom whilst Dagi's was small and alright. They were oblivious to their parents' wicked plan.

Dagi was the first to fill his container and thinking that his parents might be thirsty, he decided to go home first.

'Father and mother will be thirsty, so I'll go home,' said Dagi, as he carefully lifted his bamboo container off the ground.

'Sure,' replied his sister. 'Tell them my container is slowly filling so wait a few minutes for me.' But they never waited.

As soon as Dagi reached home, Sinegare quickly grabbed the bamboo container and told Dagi to carry his string bilum and follow them without saying anything as it was time and they must leave immediately.

'But…but what about Korai, she doesn't know where we are going,' he protested, surprised by the sudden rush and icy tone in his father's voice.

'She'll still come later and catch us!' he screamed 'now hurry up!.'

Scared and confused, he followed them reluctantly, turning around each time just wishing his sister would come quickly.

'What's taking this thing so long to be full,' thought Korai, suddenly feeling alone and frightened after waiting. Something must be wrong she thought aloud, suddenly it hit her. Her bamboo container was never full so it must be broken. And it was true there was a hole at the bottom which never existed before. Smelling danger, she threw her 'male muguhs' and was on her feet towards home. Upon arrival, she realized that her family were already gone. The house was empty and her string bilum was still sitting there. Panic stricken, she quickly grabbed it and ran after them, but they had already left Urmil by a different route unknown to her and had reached Obil, which is the next village when it was nearly dark.

Tum! Tum! Tum! Her heart began beating rapidly, her legs ached, sweat was all over her body but she continued running. When she reached Obil, there was no sign of them, they were already in Wigo.

Sinegare and Alebia were quite pleased that their plan had worked out. Dagi kept looking back every now and then, hoping by chance that his sister would eventually find them, but it was to no avail. His hopes finally faded when they arrived at Kuleka. This was the last village before they crossed the huge, fast-flowing, rough and ugly Maril-nule on the shaky vine bridge and they finally arrive at Omkolai. Dagi believed that his sister might be lost or either be killed by the so-called 'sangumas' which is quite common in Gumine, Chimbu Province.

Sandwiched between his parents, his cries and protests for his sister were ignored as they pulled and shoved him forward, frightening him with all the tales about 'sangumas'. Half walking, half running, they at last reached Maril-nule, but there was no time to rest. They briskly stepped onto the shaky bridge and tried to make their way across, holding firmly to the vines as the bridge swayed from side to side. Suddenly Dagi heard someone screaming on the mountain. Looking back and up to *humesah hul* or the "mountain of sangumas", he saw Korai running down towards the bridge.

'Mother! Father! Korai has come!' shrieked Dagi with joy and relief whilst his mother stared in disbelief. But Dagi's joy was for a short time.

As soon as they reached the other side safely, his father got his stone axe and very angrily began cutting the vine bridge. Meanwhile Korai was already in the middle of the bridge. Realizing the danger his sister was in, Dagi knew that there was nothing he could do to save his beloved sister. He was not her saviour this time.

The moon was very bright and illuminated the surroundings very clearly. The look of terror on Korais' face was her last memory, without thinking, he bluntly got his bamboo knife and chopped off his little finger.

'Korai catch this!' he screamed as he threw his finger over to his sister; luckily she caught it without knowing what it was because at that moment, snap! The vine bridge broke loose. With a thrill of fright, she frantically tried to jump to the other side but it was too late.

'No-o-o-o!' her voice was drowned by the rough waters splashing against the rocks as she mercilessly fell into the notorious Maril-nule.

'Shh,' Aibaku beckoned her loquacious husband to keep silent and come over as she walked towards a figure lying near the rocks. When they came closer, they realized that it was a young girl, her face was sallow with bruises all over her body.

'Who is she?' What happened to her?' whispered Dalabe.

But it was audible enough for Korai to hear. Raising her head slowly, she looked around and could see rocks, water, bushes and two strange elderly couple standing beside her. Shaking her head to regain full consciousness she looked across to Maril nule and couldn't believe that she had survived in this death-trap. Still clasped tightly in her hand was her brother's finger which she realized later.

'You look tired and hungry,' said Aibaku 'we'll get you home and you can tell us about yourself,' already forgetting about going to her garden.

After Korai had eaten and her bruises were treated she began to tell her story.

'My parents have always hated me since I was born because in my village, many sons born to a family tend to bring pride and fortune and not girls. I am actually the third born in the family, however, my two elder brothers died due to illness when they were babies. When my mother was pregnant again, everyone was expecting another boy, but it wasn't. She should have thrown me into the river, but my dear grandmother took me and looked after me, so they did not bother about me.'

Tears filled her eyes as she thought of her grandmother, the woman who had loved and cared for her, 'My little brother was a relief to them so they did not bother about me.'

'Anyway,' she continued, 'my grandmother died three years ago and so I had to go and live with my parents. Life was very hard living with them. I was forced to do all the dirty and hard work and they even tried to kill me many times, but my little brother was always there to save me.'

'It seems that your parents are so cruel,' Interrupted the old woman, who had been childless and had always wanted a child.

'They are', said Korai, 'one time, they set my grandmother's house on fire while I was fast asleep in it, but my brother saw smoke coming up, quickly ran in and woke me up. They later blamed me for not putting the fire out properly. I often go without food for days, but my brother always hid some food for me. My parents have always done cruel things to me. I'll miss Dagi, but his finger is his memory which I'll keep forever.'

'They must believe that I am dead already,' she finished off and sure enough Sinegare and Alebia were at last satisfied that they were rid of her. Dagi was very worried and knew that he would never see his sister again.

The next day Korai got a vine and hung her brother's finger as a necklace. The old couple were pleased to take care of her like their own daughter. Korai was so happy with them that she didn't want to go anywhere or see her parents again except she missed Dagi.

Years passed by so swiftly and Korai had grown into a beautiful young woman, a dream girl for any young man. One fine sunny afternoon while Korai and Aibaku were busy in the garden, Dalabe called to them to come home quickly as he had something important to say.

'A big sing sing in the village tonight! Sure I'd love to go!' exclaimed Korai, after Dalabe finished telling them that some young men and boys from Omkolai would come here to Bokolma to do the *'karim lek'* and *'tanim het'* with the young women and girls at the big singsing.

Adorned with the finest finery of Bird of paradise plumes and colourful feathers with kina shells hanging on her neck, her *'pur pur'* made of bright cuscus fur which shone in the night and pig's fat smeared all over her body she walked gracefully with the other young women to the sing sing. Dagi's finger which was now bones was still hanging around her neck.

At this time of the sing sing some 'karim lek' or 'tanim het' partners usually became engaged and eventually married.

Everyone was enjoying the night away. Drums beaten in multiple beats could be heard everywhere with traditional songs sung so loudly, heads and bodies were shaking vigorously to the rhythm of the beats and the huge fire even lighted everyone's night up.

The young man's eyes were glued on Korai throughout the night and finally he got the chance to dance with her. During the 'tanim het', the necklace on Korai's neck gave him a nagging suspicion whenever he turned his head towards her. After chatting with him for a while Korai agreed to go out with him for some fresh air. When they were far away from all the noises, the young man asked her out of curiosity about the necklace.

Bit by bit, Korai told him the whole story and that she was happy to be alive but still missed her brother so much.

Tears stung his eyes as he gently lifted his hand up. Only four fingers were standing while the last finger was on his sister's neck.

'You are Korai, aren't you?' he stammered, 'my long lost sister'.

Korai could not believe what she was hearing and seeing as she fell into her brother's arms and they hugged and cried.

It was a long and tiring journey but they all arrived safely at Omkolai. After hearing that their wicked parents had already died, Korai got the two now aged and kind hearted couple and they went to live with Dagi, where they settled there forever.

He Broke the Egg
Kela Kapkora Sil Bolkin

One moonlit night in April 1953 the sky was inundated with twinkling stars. Nineteen year old Apa, standing at the peak of Dua, saw the flicker of lights at Urgiai, Gor and the Bari II lands to the south and south east. The lights were an indication that people were staying indoors because of the stiff cold wind. Indeed, the rushing wind up the hill from the Ulma and Gapal Rivers made him too yearn for warmth.

'It is a perfect evening to crawl into a bed with a beautiful girl to generate some heat and squeeze out the aches in the muscles,' he thought.

He whistled a courtship song but it was whisked away by the wind. He looked at the hills ahead and saw a cane grass torch at Mebir. It was a sign that Molpa, his girlfriend was going to and fro to the pig's hut feeding them but Apa also knew that the torch was also a deliberate ploy to signal him to walk over to her home that very evening. The Ulma River separated him and the bearer of the cane grass torch that he saw on the other side of the hill.

Molpa was an innocent 17 year old Mor Baulo girl. They had been friends for a while.

He could see Molpa's beautiful body and her smiles in his mind's eye from where he stood. He wanted to sleep close to her heart and feel her maturity. Yes, he was willing to walk the distance to her home that night.

He strolled down the hill and crossed the Ulma River. He ascended the hill with speed and arrived at Molpa's home and hid in the dark shadow of the banana patch. Once in a while he had to wave off the fire flies that circled the banana patch.

From the rear of the hut he heard voices a few times and quickly worked out the occupants of the hut. Molpa and her parents were inside. The smaller siblings must have gone to their uncle's hut for the night.

That night he was convinced that he would take Molpa home as his wife for the first time and break the egg just like the other boys.

Molpa had retired to bed but was not asleep because she expected a soft whisper on the wall nearest her bed calling her name.

The week before Molpa and Apa had met at the Ulma River when she returned from her garden. They had sat on a huge boulder and Apa had told her that he would come this very night to take her home as his wife. Molpa who was determined to become Apa's esteemed wife for as long as she was alive and was keeping a vigil that evening to see if Apa would come and take her as promised.

'Close the door, cover the embers and sleep. I am already tired and am off to bed,' instructed Molpa's father, Yau and jumped onto his log bed.

His wife, Wari started to bury the embers with the ash and said, 'I am going to bed as well. I have to wake up early tomorrow to go weeding.'

In the cold night, Apa crept over to where Molpa slept and quietly scratched the wall.

Molpa whispered from inside her room, 'Apa.'

'I am outside,' said he.

'As soon as Wari goes to bed I will come out and let you in. Right now sit under the banana trees and wait. Make sure nobody sees you,' warned Molpa.

'I know.'

Apa sat under the banana trees for some 30 minutes. The damp soil and cold winds made him restless.

'Men, make her parents go to sleep quickly. I have to get in soon,' begged Apa. He prayed to the spirits to seduce Molpa's parents into a deep sleep.

Not long after his prayer, he heard the logs piled up at the door removed. He stood and looked in the direction of the door and saw Molpa emerging out of the dried banana leaves that served as the first layer of the door. Her maritas juice oiled breasts reflected the moon's light and Apa was captivated. As he moved closer he smelled the scent of the sweet forest orchid fruit that was hung around her neck.

He smiled and at once embraced her. Molpa fended him off with might.

'It is a full moon. People will see us so be quick and follow me,' she said.

They crawled into the hut together. Molpa shut the dry banana leaf door and then replaced the logs. They were careful not to wake her parents and crept into her room.

Soon they lay close to each other on her pandanus mat. Molpa rested her head on Apa's left hand as they slept and had their legs inter-locked. Apa's right hand rested comfortably on the left bulging breast of Molpa. The fingers at times stroked the left nipple and squeezed. Molpa enjoyed his hands on her. Apa wanted to slip his fingers into her fur skirt but Molpa rejected the move.

'Not tonight. Unless you take me home as your wife you will not go further down,' whispered Molpa and removed his right hand. Apa stopped and concentrated on the firm bulging left breast and gave her a few good kisses.

They could hear the wind blowing hard against the banana leaves from inside in their bed. On the opposite end of the hut they could hear Molpa's parents snoring away and Apa was sure the spirits had responded to his prayer. Apa and Molpa were happy in each other's arms and made pillow talk long into the night.

'We will leave for my home at second cockcrow,' concluded Apa.

Molpa pressed Apa's right hand in agreement.

A little sleep and all of a sudden they heard the first crow of the rooster. 'Get up and pack a few of your things,' ordered Apa.

'I already did it during the day. It's all ready.'

'What a good girl. We will crawl out and leave during the second crow of the rooster. We must arrive at Dua before the cicadas sing to welcome dawn,' added Apa.

Molpa hissed, 'I have to get into my best attire to go off for marriage. In that way I will lift your status among your people and mine too.'

She rose and slid into a new fur skirt that covered her front and loins. Then she took a possum testes necklace and hung it around her neck. Apa dozed and waited for her to finish. She then slid a band over each of her arms as far as the biceps. Finally she rubbed maritas juice on her firm body and combed her hair. Satisfied, she picked up her bilum and whispered, 'Let's go, I'm done.'

As they departed her parents were still snoring. Molpa walked a few metres and then looked back at her home. She knew that she had left her childhood behind. She was saddened and shed some tears. Apa comforted her and they never looked back again.

Apa's mother uncovered the embers and fanned the flames to roast kaukau for breakfast that morning. As cicadas sang to welcome the dawn Apa led an attractive girl into the hut. His mother reacted with disbelief.

Then she cried with joy and embraced Molpa's legs.

'Oh, it is not a good harvest season, why bring such a beautiful girl here. What have we to feed her', grieved Apa's mother.

In reality Apa's mother was proud of her son. He had brought home a nice-looking girl to be her daughter in law.

News spread of the arrival of the new bride and the women and men gathered at Dua for the grand shouting to make her a married woman.

Apa's father, Ole shouted with both his index fingers shutting his ears. After he ended his shouting his kinsmen joined in for a grand shouting. The women completed the excitement with screams at the end.

Ole faced the neighbouring villages on the eastern end of the Imil-Gapal Rivers and announced at the top of his voice that Yau's daughter had arrived as a bride to Dua.

Everyone from the neighbouring clans commented about her beauty.

'She made the right choice to marry Apa,' said some. 'She is still a young girl. She should have waited for two more years,' said others.

At dawn Yau and Wari, the parents of Molpa entered her room only to confirm their fears.

'She has left for marriage,' lamented Yau.

Wari sobbed, 'Truly she has left for Dua. It's Apa.'

The women at Dua came with bags of garden food to make a feast for Molpa. She mingled with Apa's mother and the rest of the village women. They cooked the food in an earth oven.

Apa sat with the other boys near the men's hut and kept his distance from the women. At times he looked over and saw Molpa going about with dignity preparing the food like the older women. He was pleased that this beautiful girl was now his wife. What's more, he was sure that she would not now stop him from digging into what was buried in the fur skirt tonight.

He couldn't wait for nightfall.

Now I Can Die
Kela Kapkora Sil Bolkin

The Dikne Guri Range, Gor Maia, Waure Tepe, Pil Dimna, Wikauma and the Omdara Hills fence in the Mon Maril valleys. These landscapes provided a safe haven for the Yuri tribe but more particularly for the Mama Gauma clansmen at Oldale Nilben Kowan.

The steep slopes, frequent cloud cover and low temperatures at higher altitudes sometimes made the valleys look like Antarctica. Villages were spotted in pockets and most of the land and its surrounding areas were unoccupied by humans.

Oldale Nilben Kowan was home to some 300 Mama Gauma clansmen and served as the hub of the Mon Maril valleys. The Mama Gauma sub-clan of the Kumai Kane clan had foraged between 1400 and 2000 metres in these hinterlands since time immemorial. They had no contact with the outside world. The annual rain fall there ranges between 2400 and 3700 mm, increasing from north to south.

It was around 6 pm on the evening of February 1926. White clouds snaked their way up the Maril River. Kamtai Milkn and Kap Dan, both on opposite ends of Oldale Nilben Kowan, were engulfed in white clouds and showers. Both places were hopelessly hidden from Oldale Nilben Kowan, let alone Al Ulma and Konba Sil Main. The scene was typical of the Yuri tribal lands.

Sil Olmi's family hut at Oldale Nilben Kowan was camouflaged as smoke oozed out of the thatched roof. Sil Olmi pushed two logs into the embers and fanned them to enliven the smoldering fire and warm himself. Crickets were chirping outside and the thud of rain bouncing off pandanus leaves drowned a courtship song that Sil Olmi sung with feeling in the hut.

He deliberately hummed the song to avoid hearing the groan of the labour pains uttered by his wife. Popne Ku struggled at the rear in the women's sleeping quarters with two mid-wives helping to deliver her fourth child using a cane grass torch in the darkened room.

His three daughters had gone south east to Molgime early in the morning. Dusk crept in but the girls had yet to return.

'Why have the girls not hurried back to cook for the pigs? They know that Popne Ku is with a burden,' complained Sil Olmi.

One of the mid-wives said, 'They must have run off with some men. If not, then I assume they feared the rain and took a shelter somewhere at Dini Pima Nul.'

'I am already frustrated…'

'Aah yaaaah,' shouted his wife.

'Take it easy. Stop this nonsense of shouting about. This is not your first time to deliver,' complained Sil Olmi.

'Popne Ku has delivered,' hissed one of the mid-wives with relief.

Sil Olmi jumped on impulse and looked into the rear sleeping quarters but the cane grass wall blocked his view. The smoke exuding from the burning logs also clouded his eyes.

He prayed, 'Good people, if you are all watching, make this child a boy.'

Then he shouted, 'Boy or girl?'

'It is a boy,' yelled a mid-wife.

'True…..? Thank you my ancestral spirits. You all must have seen my craving. If I were a dog I would be wagging my tail to prove my appreciation,' belched Sil Olmi.

Sil Olmi, who only had three daughters since marrying Popne Ku, was over the moon when he heard the news of the arrival of a baby boy in his family. His legs and arms itched to crawl to the rear and see the boy immediately. However, he knew it was a taboo for men to visit a delivery space. He waited with patience for the child to be brought to him and continued to sing a couple of courtship songs to pass the time.

His son was properly patched and cleansed by the mid-wives. After 30 minutes, which Sil Olmi considered a very long wait one of the mid-wives brought the child to him. She placed it in his arms and said, 'At last you have re-created yourself.'

Sil Olmi had a good look at the sex of the child to confirm what the mid-wives had said then took a good look at the nose of the infant in the faint light of the burning logs. He then held it close to his heart for a few good seconds. Sil Olmi felt his heart and the child's beating in unison and their blood running through each other. He felt like crying but held back his tears.

'Having a son that looks exactly like me from what I believe was my last seed is awesome. I will surely die a happy man,' he chanted.

'Absolutely!' replied the mid-wives.

'My son will inherit my land and carry my name in the days ahead,' said Sil Olmi.

'Surely the child is a replica of you. Your legacy will live on through him.' Sil Olmi smiled with content as the child sucked on his own lips.

'The child his searching for breast milk, come I'll give it back to his mother,' said one of the mid-wives.

Sil Olmi gave an exceptional smile to his ancestral spirits and walked in the rain to the Oldale Nilben Kowan men's hut to break the good news to his Mama Gauma clansmen.

'Popne Ku gave birth to a boy,' bragged Sil Olmi as he entered the hut.

His Mama Gauma clansmen in the men's hut all yelled, 'Ah paaaah… she has done well. Now you have a fringe or retirement child.'

'I've said it all these times that she will bear a son and she did,' said Galmai Bia.

'You said it many times,' confirmed the old men.

'To have a son you must sleep with your wife when the full face of the moon is up at Mount Wikauma. Sil Olmi took heed of my advice and now he is happy,' bragged Galmai Bia. The younger men in the men's hut smiled upon hearing this and added, 'He has studied the moon very well this time.'

'I bore three consecutive girls and kept a vigil for a son. Now, I shall call him Bolkun (a tall broad leaf tree species). He shall stand tall and repel foes on battle fields and represent our clan at forums,' said Sil Olmi.

After Bolkun's birth, Sil Olmi made sure his son was in good health. He was up early at dawn to check for footprints of both men and animals near his hut. He even shot at owls whooping in the night near his hut and chased them away.

'Don't take the child with you to Oldale, Kamtai Milkn or Kap Dan. Remain at Oldale Nilben Kowan until the child is big and strong. Take heed of this instruction. You could be in for a big trouble if you don't and the child is sick,' Sil Olmi said.

Popne Ku lowered her voice and added, 'The sanguma are very active nowadays. Their thirst for human blood is infinite. I am fearful of their weird moves.'

'Watch out for strange animals in the vicinity,' instructed Sil Olmi. Popne Ku breast fed her child and nodded her head in agreement.

She took heed of her husband's caveat and kept a close watch in the vicinity of their hut each passing day. She took the child away and avoided it being seen by men and women who were thought to possess sanguma or evil spirits.

The effort and vigilance paid off. Infant Bolkun steadily grew up into a papa's boy. He was already two years old. Sil Olmi having seen the rapid growth of his son and hearing his son calling him papa openly declared, 'I can now travel to far off lands and even die because I already have one of my own kind to stretch my legacy.'

Sil Olmi's wife had another daughter when his son was two years old. But sadly Sil Olmi's health was failing because of an unexplained illness. He summoned his wife and children to his sick bed.

'I think I will not be with you all long enough to see you growing up and getting married,' he told his children. His wife Popne Ku crouched near the fire mound and covered taro with burning charcoal.

'My wife, please take the children and go live with your would-be son in law, Kone Yalgol in the Bari land and raise the children there. I don't think my Mama Gauma clansmen will help you to raise my children,' he instructed his wife. Sil Olmi's first daughter was betrothed to Kone Yalgol of the Bari tribe further up in the west.

Popne Ku said nothing. She had pangs in her heart. Her eyes were clouded with tears. Two year old Bolkun saw his mother crying and asked, 'Mother, who beats you.' Her son's voice was shaking. She rubbed her soft but creased fingers on her son's head and said, 'Fire burnt my fingers.' Bolkun looked at his mother's fingers to check the burn. Popne Ku didn't want her son to know of his father's fate.

A couple of days later Sil Olmi felt the time had come for him to pass on to the next world. He called for his son to come to his bed side one evening. He held his son's hand and cried. 'I am sorry for bringing you into the world only to leave you so soon.' Small Bolkun did not understand what his father was saying. He looked at his father with innocent eyes.

'However, Popne Ku is still strong and I know she will raise you up with great care. When I die, I will turn into a silver beetle and watch over you every day.'

Rain was still bouncing off from the pandanus leaves and making fluttering noises outside the hut. Night birds were howling away in the trees higher up. Cicadas sang as if it was dawn. Not even a single star was up in the sky. The presence of the ancestral spirits in the vicinity of the hut was evident through these signs.

Popne Ku knew the ancestral spirits had come to take her husband away. Before late evening Sil Olmi breathed his last while still holding onto his son's hand, leaving all his five children and wife behind.

Fire Truck
Biango Buia

Bangi was always noisy in his class and the teacher Miss Sama Saki put him up with a girl called Dorrtie. Dorrtie was a "nice girl" said all the teachers in the school. She never said bad words, was never late, an obedient girl and always very clean. Miss Sama had thought that if she put Dorrtie and Bangi on the same desk then there was a chance that Bangi would quieten down and that maybe some or all of Dorrtie's goodness would rub off on to Bangi.

Bangi and Dorrtie were in grade three at the Morehead Primary School in the South Fly District of the Western Province. While they were the same age at 11, in the same school, in the same grade, and on the same desk, they were very different in outlook. Some teachers suggested that they appeared more like an angel and the devil on the same desk!

While in Grade 3 Bangi, his village friends, Wills and Boni and Mila the son of the Head Teacher were playing marbles at the edge of the school yard on a dry Saturday afternoon. After playing for some time Bangi ran into the nearby scrub, pulled done the front of his shorts and began to pass urine.

His friends heard some giggling from the scrub and ran to see what Bangi was giggling about. What they saw was quite funny. Bangi was spraying the lizards in the scrub and the lizards were running in every direction to avoid the "mighty waterfalls" of Bangi.

It looked so funny that the other boys pulled down the front of their shorts and also started spraying the lizards. It was so funny to see the whole lizard population in and around the scrub running for cover in all directions.

The boys laughed long about this situation. But sad to say the young boys ran dry of "ammunition" to the relief of the lizard population.

Then Bangi suggested, "Let us go drink more water or anything that would make us pass more urine and chase the lizards again."

Then Mila, said quite excitedly, "Hey Bangi, you know when my father drinks beer how they always go to the toilet to pass urine at short intervals."

Bangi screamed; "Yes Mila".

Mila said, "Well my father and Dorrties' father were drinking last weekend and when the Pastor came to see how we were going they hid the beer bottles at the back of our garden".

"Okay, Mila run right now and find the bottles," commanded Bangi.

Mila ran as fast as he could and returned in record time with the three bottles.

Wills and Boni were quite nervous now.

"Bangi, you are not going to drink beer are you?" they asked.

"Well, not drink but we want to chase the lizards and we need the water, so that's why we will drink."

Bangi opened one bottle and drank a mouth full. The taste was terrible but he subdued any signs of yuckiness and offered it to the other boys.

In a short time the boys had lowered the front of their shorts and were at it again, wetting all the lizards in the surroundings. It was quite funny because the boys were literally "operating on fire truck mode", with their little "water sprinklers" ahead of them.

When the water sprinklers dried up, Bangi opened another bottle of beer and drank a mouth full and offered it to the other three. Being very scared now, Wills and Boni refused to take any more but Mila joined in and they both continued spraying the lizards. The four boys were having so much fun, that Mila's sisters heard the noise and came to see what was happening. By then Bangi and Mila were towards the end of the third bottle and already Wills and Boni could see Bangi and Mila were not talking normally. They were now laughing for no reason, dancing in silly ways and Bangi was pretending to be the Head Teacher, at the School Assembly.

Bangi stood on a mound and raised his hands up like the Head Teacher and said, "My children, you must all study hard and become the best you can. Life is in your hands."

Then they all laughed loudly and Mila and Bangi did girlish dances.

Bangi stood up again and said, "Now some of you boys and girls are naughty. Let today be the beginning of a new way of life for you. Today I ......"

"Hey, what's this nonsense?"

They turned towards the direction of the voice. They could see Mila's two sisters and mother standing right behind them.

The boys ran in all directions (a bit like the lizards). Wills and Boni ran as fast as they could to their village. Bangi and Mila tried to run but to their surprise their legs were very heavy.

Bangi and Mila tried to jump over the drain but instead landed in the middle of the drain and did not stand up.

"Oh Mummy, Mila is going to die, Mummy noooo!", please where is Daddy, Mummy Mila is going to die," cried Mila's sisters.

"Well if Mila dies, I will kill Bangi with my own hands," screamed Mila's mother in the midst of the panic.

"Look Mummy the empty bottles, they drank these three bottles of beer and, oh Mummy, Mila is going to die", the girls kept screaming and crying in shock.

"Yeh but how did this son of a drunk end up here," screamed Mila's mother at Bangi.

"Just like his father, shame," she continued.

Then Mila's father, the head teacher, arrived and asked what had happened.

"Oh Daddy, Daddy, Mila's is going to die," cried the sisters. "He has not woken up. Bangi got him to drink these three bottles of beer."

Mila's father knew exactly where the bottles of beer came from. But he pretended to look very surprised, puzzled and very serious.

"Okay, let's carry them to the health clinic for the Nursing Officer's medical attention."

The Head Teacher carried Bangi and his mother and daughters carried Mila to their house. The two boys were laid on the mats outside the house, while the Head Teacher looked around for bigger boys to help carry the boys to the clinic.

When the big boys arrived, the Head Teacher and other teachers accompanied the big boys as they carried Bangi and Mila to the clinic. As the boys were being carried to the clinic the crowd got larger and larger.

A story spread that Bangi had somehow got a cartoon of beer and had drunk all 24 bottles and had fainted and was probably dead! Bangi and Mila were attended to by the Nursing Officer and after hearing the story from Mila's mother, he said the only medicine at this stage was to let the boys sleep off the intoxication. The only intervention was that the boy's "sprinklers" were going to be inserted into a waste tube to hygienically collect any access urine. That to do this he was going to put a pillow each between their legs so that the waste tube was free from possible entanglement.

"Teach this boy, he is like the father"

All of a sudden screams could be heard outside the Clinic. Mila's mother was now shouting at Bangi's mother.

Bangi's parents had just been alerted and they had run all the way to find out if Bangi was truly dead!

Bangi's father passed all the screaming women and went straight into the Clinic and sought the Nursing Officer's assessment. On hearing the assessment he was relieved and went outside to rest from the running and anxiety.

"Bangi can't be that silly," screamed Bangi's mother to Mila's mother.

"You know that, Bangi's father does not take beer. It's your husband, beer face Head Teacher. That's why even grade 3 children imitate their teachers!"

Mila's mother stood very quiet breathing heavily from the verbal "flooring" from Bangi's mother.

Bangi's father coughed and this caught Bangi's mother's attention.

"And you, your bald head is so big and clean that we cannot tell where your forehead begins and where the rest of your head is," she shouted at her husband. "Aren't fathers supposed to know where their sons are?"

Bangi's father said something like, "Ah mum ah..."

"Stop, I don't want to hear anything from your toothless mouth," shouted his wife.

The crowd was really swollen by now, it looked like all of the Morehead Station residents where there. Even the lame, the blind, the crippled and the mentally ill were there too.

Dorrtie and her sisters had by now arrived. Dorrtie was really enjoying the descriptions of Bangi's father. Because in many ways Aunty Yana was describing Bangi himself! Dorrtie laughed quite loudly when she imagined Bangi without his hair and teeth.

"What! .... the laugh?" asked Wena, Dorrtie's big sister, as she "burnt" Dorrtie with her eyes.

"Mum is going to wring your neck, if she hears that you are laughing at Aunty Yana and Uncle Wangarr.".

Angel
Regina Dorum

Missus' scrutinizing eyes passed over Angeline and rested on the new girl next to her. One neatly trimmed eyebrow over the slanted eyes rose enquiringly and moved up and down the skinny girl in slim black slacks.

'No, no, no! Not like this!' the slim matron tugged at the slacks hanging onto the girl's thigh. 'Tight. No loose. Customers happy, see?' Pointing to Angeline as an example, the Asian matron drew Angeline out of the file of girls to make her point. Angeline stood, proudly thrusting her high chin forward, dressed in a tight black leather mini skirt which exposed her slim long legs supported by high stilettos. Her second-hand top was finely cut and strapless, exposing a little bit of her narrow waist and belly. Her frizzy hair touched her exposed slim neckline and shoulders giving her fair face a soft glow.

'This good. Good? You clear? See?' Missus stepped around the barely dressed girl and spoke in broken English with the Asian accent that would have made Angeline laugh aloud if she wasn't the centre of the attention. 'More customers. Spend more money, you get ten per cent ah? Angeline, you help her dress ah?'

'Yes Missus.'

Missus completed the inspection with little exclamations and recommendations on do's and don'ts of what to wear and how to behave around the club house. She dismissed other girls and told Angeline to help the new girl.

'Hey, you are new, aren't you?' Angeline asked the obvious as she rummaged in her locker to find suitable clothes that would fit the girl. The girl only nodded.

'What is your name?'

'Donna.'

'Well Donna, don't mind the Missus, she is sometimes feisty, especially when someone pisses her off. Maybe the master *did* piss her off!' Rolling her eyes, Angeline said conversationally and pulled out a short black dress and held it against Donna. 'This should fit you right. Try feeling comfortable in it as much as you can. Don't be scared, no one will do anything to you, the club bouncers are there to keep us safe.'

Angeline let Donna get dressed and entered the noisy bar. The DJ played a latest favourite music as the drunkards cheered and shouted in unison. The crowd was rowdy as it always is on Friday nights, however not yet full as the night was still young.

'Oh my angel,' an old regular grabbed at her slim waist as he tried to finish his beer in one drop simultaneously. His fat greasy puffed up face reflected the ballroom lights and Angeline imagined steam escaping from his large ears as his flat nose flared! Disgusted, she politely pushed away his hands, as it was her job to be polite to customers as a hostess, especially a regular. Otherwise, she was done!

Looking around, she spotted the girls who were also hostesses. They were in groups of twos and threes some dancing with customers while others glanced around cheekily, hoping to find a rich customer. The hostesses were clearly distinguished from the sex workers who frequented the clubs. The skinny sex workers with their over made-up scarred faces with no sense of fashion forced their way onto the male customers with feigned intoxication. They were often beaten by both customers and bouncers, slammed and pushed around. Most of them lived in the cargo containers on the wharf and were at the club seven days a week. Although Angeline pitied them, there was nothing she could do. The best policy was to ignore them but she often bought them drinks and gave them money when she could afford to.

Angeline herself made more money than all the girls combined. Being beautiful, smart and a sexy dancer; wealthy highlanders, especially land owners and businessman preferred her company. The club rules were simple: if a customer that a certain hostess entertained bought drinks, the girl was allowed to keep ten percent, however it was the club's policy that the girls were not allowed to leave with a customer *against* her wishes. If the hostess wished to go with the customer, he would pay the club manager and each girl had a price. Angeline had the highest charge of K200. Many offers came her way but she always declined. And rule number one: boyfriends were prohibited from entering the club.

'Hey hon, can I buy you a drink?' an old, well dressed man with neatly trimmed silver hair reached out and tapped her on her shoulders. Angeline turned and smiled at him, it was rare to have a polite customer and she personally appreciated such offers.

'Sure.' She replied and sat on one of the high stools that he pulled out next to the bar. He ordered beer for himself and two young boys her age who were with him and ordered a glass of whisky for her. While waiting for their order, Angeline scrutinized her companion. He was well groomed and handsome for an old man with a certain air of authority and charm. His tight fitted faded jeans and collar shirt flaunted his well-shaped muscles toned from regular exercise. He had a cute moustache which twitched whenever he smiled under his high Viking chin. A mixed race, certainly, she thought.

'What is your name, hon?'

'My name is Angeline and what is yours?' She smiled at him timidly.

One bushy eyebrow lifted. 'Not a shy one, aye?' he laughed loudly and briefly glanced at his boys who stood away from them, as if they didn't want to be seen with the old man. The boys must be embarrassed or scared maybe? Angeline thought to herself. 'That I like, that I like.' The man said and nodded to himself.

Blushing furiously, she busied herself assisting the waitress who arrived with their drinks and turned back to the men. 'Shyness is not in my vocabulary, you know.'

'Bravo, bravo girl! Oh you can call me Ben and these are my nephews.' He gestured at the boys. 'You are a very beautiful girl, you here with someone?'

'No, I work here.'

'Oh, is that right? What do I call you, an entertainer?' he met her eyes directly which made Angeline's blush deepen.

'Sort of, but hostess would be a better term, and um if you don't mind, can I keep the receipts?'

'Why? If I may ask…..' Ben sipped his beer and asked her.

'So I get ten per cent of the drinks while accompanying you,' she said simply.

'Oh really now, I guess I have been away from the night life in Port Moresby for a while. There was never any hostesses before. Is it the same with all the clubs?' Ben asked curiously.

'No, only certain clubs like this one.'

Ben stared at her face for quite a while before laughing again, his husky laugh brought a few glances their way.

'May I have a dance with you, Angel? May I call you Angel?'

'Sure, I would like that. And yeah, many call me Angel too.' She said and stood up.

Makes me wish I was a real one with angelic life! She added to herself mentally. For an old man, Ben could dance! They were the centre of attention. People stared at the beautiful barely dressed girl in the arms of a man, old enough to be her grandfather! Women sneered at them and old men cheered. Young men and boys begrudged the old man. People who knew her line of work turned away in disgust but couldn't help staring. Although many of her friends and family had tagged this job as prostitution, Angeline took pride in it because there was never a time she had left with any men. She had been at the job since she was sixteen and this was the only job she had ever had since running away from home three years ago. Let them think what they want, I know myself, she reassured herself. And it's a means of living and her boyfriend William had never complained anyway.

William, a taxi driver, had been her boyfriend for almost two years now and they lived together in Morata settlement, sharing rent and responsibilities. He was a well-built highlander that she had met one night in the club. Although he was very drunk, he had been so sweet to her. He tried so hard to persuade her to go home with him but to no avail so he begged for her number and they kept in touch. Six months later, with no other place to go, Angeline moved in with him.

'You are a pretty good dancer, Angel!' Ben brought her back from her reverie with a breathless peck on her cheek. 'Makes me wish I was 30 years younger!'

They danced the whole night and ignored Ben's nephews who tried to look very inconspicuous. At the end of the night when the lights came on, Ben dragged her to an empty couch and sat and pulled Angeline down on his lap. 'Can I keep in touch with you Angel? You make me feel like something I haven't felt in a very long time.'

Angeline was very light headed from the many glasses of whisky that she had drunk by now and she silently thanked her lucky stars that he didn't ask her to leave with him. Ben had been very sweet and generous and it would be a shame if she refused to leave with him. No matter, nice, sweet, polite or rich, she would never break her own rule to not leave with a man.

'Yes, I would be happy to keep in touch with you, Ben.' She smiled and whispered into his ears. 'You seem to be a good man.' And I hope that William will not find out! She shuddered at the thought. Although William understood her profession, he had warned her not to leave with anyone or keep in touch with anyone.

As dawn approached outside, Ben gave her his mobile number to her with a K100 tip and left with his nephews.

The next evening was also packed and Donna the new girl needed more help. Angeline assisted her, giving her advice and guidelines, all the while keeping an eye out for Ben, however he never showed up. The next day was Sunday and her day off.

'Hey babe,' William said as he lay himself flat out in their tiny room. Although their small desk fan whirled quietly in the corner, heat from the roof was enough to melt a person. After a few minutes, he was snoring.

That Sunday evening was very quiet and bright with a few church goers returning from the church, a few vendors selling buai and cigarettes where gamblers swore loudly as they lost their bets. Angeline sat outside in the shade in the hope of a cool breeze which hardly came. She stared at her phone and after a swift decision; she made the call that had been nagging her before she could have a change of heart.

'Hello?'

'Hi, is this Ben?' She asked with butterflies in her stomach and fingers crossed.

'Yes it is. And you are?'

'Oh, it's me, Angeline. I mean Angel, you remember me?'

'Oh yes, yes, my angel! How are you, my dear?' He said, sounding genuinely happy to hear from her.

'I am alright. I am just trying to check out your number.'

'It's good you called, can I buy you lunch today? If you are free that is......'

'Can I trust you?' she said firmly and hoped that it should clear his mind about what sort of person she was. She was neither a whore nor a gold digger!

'Yes, come on honey, you know I'm an honourable man you know.'

And so they had their first lunch date at Ela Beach Hotel. After the lunch, true to his word he was a gentleman and dropped her off in his brand new five-door Land Cruiser. She found out that he was married and currently with his second wife who lived in Brisbane, Australia. Ben said his first wife had left him with their three daughters and had remarried again. He was in Port Moresby for business.

Ben's father was an Irish Priest during the colonial times in the remote highlands area and had Ben with a local woman during the time when his faith was tried! Ben was a self-made business man and enjoyed the company of young people.

In the following weeks, they kept in touch secretly and Ben frequented the club. And during these times, Ben never for once asked her to leave with him. He started bringing her small expensive gifts of jewellery, perfume and once, lingerie! She never asked him for personal favours nor would she ever use him for his money. They simply enjoyed each other's company, danced and chatted about current issues and their personal lives. She was glad he never asked about her family or her background.

After their third Sunday lunch date; William was waiting for Angeline when she returned home.

'Where have you been?' he asked lightly as he busied himself cleaning his car.

'Ela Beach.' She replied half truthfully, her heart in her throat. If he found out about the date with Ben, she was as good as dead! Thank goodness it was the Ela Beach Hotel because the beach was often packed by young people on Sundays for a swim, sports or just to hang out and true to it, William believed her.

'I hope you just went for a swim babe, otherwise……' he cut off and sat behind the wheel. Otherwise I am dead she concluded for him and made a mental promise to be more careful.

'Maybe next week we will go together,' he said as he drove off.

Next Friday the club was packed with a rowdy crowd as usual. It was already past midnight and Angeline sat next to Ben on the sofa, her head resting on his shoulders. Conversation was a bit difficult with the loud music and crowd. Angeline was dressed in a very short evening dress with knee-high hooker boots - all second-hand of course. She fingered the golden necklace crested between her small breasts and looked up at Ben. It was 18 carat in heavy locks of chain with a heart-shaped cubic zirconia blinking like diamond.

'Thank you again, Ben. It's very beautiful and right now all the girls envy me,' she told him for the tenth time that night. Ben smiled and caressed her chin lightly with his small finger.

'You make it look breath-taking!' He smiled teasingly. 'When I first saw it, I pictured it on you. But damn girl, it looks more beautiful now than what I pictured though.'

Blushing, she rested her head back on his shoulder but sat straight back up when she spotted someone who looked like William. Heart hammering against her chest, she prayed. Oh dear god, William! Yes it was him alright. He was shoving his way through the crowds, eyes blazing and feet staggering. Oh lord, he is drunk, she thought. William was naturally a good drinker and would still be standing while all his mates had passed out! If he is staggering now, he must be very *drunk*!

It was like slow motion. When she stood up, William was already standing over them, glaring down at her face, red eyes giving off heat like a red furnace and a balled fist!

Angeline heard her chin gave a sick clink as William's balled fist slammed under her ears, giving her an upper cut! Her body collapsed like a rag doll heavily onto Ben who was in the process of rising and they fell in one heap on the sofa.

'You f-fucking sssick sssslut!' William was screaming in a slurred voice. The music had stopped and his voice carried across the room and bouncers pushed their way among the crowd to seize William. 'And you sssay that it's just a job, layin' so close to one grandfather you call customer! Your father abused you and-and I took you in!' Angeline felt as if she was watching from the side and right now this was happening to someone else as William shook like a bear, beating his chest to make his point.

William, she pleaded silently, please don't go there. Please don't. Everybody would know. She prayed, let me die, let me die.

William, now seized by bouncers, continued with his verbal abuse, giving away her greatest secret to her work mates, bosses and customers.

'Your father raped you, tortured you!' William screamed as he was dragged out. 'You bloody bitch! How many times did you do the abortions? No one will take you in the way I did and you still fuck around, you little slut! I will hunt you down!' his screams faded out into the exit.

Angeline stood up slowly in a daze and allowed a bouncer to lead her to the dressing room. Her chin felt as if it would fall off her face and her tongue seemed to stick to her palate. Her eyes watered as she tried moving her jaw up and down. Her ears still rang with William's heated voice and her heart beat tripled! She had trusted William with all her heart when she had told him of her father's treatment towards her. William had been so kind and understanding then and she had never believed that he would betray her like that!

Donna, to whom Angeline had grown close, gave her an assuring hug and waved others away as she wiped away her friend's tears and swore at William in different languages simultaneously.

'I told you! NO boyfriends! In here?! Remember!' The voice of the matron's accented voice thundered around the small dressing room. The fat Asian woman stood rigid at the doorway with her chubby arms folded under her chest and eyes blazing. 'Go, go! Leave. You finish! Okay?'

'You know, you sound like a gorilla?' Angeline stared at the matron in the doorway and placed her hands on her hips. The room fell in a shocked silence and the matron's mouth fell open wordlessly.

'You sound like my ass farting in breaks but with an Asian accent!' Angeline continued loudly, her eyes filled with tears as she laughed aloud foolishly. By now, the matron's eyes doubled in size and her small lips opened and closed like a fish.

Shocked by her own words and by the events that had happened, she grabbed her bag with shaky hands and pushed the stunned matron aside and walked out past the bar and into the cool dawn with the bouncers closely flanking her.

Opening the door of the first cab she saw, Angeline sat and closed her eyes, trying to settle her jumbled thoughts. The loud rap on her side window made her open her eyes in fright, envisioning William's angry face glaring at her.

It wasn't William but one of Ben's escorts telling her to follow Ben's car. Nodding in response, she silently thanked her lucky stars that Ben had not neglected her at this time when she really needed someone. Where was I going to go when I hopped into the cab? She asked herself, William is at home waiting to kill me! She shuddered and hugged herself.

She had nowhere else to go and she could not go to her parents' house. She would rather be dead than see her father's face again. The thought of her father brought on unsolicited memories, the hurt, shame and anger she had tried to forget over the last two years. Tears flooded her eyes as she remembered the two abortions she had performed on her by the old dirty hag from the settlement and the looks she had received from the community.

Oh William, how could you? It would be the same old feeling all over again. Hatred of her father filled her soul and made her feel the pain physically all over again. Angeline closed her eyes and tried willing the memories away. The cab came to a stop at one of Ben's sea view apartments.

Ben's escort paid the cabby and gently led her into one of the rooms.

'Boss says you can stay here for the night,' the escort said. 'He will call on you later.' After the man left, she sat down heavily on the chair until the dawn broke and the morning sun streamed past the window curtains. The sea was serene with morning sea birds crowing above in search of food.

In a trance, her hands calmly reached for the silk bed cover and pulled it into a slim long cord shape. She wound it around her neck and tied the edge to the high veranda and threw herself over the edge and darkness took over as the oxygen was cut off from her lungs and the light faded from her eyes.

News flash: A young woman was found dead in one of a business man's flats. Believed to be suicide. Comments from the owner, Benson Roth, were unsuccessful…

Two weeks later, a single wreath of flowers was placed on Jane Doe's headstone at 9 mile cemetery with a single card reading:

I am so sorry, My Angel, you could have told me. RIP.

Oh, it's the songs they sing
Jeffrey Mane Febi

"We see; you've come with the flower of the mountain; that blossoms a pleasant red and dances in the wind while the stars look on. We see; you've adorned yourself with this flower and come with a determined purpose; and our attention you've courted. But before you tell us the reasons, let us show you where you'll rest your head. Let us bring you firewood. Let us fetch you water. And let you rest for a while. For the night will be querulous and wearisome", so sang the welcoming villagers.

"Oh so you've seen! Well, we cannot hide it, can we? The wind had spoken about it long before. And the earth has brought forth the dancer on the mountain. We came here for a purpose! We will tell when we've rested. We will tell when we've drank! We will tell when we're fed. But for now we say thank you that this place may welcome us too", sang the visitors in reply.

It was a pleasant surprise for Oromo, the tired and weary traveller, who stood and watched his fathers, mothers, brothers and sisters; all singing together in unison; chorusing a sound that captured his ignorant spirit. Not a word he uttered, not even a sigh. Mouth half open, he gazed blankly with his mind's eye and listened attentively, trying to capture the lyrics; those words that were trampling all over his heart.

But it ended so soon; and ushered to a sitting spot, Oromo could not but wonder at those echoing words of the songs. He has missed a lot, he realised. Even the younger ones knew the songs; they knew these songs are usually sung only on such occasions. How could he have not known this kind of *singsing* existed? Did they do this just for him? People at home sing for different occasions; but this? Welcoming a visitor with a song, and then the visitor responds in song too, it was totally new to him. He glimpsed the world of his grandfathers that day and it found a place deep in his heart.

He was shamed by the younger ones; those cheeky companions. They knew things he did not know and his heart despite the fatigue, yearned for this precious knowledge and more. In these forgotten lands, where the government's presence continued to remain on the distant horizon; the traditional treasures were truly valuable. And row upon row of dusty shelves and more rows had yet to see the light of day.

The darkness gradually set in and the fire's glow became brighter. With every additional piece of wood shoved into the heart of fire, the hotter it became. Oromo turned and noticed the house was full; every inch of space taken up by inquisitive souls. Souls that had gathered with wide open ears and welcoming hearts to listen and learn of things they did not know about.

Then a drop of sweat slid down over his eye lashes and he knew the place would get even hotter, but no one would feel it except him, for they were used to such gatherings. People had been steadily filling up the house for the last hour or so. Fatigue and the soothing words of the songs had rendered him oblivious to his surroundings, lost in reverie, letting them take him where they would in this enchanted world.

It wasn't long before a new song started. Abruptly; his heart woke from its hibernation and he prepared to savour whatever the night offered. He knew his educated mind needed this precious knowledge in order to be complete. He knew he had to learn fast to blend in. He knew that this was to be his first time to be in such a *singsing*. He knew it wasn't an opportunity to be missed.

The hosts started singing praise for the flower of the mountain; detailing the adventures of many a dream that had failed to return with the flower. Many dreams had soared to the top of the mountain, only to find the flower unwilling to return with them. Many had waited for the moment; the time they would meet the flower. And how happy they were when it had happened. But the question is why? Why come now?

Then Oromo tuned his ears to hear his tribesmen reply. It didn't come! He grew anxious! Why didn't they respond quickly; he couldn't wait. His heart was pounding; he wanted to know what the answer would be. And they'd sing it to their host. As whispers continued, presumably discussing the response to the question, the wait seemed long and he steadily grew uneasy. And the heat that he had forgotten began to take its toll. "Water!" he whispered hoarsely to his closest companion. "Please hurry!" He gulped the water from a plastic container with determined haste. Then his throat closed suddenly on him. He coughed abruptly towards the fire and water from his mouth and throat went scurrying into the flames.

Then a voice; a familiar voice! High pitched and with authority; pierced the dimly lit and smoky interior. The thick lazy smoke hovering just above their heads seems to part as if to make way. The voice reminded him of his childhood. Those yesterday's when he used to hunt lizards and insects with his tiny bow and arrows; those days when his papa would challenge him to a playful wrestle. Oh the unmistakably commanding, yet adorable voice of his mama. The one and only woman who best knew her son.

It echoed into the night while others waited for their turn to join in. Oromo too waited. He wanted to know when the others would join in the song. Then all his companions, old and young alike, joined in the chorus.

But his father's voice, raised up from the dust ridden depths of his heart, was a mere whisper, drowning rapidly into the abyss of the chilly night outside.

"…so with your great voice, you've asked why! We have walked over hills and rivers. We have brought the flower of the mountain. To you now we present it! So tell the others about this. Tell the others about this".

And on the two groups discussed; disputed each with other; then compromised on certain things; all in song, poetic songs only. And Oromo in his bewildering excitement, listening hard to learn as fast and as much as he could, dozed off into the wind and was carried to the mountain of the red flower.

When first light appeared and the sharpening orchestra of early dawn had begun the members of the two groups, having exhausted themselves, succumbed to their harassed bladders. It was time to depart for the next village. Pots of kaukau were brought in and served quickly. They must make haste in order to cross two fast flowing rivers and clamber over an ugly hill before the clouds started roaring and the rain began pouring.

Love When Bought
Eric Gabriel

She stood there staring at me, unsatisfied and sobbing as I offered my last words of comfort. Grieving tears rolled down her face. She no longer looked like the beautiful girl I knew from childhood. Her beauty had vanished; devoured by the ugly pain. I cleared my throat, as if it was the only thing to do, and stared into the approaching darkness. I wanted to be strong because that was what she saw in me, and if there was anything I wanted her to remember me for before we parted for the last time, it was this attribution - the one she adored.

Tide was already coming in. The surrounding palm trees stood still as if saluting the approaching night. The wind had ceased and the shrieking call of crickets and the faint buzz of night insects suddenly seized the silence. Sea birds in thousands crowded the beach pecking at one or two unfortunate fishes. Suddenly, I envied this liberty nature had bestowed upon the wild – the birds had the ability to soar high above earth in limitless freedom unknown to mankind. The serenity of the atmosphere drew upon me, it was getting late, and we both knew we had to part.

Seeing she was adamant to leave, I reached out to her and gently stroked her shoulders. She did not move. "We are born, but into a society". I spoke gently. "For us the society must labour. That is its essence, so we become one of them. Owned and attached to them in a web of invisible values. Our will must correspond with our traditions, which in turn control, determine and even attempt to establish love between partners. You and I are victims of our own ways of life, you see", I explained.

"I wish I had the power to change the course of everything". She whispered, almost to herself.

I looked at her sympathetically, "You should not despair; love rejuvenates. Like a tree felled, it will always grow back to regain its natural shape and beauty. I will be gone, but for him, you will still have the same kind of feelings you have for me…who knows you might come to love him even more…" I added, hoping to make it sound convincing"

"What if I hated him?" She cried out. "What if I ran away? What if I hang myself? What if I …"

I wrapped my arms around her and held her close, "Take it easy," I soothed, as she collapsed into my shoulders and wept bitterly. I tried to comfort her. "Nothing is perfect. Forget what has happened today; tomorrow will tell us a different story. You know, it's a short life we live, be strong and be content with what has already become of us".

She turned and looked at me questioningly, "Why do you sound so indifferent. Isn't this between you and me?

For a short while I did not answer, then I replied "Yes, but we have to accept what is before us and move on. You will go your own way and I will go mine. See…you wish you had the power to change the course of everything and I wish I had the money to pay the amount your people have demanded."

The sun was turning orange over the horizon. Weakening like a huge ball of fire, rolling over a battle field. Its reflection grasping and transforming everything it met along its path. Night was fast approaching. Soon her name would echo through the dark, to declare the end of us and whatever we thought we had as friends, partners or couples.

For the first time in my life I felt rejected by my own people. A girl I love had to be taken away from me, uncompromisingly and unjustly. Even if I proved my higher love for her, to them I would still appear weak, a weak man. It had to be money. And money was not what I had. Only love, genuine unconditional love that would protect her, feed her, shelter her…I pitied my people's foolishness. Money was all they wanted, the ultimate reason why they would not think humanely. I was sorry for Lekwa too, my successor; the man who would become the bridegroom in place of me, the man who was stronger than me. I tried to picture her holding hands happily with Lekwa, but the image kept falling apart, like a million pieces of puzzle that would never fit together. If only Lekwa saw the true meaning of love, he would have dismissed everything in my favour.

Then it came, the moment we feared, her name echoed through the night, piercing through our hearts like a sharp blade and numbing our veins. Ahead, lights from torches and hurricane lamps lanced through the already dark undergrowth. Distant figures wavered towards us.

"My love this must be the end…I will miss you". She let out a muffled cry of bitterness as she gave a final squeeze to my hand and moved away reluctantly. My heart froze as I felt the passage along my throat constrict. I fumbled in the darkness for a last hand shake or hug or whatever my heart instantly longed for, but I could only hear her sobs getting louder as she staggered towards the approaching figures. Immediately I missed her presence. I wanted to run after her and grab her, whisk her away and mend our heartache forever…but I could not, it was impossible.

The lights had come closer. "This is it" I thought, "This is the end". I turned and paved my way silently through the palm fronds and shrubs, trying to glance back, but fearing.

I was numb to the ferns and under growth that pushed past my legs or occasionally brushed my face. A while later, the night sounded still, I could only make out the faint thud of my own footsteps. I halted and glanced back where I had come, hoping as if to see her face one last time, only to be reminded of the dullness and darkness of the night around me. I looked up into the dark sky and felt the universe looking down at me like a mother to a heart-broken child. Like me, many had taken this journey before and still many will take this journey – a journey of an uncertain destiny. I forced a smile to my lips and welcomed the bitter tears that welled up in my eyes. "Will her heart ever heal; will she ever find happiness again? Will they ever see what they had done to her - us?" And it dawned on me; only time held this answer to the mystery of love when bought.

The K50 House
Ian Dabasori Hetri

Afternoons in the highlands of Papua New Guinea are characterized by a special kind of light. In the mid-afternoon, the light softens, dimmed by a golden then mauve haze. The tree–lined streets are littered with betel nut spit, cans and bottles. Shopping plastics are scattered, some swept up in mounds against fences and gutters, others swirling in eddies. I live in the heart of Kainantu town with my Dad who works with PNG Power Limited.

Like any other highlander who had never been to the coast, I dreamt of seeing the sea and sailing ships. I had worked very hard to save enough money for my holiday trip. I had decided to spend my holiday with my uncle Peter Angra, who is a renowned business man in Lae.

One afternoon I went on my usual trip of selling my cabbages. The weather was chilly. I walked past the town gate and headed to the nearest village on the outskirts of town. My family and clan were well known so I feared noting. It was almost dark now and I wanted to be indoors but I had to sell the remaining cabbages.

This time I decided to visit the house of an old man and woman. I didn't know well this couple but they seemed strange to me so I just decided to pay them a visit. Who knows, they might have children in town that had sent them a lot of money. Besides they were too old to garden so they might as well buy my cabbages. With that thought I gave a knock on their door.

A small, spritely, elderly woman with startling eyes answered. I could tell immediately she was the sort of person who was happy to talk to anyone. If she knew them, then good for her; if she didn't she would prattle on all the same. But I didn't mind. She invited me in and I accepted. When people open their doors to me I always feel privileged that I am allowed a glimpse of their lives. It was one aspect of my selling activity I enjoyed the most.

The passage way was very dim. Unlike the common highlands round house, this house was a bit more rectangular than I had seen from outside.

I could smell kerosene from a burning lantern at the far end of the house. The house had two partitions connected with a walkway in between. As my eyes adjusted to the light I became aware of K50 notes, hundreds of them, all over the walls. The woman ushered me into an equally dim room. Here the smell of kerosene was much stronger. An elderly man sat huddled in a cane chair near the orange glow of the lantern. He offered me a creaky old dusty chair. His voice sounded weary and his eyes, unlike of his wife, were dull.

This room was also filled with K50 notes - all over the walls and on his old table. 'Do you save all your K50 notes?' I asked, thinking this was certainly one of the oddest houses I had ever been inside. 'Oh no!' the old man protested. 'I couldn't do that; it would make me and my wife very poor'. 'Life would be cruel if we did, wouldn't it?' I had to simply agree with him realizing how rationale he was. I looked closely. There were K50 notes artistically painted from papers. Some cut out from advertisements in newspapers and magazines.

The woman was keen to see my cabbages and she sighed in delight as I drew each one out of my wool bilum. I knew too well not to try to entice the old couple into buying my cabbages. I doubted anything could upstage their K50 note collection. So I settled for a conversation with them instead.

The old man was pleasant but seemed unmoved. 'Life has no meaning for me, I'm afraid', he said suddenly. 'I'm merely living my days'. I was momentarily annoyed. I had experienced this 'one foot in the grave' attitude before; perhaps it was the onset of another dreary night that made people dour. A gentle touch of humour might help. But before I could speak, the old man began to tell me about his son, Yakarambi.

When Yakarambi was old enough to go to school, his parents sent him to the coast in search of education. They believed that if Yakarambi got educated and got a job he could earn money and later look after them. Yakarambi attended Bugandi Secondary in Lae. All was well for Yakarambi until one day his cube mate stole his K50 that his parents had sent to him. Yakarambi was so mad that he chopped off one of his cube mate's finger. The relatives of the cube mate who lived in the nearby Zero Block Settlement retaliated and beat Yakarambi up severely injuring his spine and paralysing him for life physically and mentally.

The man described how he and his wife had fed, bathed and changed their son every day of his life afterwards. Well into their seventies, they were still caring for him at home. They never had a sign from Yakarambi that he knew they were his parents. On occasion they sought respite care for him and discovered that they had some mysterious bond with their son. If someone else looked after him, he would become inconsolable.

The old man faced a terrible dilemma. Both he and his wife were growing frail and he feared that if one of them died the other one wouldn't be able to cope with Yakarambi. Institutional care for their son was not an option because they were too poor. The old man had heard about how arrogant the staff were at the hospitals in big towns and he refused to send his son away, fearing he would die of mistreatment from the selfish hospital staff. Calmly, one night he made his decision. 'I put my son to sleep', the old man confessed.

I felt my body stiffen: No breath, no heartbeat, and no movement. My thoughts became crowded. Here I was sitting opposite to a man who had killed his son. The shock of confession, however, soon dissolved into great compassion for the old man. He had only freed his only son by suffocating him. To him it was an act of immense love and kindness, not malice, yet in the eyes of law it was murder.

'It was in all the papers,' his wife said excitedly, handing me a bunch of clippings. Yakarambi's death and his father's subsequent trial for murder in the Supreme Court in Port Moresby has been a landmark case. The plight of thousands of the carers who sacrificed their lives to care selflessly for their disabled children had finally been thrust into the open by this tragic yet courageous act.

A small chill ran through me as I read the clippings. Yakarambi and I were the same age if he had been living by now. The cruel irony of his captivity and my freedom didn't escape me, nor, I suspect, did it escape the old man.

I also understood why life had no meaning for him. Despite his severe disabilities, Yakarambi has been the reason for his living and now he was gone. The old man was content to live out his suspended sentence for manslaughter in a cane chair in an airless room.

Walking out into the dark road some time later, I was greeted by the dry grass rustling under my feet. I felt revived as the cold air hit my face. But I felt changed. I knew I would never forget my chance encounter with the onetime famous couple in their K50 money house.

I worked hard and raised enough to go for my holiday in Lae. While in Lae, I asked my uncle to drive me to Bugandi Secondary School where Yakarambi went to school. I visited Voco Point where I saw huge and small ships of different types. I felt the sea and even tasted it. It was the most memorable trip in my life.

Diary of Phoenix
Peter Jokise

The rough waters of the Solomon Sea crashed against the aging hull of the ill-fated MV Rabaul Queen with the promise of bad weather as the old beast sliced across the oceanic territory of West New Britain into Morobe Province. The crowded ferry had almost 500 passengers, some returning home from the New Guinea islands while others came to work there, study or just visit the city of rain, all without any clue of what nature had in store for them.

Phoenix Dambui sat on the barren floor in the corner of the lower deck reserved for the 'low class passengers'. In his twenty-one years alive, his deepest thoughts involved a fascination with psychology and religion, even though his major was biology. Looking out of his window he could see the waves protesting as he flipped open his diary, a useful hobby he had picked up in high school. His father once told him that memories are too important to lose so he kept these precious memories inked and treasured in his diary.

On a clean fresh page, his heading read; *Date: February 1, 2012, Time: 1145pm, Title: Is God Fair?*

Dear Diary,

I'm having a bad feeling about this unpromising weather. So many times I used to wonder; is there really a loving and graceful God out there watching as disasters and diseases keep killing people in thousands, disability mutilates them and grief weighs them down? Why couldn't this all-powerful God at least pay attention to men's agonizing prayers? Have mankind ever deserved such injustice, hurt and suffering from God? Had mankind even asked God to create them in the very first place and leave them stranded on this unloving planet? My deepest conscience tells me that God created mankind for the sole purpose of receiving glory from them but in the meantime, does mankind have to go through all this undeserving misery? All this is claimed by God to draw mankind closer and bring greater glory unto him. My god, what kind of an egocentric maniac would toy with his creation for his glory, imposing a death penalty on human descendants to begin with and then banishing them to hell for not worshipping him? He himself claimed to have given them free will, hence mankind has the right to choose if they want to worship Him or not. Why would He punish mankind when all that mankind did is simply exercise its free will? Or the question gets more even mystifying; if this God is all-knowing, does man really have free will? Can free will co-exist with omniscience? Or is free-will just a divine illusion from this God, an illusion that only exists in a man's mind when in reality, his very destination from birth has all been conspired?

The time on his cell phone showed February 2, 1:53am as Phoenix shut his heavy eyes and retired in a deep sleep barely aware of people snoring calmly, some tossing and turning, others just lying completely still with their eyes open, not sure whether they were awake or dreaming. His last question alive was: "will somebody please give me the answers to my questions?"

He dreamt of that sad, beautiful girl he saw during the day and he longed so much to be with her and make her happy. He thought, if God couldn't make her happy, I will.

Slowly, he opened his eyes and he was standing in a long marbled corridor, magnificently ancient but yet alive with energy. A shining white figure approached him and called unto him, "Mortal man, do not be afraid, I am Lynx, the Ancient Eyes and I will show you to the chambers of my master. There you will be able see the reality of the unseen world that took place in the year 0, the mysterious year between BC 1 and AD 1 during which time and space had frozen; you must write as I translate."

A shocked Phoenix then asked, "Am I dead?"

"No, what you are experiencing is called astral projection. Your spirit simply departs from your physical body to explore the realms of the unseen. If you choose to remain in this realm, your physical body as a rule will perish and live no more,"

Phoenix was led away by Lynx and they came to a towering double door with two angels guarding the entrance. The doors flung open and they walked in; further across the hall was a shining throne. As Phoenix approached the throne he gawked at the majestic angel seated on the throne, the most elegant being ever created; his mere presence made Phoenix weak to stand yet frozen in his posture.

Lynx calmly declared, "Behold, Lucifer, the son of dawn, the Bearer of Light and the Giver of Knowledge!"

In an instant, all those evil pictures painted of Lucifer just vanished as Phoenix's heart stopped and his throat became dry. Then his thoughts were cut short by a melodic yet powerful voice speaking, "I see, you are troubled by my appearance, you have nothing to fear, mortal man. Here take this and eat, for this is the fruit of knowledge, your eyes will be opened to the answers of your questions."

Phoenix reached out and took the fruit and bit it. Miraculously, he became aware of Lynx taking him back into time to the year zero. The highlights of the unseen occurrence in history played out like three dimensional movie scenes as Lynx urged him to write and began to translate.

The fresh page read; *Date: Year 0, Time: unknown, Title: Questions Answered.*

Dear Diary,

And I see before me, Lucifer conquering the city of Zion and gaining possession of the covenant chest which holds the stone tablets (laws to mankind) and the divine 'blueprint' of Hashem's sovereign plan of salvation. The blueprint is what Lucifer is after and now I see what he saw and now I know the answers to my questions.

The blueprint outlined Hashem's plan to create immortal angels and mortal mankind; the latter would have to endure evilness, pain and suffering thus relying on Hashem's promising words to eventually bring torrents of glory to his name, feeding his ego and making him invincible while those pains and suffering by default become the fault of Lucifer. Lucifer was framed by Hashem right from the very beginning therefore he has been fighting Him for justice for his tarnished reputation and also for mankind for all the pain and suffering that they never deserved from this self-centered tyrant.

Then Lynx took Phoenix back to the throne of Lucifer and Lucifer smiled at Phoenix and spoke, "Mortal man, now that your eyes have been opened, would you give up this courage to live eternally to glorify an egocentric being that had caused all misery or would you live free and die free; to join me in my quest to fight for justice as we advance towards Armageddon?"

Phoenix turned to Lynx, gave him his diary and said "I will die in those dark waters but in return I want to save a life, a life that God cannot save. Put this diary in my metal box and let that pretty girl find this box to float on to safety".

He watched as the MV Rabaul Queen sank into the hungry waters of Solomon Sea. He turned to Lucifer and smiled "I am Phoenix, I will be reborn to freedom from the ashes of my mortal body and I will live free and die a free man."

Gemma Velekiri sat on the grey sandy beach of Tami Island watching the waves roll by in the morning of February 5, 2012. She had been floating for three days out in the sea, on a metal box which now lay open on the sand by her side. In her lap laid open a black diary belonging to a boy she had never known called Phoenix Dambui. The opened page in the diary read: *Date: Year 0, Time: unknown, Title: Questions Answered.*

And as the calm island breeze caressed her sticky, salted-skin, a shy, guilty smile played across her lips, she picked up a shell and whispered: "You gave up your life to save mine Phoenix, wherever you are, may you find the peace you have been searching for all your life." And she threw that shell into the sea.

Out on the horizon she saw a boat coming to her rescue. Clutching the diary in her right hand, she waved with her left at the on-coming rescue boat from the Royal Australian Navy.

Nightmare
Ruth Kamasungua

Things happened so fast and he still could not digest all that had happened. He had walked down to the street near his cousin's house to buy betel nut. It was sometime past six when he crossed over to the other side of the road and bought two nuts for K2.00. After he chewed the meaty fruit he threw the skin at a passing police truck. The truck stopped and a policeman came out of the back of the Land Cruiser with a rifle. "Did you throw a stone at the Police car?" The officer asked. "No I swear I didn't." The policeman cursed and swung his rifle at the head of the man. He felt a thud at the back of his head and fell. That was the last he could remember. When he came back to his senses he was rolling about on the floor of the police truck with his hands cuffed. He couldn't gain his balance. He was rolling like a ball with the movement of the vehicle as it made its rounds throughout the city. His head felt like a heavy stone and he could hardly open his eyes for they were swollen and his lips felt as if they had doubled their size. He felt jabs of pain coming from his ribs and he could hear cursing and swearing coming from those who were sitting in the car. The smell of alcohol filled the moving vehicle and voices of drunken men talking and laughing. He tried to open his mouth in vain. Somebody stepped on his head and another kicked him in the guts and he passed out again. When he came back to consciousness, he could hear the sound of laughing men who used curse words at each other. Suddenly the car came to a halt and someone poured what seemed to be a bucket of water on his bruised head and body. The water was freezing cold and he was completely alert by then. Maybe that was the purpose; these brutes thought that they could wake their victim up with cold water. He felt ice-cold water penetrating his bruised face like a slicing knife and tried to lift his head in vain. His right eye was completely shut and he tried his best to open his left eye in vain. "Throw the pig out now," someone ordered from the front of the vehicle. "Give me the key to the hand cuffs," said someone else who sat closer to him. He was rolled roughly around by someone's heavy boots. He could hear the key clicking open the merciless cuffs which had bounded him all night. Someone else set him up on the vehicle and the door of the back van opened and he was pushed roughly off the truck onto the ground. He fell badly on to the ground and got up. Someone from the vehicle fired a shot into the air causing him to run like a wounded animal slowly away from the vehicle. He tried to focus his good eye on where he was but in vain because it was also red and stingy from the punches that he had received. "Keep moving, you @*%%@, someone swore at him from the police van." It was probably the men who fired the shot. There was another shot close behind him and he accelerated his steps into a run and because he couldn't see properly, he didn't know where he was going. All he could see was a blurry vision of a street which may have been Gordons Buai Market Street accept that this street was cleaner than Gordons Buai Market street where he last remembered strolling to find betel nut. Then he remembered his dear wife who had sat outside the police station at Gordon breast-feeding his two month old son. He remembered her beautiful face as she said "Where are you going?" He had replied "Just across the road to get some betel nut." His father-in-law, a real gentleman was grinning his usual 'approval grin' as he regarded him as his own son even though he was not an ideal one. Suddenly, something occurred to him. He remembered taking his father-in-law's wallet. He said he would keep it for him and in it was a thousand kina in hard cash. He quickly put his hands into his pocket to check the wallet, it was gone! He was alarmed – by now he was fully alert. As he tried to figure out what actually happened to the money, there was another shot and this was a close one that missed his feet. He ran for his life – he ran until he came to a big building. His feet grew tired and he was perspiring. He realized that he was running barefoot. His shoes must have been taken with the rest of his stuff. He rubbed his good eye and tried to figure out where he was. He stood there for a while and tried to read the sign on the building. It read 'Able Computers'. Right away he knew that he was at Rainbow, Four Mile. He didn't know what time it was since everything including his two mobile phones and his shirt had been taken from him. He guessed the time to be around 6.30 in the morning and the road was already busy with buses and cars. He checked his pocket to see if there were any coins so that he could catch a bus to Gordons. There was only thirty toea in his pocket. He dragged himself across the road to the other side and waited for a bus no. 17 or 4 to come by. A bus number 17 came and stopped and he jumped in and sat behind the boss crew. He could feel that the passenger's eyes were scrutinizing him, which meant he must have looked like a zombie with his badly bruised face and without a shirt. The bus stopped at Gordons and he got out and walked to the house. His wife was bathing the baby when he walked in and he went straight to the *patapa* in front of the house and slept. His cousin-in-law, Josephine and her two daughters were outside marketing when he walked into the front yard. They took one look at him and guessed that he had been drinking in the night. Thinking that he was in a drunken stupor, they did not ask him about his bruises and let him sleep while they went about doing their marketing and other home chores. He felt a hand on his arm and woke up. There was his mother sitting next to him on the *patapata*. "Henry, did you have a fight? How did you get your face swollen and those bruises all over your body?" asked his concerned mother. He sat up and was trying to explain the whole situation to his mother when his father and sister arrived. "Henry, your face! What happened?" asked his sister as she sat next to the elderly woman. His wife came out with the baby and joined the rest of the family on the *patapata*. As they all crowded around him, he explained to them what had happened. His parents thought he was lying while his sister believed him. His wife looked at him with a sad face. "Why would Police Officers do that to you, they are supposed to uphold the law?" complained his sister. As they were talking his father-in-law arrived. "What happened, Henry? Did you have a fight with somebody?" His daughter nudged him aside and whispered to him. "He drank last night with his mates, can't you see, and he is trying to cover it up by telling us and his parents and sister that he was beaten by police men." "Oh, my money! " The man's voice quivered as he looked at his daughter. "Dad, I told you not to give it to him, why did you do it." "Well, he said he would take care of it and I trusted him. I'm pretty sure that somehow he has kept it safe for me somewhere in his pocket." He walked to where his son-in-law was sitting and asked, "Henry, can I have my money back now?" "I'm very, very sorry; the policeman who hit me last night must have taken my money. They've taken everything that was on me, my watch, shoes, the wallet with your money and mine, and my two mobile phones." His father-in-law stood shocked as he looked from

Henry to his daughter and back to Henry. And for the first time he regretted having Henry as a son-in-law.

An Adventure with Potholes
Hogande Kiafuli

In Memory of the lives lost in Airlines PNG Dash 8 Plane crash in Madang, and the MV Rabaul Queen ferry sinking off the Coast of Finschaffen.

The lone hostess hurried up the aisle to the front, and buckled herself into her seat. It was take-off time.

Then there was a small push, as if a giant thumb has slightly tapped it, and the Airlines PNG Dash 8 moved forward, gradually gaining speed. Leaning comfortably back in his seat, Tunude peeped through the oval window and watched the buildings and parked planes move past. He knew that the plane was speeding along the runway of Jackson's airport.

Suddenly, a wave of frightful, yet pleasant sensation conquered him. He thought his heart was sinking. He held his breath briefly, but let go in a sigh as the sensation disappeared. He looked out the widow again, and saw the runway dropping back, waving goodbye to the plane. Have a pleasant ride, it seemed to say.

The sun smiled at the plane cruising through the cloudless sky. Trivial winds blew against the plane, vainly slowing its speed. For a moment, Tunude thought he was sitting on the sofa in a hotel room. Even the beautiful flight attendant serving him a glass of juice brought to memory the waitress who had served him at the hotel a few days ago, though her face makeup reminded him of a human toy that he had once owned as a child.

He took a sip from the juice, and was meditating the tasty orange flavour when a sudden jolt splashed some juice onto his trousers. He peeped out the window anxiously, but vast clouds of pure white stared back. He was inside a tiny blue capsule that was attempting to come out of thick white cotton.

The plane jolted, jarred and jounced as it pierced through the huge ball of clouds. It swayed, shook, and slowed as it turbulently battled with the clouds for a clear sky. The engine even made strange, scary noises that propelled fear into Tunude's heart. Not of clouds, or death but the fear of the unknown.

After a good three minutes, the clouds disappeared, taking the turbulence with them. Tunude sighed in relief as blue sky reappeared. The cry of the engine was now soothing, but fear lingered in his heart. As if complementing the relief, the 'Fasten Seatbelt' sign illuminated and the plane dived towards Madang airport.

Landing was smooth, but the plane vibrated as it taxied along the runway, and to a stop. Finally it was time to disembark, so Tunude unbuckled, picked up his hand luggage and walked out. He forced a smile at the attendant, who parted her painted lips into a beautiful smile that vaporized all traces of fear.

Where was that wonderful smile when the plane jolted through the potholes in the sky, Tunude thought, *to sedate my pounding heart and slow my speeding blood?*

The driver of a white bus was waiting for Tunude. He placed his two green bags and his blue umbrella into the bus and slid the door shut. *Lutheran Guest House*, which was painted on the side of the bus, was revealed as the door slid shut. A few minutes later, they arrived at the wharf, where *LuHealth* was waiting to take him across the ocean to the small island he was headed to.

With Tunude now on board, *LuHealth* slowly pulled out of the wharf and headed for the open. The sky was empty, with only a few thin clouds scattered against the blue background. Straight above, but heading west was the lone sun, vaporizing the clouds that stood its way. *Fixing the potholes in the sky, aren't you?* Tunude mused.

The sea was also blue, but slightly darker than the sky. It was as serene as a child in the womb, but with the few low waves, not as smooth as a baby's bottom. The boat cut through the waters, leaving waves and bubbles in its track. It looked as if the boat was creating clouds on the sea, where it traversed.

It was an enjoyable ride, surrounded with magnificent views that Tunude's camera could not resist. About half an hour later, the silhouette of the destination island appeared on the horizon. It was a shade of green between two blues; the island sandwiched between the sky and the sea. In a few minutes, he would be it. The thought of stepping onto the island that he had heard about since childhood made joy leap in his heart.

But joy was silenced by a sudden gush of sensation, like that which he felt when the plane lifted off the ground. He quickly realised that a big wave had forced the boat upwards, and the boat was now free-falling behind it. With a loud thud that shook his heart, the boat landed on the water. He looked around to see if anyone had noticed his fright, but everyone seemed as calm as before. Fright, fight or flight, he chose all.

The sea was pregnant with waves as they neared the island. More armies of waves met them, as if to prevent them from reaching the island, but they submitted to the boat as it glided over them. Some revolting waves however, sent the boat flying into the air, as if spitting it out of their mouth. Some splashed against the boat, forcing showers of sea water to rain over Tunude's face. The waves rumbled under his feet, as they rocked the boat with their natural strength. Fear rose with the waves, and evaporated every pint of peace. *It's a seaquake to drown ya,* fear told him.

The boat finally reached the shore, triumphant. Tunude was first to step off and onto the sand. He was greeted by a local, named Sumerg, who had come to pick him up.

"Welcome to Karkar Island," smiled Sumerg. "I'm sure you had an enjoyable ride here!"

"Sure, it was wonderful!" Truth fled. "But the potholes in the sea rumbled my heart to fear, and deprived my bladder of tears!" Truth returned.

Missed by the Wielding Axes
Peter Maime

It was in the year 1982 that I did Grade Eight at Minj High School in what is now Jiwaka Province. I don't know what the school is like now because I haven't been back since completing Grade Ten in 1984.

During my time there were no dormitories for the boys. The girls had one small dormitory. This building for the girls was an old converted administration office. The boys who came from distant areas were given land on the school grounds to build their own houses to live in and go to school. My two cousin-brothers, Alki Tine and Du Kunagel, who arrived there before me had a house and I was accommodated by them.

Alki had left at the end of 1981 and gone to Goroka Technical College. I was with Du who was doing Grade Nine.

We had to find food ourselves. Du and I were unfortunate because we were cut off from home due to tribal fights. Our home was some 30 kilometres away from the school. We depended on Du's sister for food since she was married to a man from Kudjip, at that time a 50 toea bus fare trip away.

Our staple food was kaukau. We would cut flat kaukau and fry them on a heated drum oven. If we were lucky we would have them with tea. Most of the time we just had to be content with kaukau. The school only provided lunch and we had it with the rest of the students. Lunch was mostly rice and tinned fish.

One weekend I decided to go home and see my family because it had been almost a year since I had seen them. The tribal fights at home had stopped and people were now moving around freely. I went on a Friday. My mother wailed and cried because she was happy to see me again. I am her first born son. My other family members were also happy to have me in their midst.

On Sunday it was time for me to return to the school. My mother filled an empty rice bag with some kaukau that she had dug and three round cabbages from my father's vegetable garden. Then my parents walked me to the next village to catch my transport. The distance between my home and the next village was about three kilometres.

I was lucky. There was a car ready to leave with some passengers for Minj when we arrived. Our neighbouring Golekup clan owned the car, a green Toyota Stout. My parents put me on the car and saw me leave before they returned home.

When we were halfway to the main Highlands Highway the driver stopped to collect our transport fees. I paid mine. It was about two kina. But the other passengers refused to pay because they claimed they were all owners of the car. The driver's facial expression indicated that he was not happy with the reception he got from the passengers.

However, he got in the car and drove until we finally reached the main highway at Ganigle. Now we had to head west. Our home borders the Kerowagi District of Simbu Province. Minj would be about a 30 minute drive from the junction of our trunk road and the main highway.

The driver was speeding on the highway and I began to sense that there was something abnormal about the mobility of the car. We had travelled the longest part of the journey and were close to our destination. Then the worst thing happened.

The driver lost control and went off the road. The car hit an old woman who was sitting on the side of the highway. The accident happened at the Wahgi Bridge just a few minutes' drive from Minj town. There were about ten of us on the car, six males and four females.

The old woman who was hit by the car was from the area of the accident. The story of the old woman got to me some hours later. Though I was travelling on the car I did not know that the car had hit the woman.

All that I remember is that stones, sticks and axes were swung at us. I did not know what had happened to the other passengers. I jumped off the car and ran into a big kaukau plot. Some men followed me with axes.

Now I realised that my life was in danger. I got out the five kina note that my parents had given me, put it in my mouth and clamped it with my teeth. I plunged into the Wahgi River and started swimming. I was struggling with the rushing current because it had rained heavily the previous night. I put the money in my mouth because I did not want the water to wash it away from my shirt pocket.

I managed to reach the other side of the river. When I looked back the men who had pursued me were searching everywhere among the pitpit thickets to locate me. There was a man and a woman with their dog on the side on which I was standing, but some distance away. The men who had chased me called to them to track me down.

There was a bush track close to where I was standing so I took that and started to run. I was not familiar with the place. I knew I was being followed so I had to run as fast as I could. I was exhausted but I had to push myself to get out of danger.

I finally reached the top of a mountain. I looked down and it was clear to me that no one was following me now. But I did not stop there. I ran from the mountain until I reached the Minj River. I followed the river upstream. It was quite a distance to walk alongside the river before I arrived at Minj town at around two o'clock. I had left home at 10 o'clock that morning.

I saw the town buildings. I could see the high school from town. There were people walking around in town but none of them knew what had happened to me. My five kina note was still with me so I settled down with a packet of chips and a bottle of Coke. But the experience of being chased by the armed men just a while ago did not disappear.

From town I walked slowly to the school. Before reaching the high school the road passed the town hospital. When I was closer to the hospital I saw someone I knew walking out of the hospital gate. She mentioned to me that some people had been in an accident that morning and were admitted to the hospital. I then went in to check.

In one of the wards the driver of the car in which we had been travelling had white bandages all over his body. Two other male passengers who had travelled with us were also in the same condition. They told me what had happened. Armed relatives of the old woman clobbered them with fence posts but they were fortunate to be rescued by a highway police patrol. I thought to myself that it could have been fatal for me.

After visiting the hospital I walked back to the school but without my bag of kaukau and cabbages.

When at school I got the news that the old woman had recovered at the Kudjip Nazarene General Hospital. One of our clansmen, who was a passenger was killed and thrown into the Wahgi River. His body was later washed ashore in a whirlpool downstream in the Gumine District in

Simbu Province.

If I had not escaped the wielding axes of the pursuing men the fish in the Wahgi River could have feasted on me.

I was just another human being but fortunately the axes did not have the mobility and speed to bite and tear on that day.

Father of the Man
Grace Maribu

Dedicated to the memory of all those who perished on MV Rabaul Queen in February 2012

The land, the sea, and the sky are swathed in deep orange. The sun is on its final leg of descent as the boy finds him sitting on the beach - legs crossed, arms folded in front, staring blankly at the masterwork. He sits down quietly next to him.

They stay like this for long moments; watching the spectacle, not speaking.

Eventually.

"I should have gone with her," he whispers. The boy turns to him, then turns back to look over the sea.

"I should never have let go of her hand,"

Silence.

"I think they're dancing and singing now; just there, on the water's edge," the boy pipes up.

"Who?"

"The angels. They are dancing - right there where the sea meets the sky." The boy picks up a small driftwood branch close by and points it at the descending glorious sun.

"Hmmff." He scoffs then falls silent, ignoring the boy.

The child continues, unperturbed by the condescending reaction from his companion. "They like beautiful lights, like sunset light, because their bodies are made only of lights."

They both fall silent, each in their own train of thought.

Minutes go by. Out on the reef's end, the surf is breaking softly, signalling the changing tide. The scorched reef - a good three quarters of a football field - is caught in the kaleidoscopic lights, bringing momentarily to life its corals and rocks and whatever else that is now exposed. The white-sandy beach is bathed pink as it continues unbroken down the south coast of the island. The minutes go by.

He comes to and shakes his head. "I should never have let go of her hand, should not have, never have…..But everything was happening all at once, so very fast."

"Three big ones hit us, one upon another too quickly. Suddenly, we were going down into the water – people, cargo, everything! It was very, very rough. She was saying a prayer as I reached for her hand and still saying the prayer when we jumped," he pauses for breath.

The boy stares at him, daring not to move a muscle, lest he change his mind and stop talking again.

"The rain was pouring down heavily and the wind …. kept on crashing, one huge wave onto another. She was still in my hand as we surfaced, but not for long; another big wave swallowed us, and when we surfaced again, I realised she wasn't with me.

A pause.

"I don't know what happened, why her hand wasn't in mine anymore. I tried to find her but…," he trails off, his voice cracking at the seams but he successfully finds the handle and steadies it.

He shakes his head.

"I couldn't find her. It was just too rough, too much panic and confusion, and the dawn light wasn't good. There were many, many others too; the rescuers just couldn't find them. And they spent days searching."

He falls silent eventually. The boy waits for more, but nothing else issues.

Out over the sea, the perfectly-round luminous sun has dropped onto the horizon, rendering the world the deepest crimson and still and dreamlike. The boy stares, enthralled; even he pauses in his faraway thoughts and pays some attention. They watch as the sun drops past the water line.

"They are very strong. I don't think the wind and rain would have stopped them," the boy says finally, looking up into the sky.

He glances with some confusion at the boy. "Who?"

"The angels. Mum's angel and the angels for all those other people."

"Hmmmf."

"Why do you keep saying that, Daddy?!" The child turns to him with open bafflement and a touch of exasperation, and as their eyes meet, a flash of memory crosses his mind. The man sees himself at home - at another time; a lifetime almost - his head bowed in prayer, his wife and son with him. He looks away across the sea, shamefaced but not really caring either.

"They would have flown straight down and picked them up, then flown up again… to Heaven." The child continues quietly.

A minute goes by.

"I should never have let go of her hand," he whispers again.

The boy turns and stares at him for a while. Then turns and picks up the driftwood again and starts digging the sand beside him. Refusing to look up, he mutters: "That's all you ever say!"

"Uh?!."

"You never say anything but that! Ever since you came back. Just now, you said some things, but I know when we go back to the house, you'll just sit there and whisper that same thing over and over."

The father stares - immobilised, tongue tied.

"You don't piggyback me anymore. Or hold my hand. You don't even call me by my name." The white driftwood now turns into a full earth-drill flying up sand as one thrust becomes more pronounced than the last.

"I know you are very sad because Mummy isn't here. I am too, Daddy." The child's little voice breaks so dangerously he almost loses it, but with visible willpower beyond his years, he steers it back on course. The driftwood drill, however, keeps its onslaught.

"She is gone and it's like you are gone too! I see you but it's like you are not there too! You just sit there …. I am waiting for you to call me but you don't even call me!"

He notices his son sitting there, on the sand next to him, really notices him this time – his little frame, how his small shoulders have drooped, his bowed head, the little right hand clasping and driving the stick – and he realises the last time he looked at his son this way was some six months ago, when he and his wife were farewelling the boy and his grandmother at the Buka wharf before they boarded the ship for Rabaul. He realises the boy sitting next to him looks different from the child he farewelled; this one looks older and weary and very sorrowful. Suddenly, something akin to lightning or an electric shock cuts across the pit of his stomach and he feels a familiar tightening around his throat.

"Why don't you call for me anymore, Daddy?," the driftwood takes its most violent plunge and stops erect like a dead mini tree stump as the first sob escapes from the little body.

He can't take it anymore. The lightning has forked and re-forked by the hundreds inside of him, he feels his stomach filling and heaving with torrents of grief and remorse and sorrow, the flood pushing mightily against his already-constricted throat. His eyes burn with boiling tears.

"Oh, Joshua!"

He lunges for his little boy and crushes him to his chest as the first wave of violent sobs, guttural and from some hidden place beyond his stomach, slams into his body. The sobs come, wave upon tumultuous wave, ferocious and furious and uncontrollable. He lets himself go to the mercy of his storm, allowing it to burst forth, rage forward, to roar freely. On and on the tempest rages, as he clings onto his little boy until, finally, the gale abates and, soaked and exhausted, they settle into a slow-rocking, hugging, sniffling cove.

He looks up at last, wipes his face, then his son's. On the boy's face, he lingers - touching this gently, wiping that softly as he peers into his only child's visage.

"Josh.u.a." He lets the name roll over his tongue, syllable by syllable, so deliberately that he feels another tide of emotion well up and his eyes blur again.

Through his tears, he picks up his son's hand. The palm is purplish and the young skin tender from the violence of the digging. He holds it to the left side of his chest and, still searching the little face, feels his heart rise to his mouth. "I promise never ever to let this one go." The tears drop and he lets them.

Then he turns his son around, sits him on his lap and draws him to his chest. They stare out over the blackening sea.

"Do you think I have my own angel too?" he asks after a while.

"Yes. Mummy said everyone has their own angel. You have yours too."

He looks up into the night sky, lost momentarily in a faraway thought.

"Do you think Mummy is up there?"

"Yes, Daddy."

A pause, but only the smallest one this time.

"Thank you, Joshua."

"For?"

"For giving me your hand."

"What's that mean, Daddy?"

"Someday - when you're older - I'll explain it to you."

Up in the sky, the stars burst forth, in unison and in such multitudes that it seemed someone had just sprinkled the sky with twinkling, sparkling dust for a show. He closes his eyes and inhales the salty sea air deep into his lungs.

"It will be a bright, sunny day tomorrow; a good day," he says.

Then he whispers into his son's ear. "Are you hungry?"

Joshua nods.

"Then, time we went in."

They get up and, without another word Adam hoists his son onto his back and piggybacks him up Kesa Beach toward home as the sea lays quiet and docile beside them.

Third from the Fourth Marriage
Dilu D. Okuk

To listen to advice had always been something that Nema always did with ease and with almost too much enthusiasm sometimes because he saw it as a way of schooling because he only had education up to grade three. But the sermon that was directed at him that morning as he was raking the garden bed was too awful for him to bear.

It had only been his fourth day working for Dr Lapiso, who lived with his family on the university campus. And Nema was quite excited about his new job as the *haus boi* for the doctor because he imagined the many things that he would learn from the doctor and his family through their daily interactions.

Nema had never had a real job before this *haus boi* job. He had worked part-time tree lopping, mixing cement and cleaning roadsides for small contractors. Other than that Nema was a full-time villager. But this, according to the doctor, seemed to be the real deal, 'full-time' he said.

Nema lived in his wife's village as there was no land for him in his father's village because his ten older step brothers from his father's first, second and third marriages had claimed all the land. It was out of the question for him to go to his mother's village because her mother's brothers and uncles disapproved of his father's exploits and would not shoulder his burdens and, besides, they had many sons and there was no land to give.

Nema's father was a *politic man*, as they would say. He was involved heavily in political parties and candidates and their campaigns but Nema felt that he had nothing to show for it. In fact, the only benefits that Nema could acknowledge was the crappy semi-permanent house that he built with the *lep-lep* or left-over politics money that he and his fifth and current wife and their four children lived in and the old Land Cruiser that sat idle outside it that ceased to go only a year after some candidate gave it to him. Nema was not so much angry with his father as he was disappointed at how he led his life.

While in town one weekend looking for a job Nema attended church on

Saturday and he was randomly nominated by the church pastor to be one of seven people who were to give a testimonial before the divine service that Sabbath. The church that Nema attended that weekend happened to be the church that the good doctor attended and as a result of listening to Nema's testimony the doctor made a proposition to Nema. "One hundred kina a fortnight", he said to Nema.

"The Doctor's family are very humble and nice," Liti whispered to Nema as they lay in the darkness of their hut later that following Sunday evening after meeting the Lapisos'

"Yes and I will work hard for them and we must never ask them for anything or take advantage of their generosity, I don't like that, it's a sin," said Nema as he yawned from the hard day's work that he had pushed himself to do that day.

The doctor's house came with a big gardening area and in the first couple of days Nema managed to make six garden plots and plant a whole range of crops that the doctor and his wife wanted. By the fourth day Nema had redesigned the whole flower garden by erecting wooden barriers around the flower beds. That day he thought he would fill them with soil and all kinds of plants.

He had completed constructing the last barriers and was raking the soil that he had filled the garden beds with when from out of the side of his eye he noticed a figure moving up the driveway towards the doctor's house. As he turned his eyes met the lone figure. It was an old man in a cowboy hat in his sixties. Taking no notice of Nema the old man proceeded past the garage heading for the main door.

"Hey! You! Where do you think you're going?" Nema roared. His voice was so loud that the old man jumped with shock and stepped away from the door. Nema moved closer as he spoke and just as he reached the garage the doctor's wife burst out of the front door.

"Nema its okay, he is family, Nema please meet papa, Papa this is nema our *haus boi* and now our security, ha-ha," she laughed. As Nema got closer he caught a clearer view of the intruder's face and was struck by terror and froze as he recognised the old man's face.

The doctor's wife took the old man upstairs and Nema went back to his work baffled and confused. Nema could not understand how his father was involved with this nice family. Maybe it was by some political association he thought.

Nema had slowly gotten his concentration back to work when he heard the sound of footsteps behind him. The steps stopped several feet away and Nema could sense the old man's gaze on him. After a while the old man started to speak.

"Is your mother's name Winito?"

Nema turned his head slowly around as he heard his mother's name and glared at the old man without responding. The he turned around to continue his work. After a long pause the old man spoke again.

"In life there are two kinds of people … there are those that wait for handouts and there are those that go and work for their keep … there are the corrupt … and there are the honest … there are the heathen and there are the God-fearing …" Nema continued to rake the soil as he tried to understand what this 'mad man' was on about. "There are the blessed and the not so blessed and like Cain and like Esau of the Bible, the lazy, corrupt heathens always try to steal the blessings of the blessed. It has happened in history and will continue to repeat itself until the Lord returns." Nema grimaced to himself with disgust.

The horn from the doctor's car at the gate interrupted just as the old man was steaming into a long-winded parable about good and bad fruits. Nema dropped the rake and moved swiftly down to the gate while the old man was in mid-sentence.

After closing the gate Nema walked slowly up the drive. The old man stood holding the doctor's right arm and was saying something to him and his wife in the garage. They all turned and looked in Nema's direction. All of a sudden nema felt an overwhelming sense of embarrassment.

"Your mother is a witch and you have her blood, that's why you are here to kill my son!" yelled the old man. "All my sons that have my blood are successful and are 'big men'," the old man screamed coming out of the garage towards Nema and pointing at him before the doctor and his wife could get hold him back. "You have your mother's blood that's why you are rubbish, well get out! Get out!" Nema stood confused with his arms folded behind him as his head swirled. He could not breathe as his eyes, filled with tears, searched the ground beneath him.

"Do … Doctor ..?" Nema cried, "Doctor, are you my brother?" Nema's voice broke as he asked the question. He couldn't stop the tears from falling. The doctor nodded as he walked towards Nema, "Yes, I am your brother Nema." Nema tugged at his shirt tearing it from his neck, "I didn't come to kill you Doctor; I don't know you or most of my other brothers and sisters." Nema sobbed as he fell to the doctor's feet.

The doctor put his hand on Nema's shoulder and turned toward their father as he spoke, "Nema is the third born from your fourth marriage, had you given him and his mother care like you did with us maybe he could have had a better chance to be someone too. This is my house …, he is my blood … and he will stay."

Watching the silhouette that his only child made playing against the setting sun that evening Nema gripped his wife's hand. She instinctively but curiously turned to him. With tears in his eyes he cleared his throat and spoke without looking at her.

"Liti … we don't have land … we don't have a coffee garden … we don't have money … we don't have education … and we don't even have a 'name' in your village … I am a haus boi … but I want to tell you this that this beautiful child that we have … she must have all of us." Turning to her he continued, "Do you understand? Annabel will not be sharing either of us with someone outside of this marriage."

Liti nodded as her tears fell freely as she cried silently under her husband's words; "That's the best we can give her; it's not much but … she will be better off that way, she will be happier and healthier."

Liti and Nema made a pledge to their child that evening that they would always be together for her.

Burnt
Gelab Piak
A true story

I walked home slowly with kerosene in a plastic bottle in a plastic bag in one hand, retreating home after a hard and very tiring day at the construction site where I worked. I felt tired, thirsty and hot; my shirt was soaking wet with sweat that ran like water down my body making me look like a fool who might have had a shower with his shirt on.

After walking for about thirty minutes under the sun's burning rays going down in the west that made everyone think they were in on an open oven I finally reached my home and was looking forward to a long relaxing night with a few friends.

As I came nearer to the house, a semi-permanent type but mainly bush material, at the foot of a valley, I realized that the house was lonely and deserted. There was no one home. The family's gone out, I thought as I jogged down the dugout stairs of the hill, and then climbed the stairs of the house in one continuous motion. "Where'd they all go", I said to myself under my breath.

The house was built at the foot of a hill and darkness was already creeping in fast. I looked around for our little red lamp and found it. Rushing, I grabbed it and hurried over to the house-cook, built separate from the house about a metre or two away. I was so hungry but I knew there was nothing to eat and I had to cook. I hadn't eaten in the morning when I left for the construction site, and I didn't eat at lunch time and now I was very hungry.

I was used to it but today we had worked hard and so I was weak and worn out and that aggravated my hunger. Also, eating lunch was a luxury I couldn't afford. This town was growing with people and companies rushing into Kiunga as the black gold called oil attracted them. Others were here for the gas, while others for minerals, and in town many shops and business offices opened like hot cupcake stalls every six months or so.

Business was booming. Yet the prices of basic goods in the stores didn't go down. A can of tinned meat costed K6. That was for the smaller ones, the larger ones cost K8-9. The prices were soaring higher and higher and the people struggled more and more to make a living and put food on their dinner tables. Families who had children in higher education institutions were burdened by the high fees they charged. Many in the town blamed the Chinese for running a monopoly of trade stores, and some thought of it as a takeover by communism. It was like a conspiracy that was going round. But the Chinese were only here because they saw the huge business opportunities in the mineral rich town.

The fire was slowly dying. I put down the lamp, and then I put down the plastic bottle of kerosene, which I had just bought and wanted to test. I was told it wasn't the normal type of kerosene usually sold; it was a new one, it was a mixture of 'F' gas, a gas sometimes used in aviation. I moved the lamp closer to the fire, and added a few pieces of split wood to the dying but hungry fire. As the flames grew bigger, light spread into the room. I wanted to use the firelight to see. I opened the tank of the lamp, then turned and got the kerosene bottle, opened its lid and poured it into the lamp. As I was doing so, a small drop spilled onto the fire.

I saw the flames taste it and grow. It was as if they liked it. The flames grew and leapt and in a split second linked with the lamp's tank. It all happened in seconds and I couldn't escape. The tank of the lamp exploded. The left-over kerosene in the plastic bottle also burst into flames. All this happened in seconds, and when the lamp's tank exploded, it threw flames in all directions.

The flames surrounded me as if they were trying to eat me alive. A dreadful feeling of being burnt alive gripped me, I thought of myself being cooked like meat. I ran in frenzy, thinking of only one thing; water. With flames dancing all over me, burning my clothes and eating my flesh I ran for the creek beside my house. The pain was excruciating, and it hurt like millions of bee stings.

I ran straight to the creek and dived into it. The creek, by God's grace, had been flooded on this fateful day. As I jumped into the water, the pain grew from just painful to unbearable, such a cruel pain. At this point I was screaming for help because I couldn't bear the pain anymore.

Suddenly, I felt a hand grab me and pull me up. I turned and saw that it was Rodney, my nephew who visits us regularly. Then another pair of hands gripped me, I didn't bother to look because I knew they were helping hands. The pain was unimaginable as the water forced the pain to burn me up, completing the job of the fire. I shut my eyes but that didn't shut out the pain.

I was then carried by the group of three strong, helpful and organised boys to the roadside, from where I was then rushed in a truck to the hospital where I was admitted to the intensive care unit. I had burns all over my body; hands, chest, parts of my stomach and my thighs down to my knees and also my neck and face regions. I was pretty messed up.

It has been two months since I was admitted to the hospital unit. When I come to think of it I was lucky that the creek was flooded, and Rodney and his two friends came along to visit us that day. Otherwise I doubt that I would have lived and I cannot imagine what it would be like. Tomorrow will be a beautiful day for me, because I will leave this hospital a whole new, repaired man. Healed by, not only medicine, but love and care given by the nurses that took care of me.

Yet every time I sit and look at every scar, as I have done in the last few weeks, I recall and remember every bit of that terrible day; a day I would never want to re-live, a day when life was breathed into fire and I was swallowed into its jaws. The scars hide a secret now, a story filled with pain that reigned with absolute terror, and shameless weeping; during which my body cried tears of blood for several days - a pain that was much closer to me than even my wife.

Dancing in a Redskin's Arawa
Leonard Fong Roka

Ami'au listened attentively to the sound of crushing dried leaves and twigs littering the forest floor. Is this another silly wild dog wandering about she wondered?

'Bekenenu, is it you there?' she called out to her husband who she had just left further uphill inspecting their cocoa plot.

No answer came so she ignored the strange sound that was now gone and lowered her body into the hole she had dug tracking the huge yam tuber.

Now, a heavy foot was approaching her, crushing the dried leaves of the galip-nut and cocoa trees that hosted her yam. She ignored it. But exhausted with strained back, she dragged her head carefully out and spotted through her armpit not a black foot but rather, a muscular red-skinned foot of a New Guinean about to attack her. A rapist!

'Oiiiiii, Bekenenu! Bekene…nu, ere'rengkong mosika*,' she screamed hysterically for survival.

They rolled holding onto each other downhill under the consoling shade of the cocoa trees. Ami'au's muscular body was determined to liberate her from her New Guinean rapist who was struggling to strip her.

As they hit a rotting bole she removed the infiltrators sweat ridden palms and yodelled: 'Help! Someone help!'

'Where are you?' Bekenenu called.

'Here!'

To Ami'au's relief, the Redskin darted off as the sound of running feet crushing dried out cocoa leaves littering the ground drew nearer and Bekenenu swiftly approached the scene angrily and ready to attack.

'Did the infiltrator of Solomon touch you?'

'No,' Ami'au sobbed in shock.

Bekenenu tracked the foreigner with his bush knife down Kirokai Creek but withdrew early in fear of been killed by the Redskin strangers in the land.

'Did you see or talk sense to the Redskins?' old Taruko asked, with sympathy as Bekenenu returned with sweat freely rolling down his balding face.

'Ee, send me not into the red ants' camp for I shall return to Doko'toro as a firefly, uncle,' Bekenenu sniffed brusquely as he sat on the mat of dried leaves.

Taruko eyed the couple thoughtfully. With the sun burning above their heads, their anger and self-pity was like magnesium burning in the night sky.

The Redskins' town below was booming with heavy traffic. Taruko's aged eyes were locked on the great Arawa General Hospital. Slowly, his blinking eyes left the hospital and crept up Siopa Place and then settled at his feet.

'This was our land when I was a child,' he said, wiping off tears, 'but today it is the Redskins' land, not yours.' The couple listened like children adsorbing every bit of parental advice. The grey haired prudent one sneezed and continued, ' When their government muddled us and impertinently began the Panguna mine, planes and ships brought them day by day into our land. Here they make the money to build their country that is so far away across the sea.'

'Really true,' Ami'au spoke after a long silence, 'all schools in this town belong not to us, all is for these foreign rapists, looters and terrorist of Bougainvillean harmony. At Toniva, Kieta, down here, at Loloho and Panguna, it is they who roam with absolute freedom and we are the dogs having our tails glued to our bellies.'

'That's why I often say don't be a lone bird in the tree for a sick dog to harm you. This race of people is parlous to our Solomon ways,' Taruko said, and skinned an areca nut to ease his mind. 'You are children, I saw that fading sun before you; as this town was developing the Whiteman feared not the Bougainvillean but rather was afraid of the Redskin that raved in the night like the bats.'

The trio climbed—a troop of defeated warriors—up the Sirovii brae for the ridge so infested with swaying orange trees. Like those fruit trees, fear was snarling and scurrying in the air that they breathed into their lungs. Bougainville was not theirs.

Taruko spat reddish betel nut phlegm into the bush with a sigh and calmly called out to the couple, 'As long as the New Guinean is on your

land, there will be fear and tears.'
   Red skinned dog

Dominoes of Love
Peter Sevara

The drunk's eyes are molten red as he sets out to grab innocent females in the evening dimness. The female's yelps of fear are drowned by the loud music blaring from the taxis parked leisurely at the bus-stop.

The cop-shop is all but empty and deserted. It's Fortnight Friday at Boroko bus-stop at its peak hour. Hova is among a handful of late passengers heading for Waigani. She checks her phone. *Why isn't he answering my text messages? Darl I need you.* Fear creeps up her spine. She logs into facebook: *dayumm…stranded @ bko bustop 4 2 hrs nau!* Log in time: 5:30pm.

The sun glares down at Ela Beach. Haivavu is sweltering in the 38 degree heat; He brushes off the droplets of sweat on his "goaty" and tucks back his sharp jaw in a yawn. His brown deep eyes scan the sea for some peace of mind. His tall lanky frame steaming under the heat!

The beach is mostly filled with teenage love-birds, street vendors, and a handful of public servants boozing away. He walks towards the Okari trees lining the beach. He is playing patience because Hova is late - again.

Hova wipes her broad sweaty brows as she waits with her cousin-sister, Uaopou at Boroko bus-stop. The buses are all full. Her dimples show because she knows that Haivavu is already tired of waiting. Her full lips sucked in. It's been two hours now and she still hasn't got a chance to get on a bus. She looks around at the raskols sneering for an opportunity, pushing amongst the passengers to fish out a phone or wallet. She shivers. No! She would rather wait for an empty bus. She turns to Uaopou.

"Sorry for keeping you with me tita."

"Nah it's okay, you just worry about your bf ok?" She offers kindly.

She gives her a weak smile and logs into facebook: *oi osem wanem? PMV short ah? Kasssttt!!* Log in time: 2:00pm.

Haivavu tires of waiting. Two hours is too much to wait. He ignores her messages and leaves town. An hour later as the bus rolls into Tokarara Service station, Haivavu checks his phone and sees a new message. It's from Hova.

"Wer r u? m @ town alredi. Walkn 2 ela beach nau. Wer r u?"

'Ye lon taim yu stap lo wer? Wari blo yu.' He ignores the text and sets the alert to silent. Its 3:30 pm.

He gets off for the main market. As he walks toward the market he senses eyes on his back. He turns around and hears Hirisi calling his name as she crosses the road.

"Hi sexy?" she drawls.

Haivavu can tell from her watery eyes that she had a little too much.

"Upla drin ah? tokaut tokstret! Haha!" he asks smiling, taking her hand into his.

"Darl I'm sure you wouldn't be bothered. And of course…I kinda get hot when I'm oiled up ya know!" She laughs a deep throated laugh.

He feels his face get warm and manages a feeble laugh through clenched teeth. He checks his phone to avoid her directness. Nineteen missed calls, seven messages and five voice messages! Hova is at Boroko. What the fuck? I thought she's already at her house! A look of concern crosses his face.

"Who's 'at darl? Hirisi, easily picking up his worried look.

"Ol hauslain yah" he lies. Damn! All this time I thought she was already at her house. He changes the phone alert to vibrate. Its 5:00PM.

Hova rushes at an empty bus nine. Her heart sinks as she hears the dull thudding of the seats in the isle. She sighs and trudges back avoiding those threatening eyes. She posts on Facebook: *"waitin 4 bus @ Bko. Its getin 18 n scary wit al dis drunkards walkin and swearin."* Log in time: 5:30pm.

Haivavu is in a dilemma. How can he slip off to save Hova without offending Hirisi? He has to make a choice. One move in any direction causes a chain reaction, displaying a certain picture or message at the end, depending on where and how you start it. Like a game of dominoes. But this is no game. No! This is for love! So what would be his move now? Devour Hirisi while she's ripe and keep Hova dangling? After all Hova kept him waiting so why should he be such a wimp to respond so quickly to her wants? And if he runs off now, what are the chances of having Hirisi so wanting like now? Waste her in the back of the rusty old Nissan Vannette, and while she's soaking in sensual bliss, he should be in a cab racing along Waigani drive for Hova, and yes of course…with a clear conscience. Hitting two birds with one stone, at the right spot, at the right time…with just one move…He smiles. Hirisi coils her moist fingers around his thumb and jerks sexually, provoking a flare of emotions. He ushers her into the shadows. It is 5:40pm.

Hova is accosted by a pickpocket. She sidles close to an unknown but kind looking man. The pickpocket falls back but keeps an eye. As they struggle for the bus, the man noticing her predicament offers to help. The pickpocket moves in, tentatively at first then quickly as the struggling gets rough. Hova struggles but keeps a side eye on the pickpocket. As she moves in, the pickpocket bumps roughly against her and she pulls out of the struggle. She looks up at the man who tried to help her. A look of concern pervades his face. Her heart sinks. Where is my Haivavu? The pickpocket curses and falls back into the crowd. She logs into facebook: *folowd by a drunk a**hole. Haivavu wer r u?* Log in time: 5:50pm.

Haivavu's sense of responsibility kicks in - fast! He races to his house and without much of an excuse, makes off with his mother's purse, hailing a cab on the way. It is 5.55pm.

Hova's attempt to seek refuge in the nearby kai-bar is futile. The guards bar her from entering. On the Asian shop-owners command they toss her outside. Hopelessness fills her being.

Oa--eh! Lou--eh!
Orova karu aeve ve otivoa eh?
Oa--eh! Lou--eh!
Orova eukoro haikakare!
Oaa--eh! Lou--eh!
Meaforoe! Ororo o moiti! Oh-haieh!
Oa--eh! Lou--eh!

Fath--er? Moth--er?
I am in someone else's land?
Fath--er? Moth--er?
I love you both!
Fath--er? Moth--er?
Please tell me? Oh-haieh!
Fath--er? Moth--er?

She is immediately pulled by the hair. The attacker rots like hell and has a greasy iron grip. She struggles with him. Another powerful figure joins the attempt. The public seem ignorant.

Lou—eh!
Ereva orove toruipi karu
Lou-eh!
Orove opoumorovira, oaura, kakeura
Lou-eh!
Iofeare mai voa eva ororo moferae mai leitepea?
Lou-eh!
Orova naria kaiae ro loi?
Lou-eh!
Ereva orove mea kakapusu ioveitipea eh?

Mother?
These are my countrymen!
Mother?
These are my brothers, father and uncles.
Mother?
Why are they doing this to me?
Mother?
What wrong have I done to deserve this?
Mother?
Can't they see how helpless I am?

She looks at the road expecting someone...something…Oh darling where are you? Hands claw her brown skin. Search under her jewelled pockets. Scrap her sea of hair. She searches for hope.

Haivavu? Haivavu?
Iofeare mai kofa voa
Ava araro okofa moi-ti kau
Ai ovira ava araro hai-arara

Haivavu? Haivavu?

Tell me the reason why
   That you haven't been honest to me
This must mean that you don't need me anymore

She searches between the groping foreign and black hands for help. Her screams echoes off the nearby padlocked gates and tall *kapa* fences. An empty bus arrives. She attempts an escape but a boot hammers her back onto the pavement. The other passengers rush without restrictions. It is 5:58pm.

Aita eva povi ofare-kau ou iyove re?
Eto eve ofare kofa voa leitepea!
Orove hairi hai foroe aia fiopua!
Aeata ororo lei napesi leitepea!
Usoso arava karu aea feare?
Iofeare lei eva ororo kou toa epea?
Arava heafo oaharo kofa aeata haiafarapai
Arava sesevitepera-soa usoso kakou!
Eve povi ofare haria ou iovetepea
Eva mea-mariti kakou eh?

So you'll just stand there and just watch?
It's happening right in front of your eyes!
My heart is crying!
They are swearing and rubbishing me!
Am I not one of you?
Why do you turn you back on me?
I am really struggling here
I find it hard to believe
That you would stand there and look
Have you no shame?

She passes out momentarily and comes back. Her eyes drain white. Her head spins. Her hands grab the air for support as her hair is tugged at its roots. Hot tears sting her eyes. And roll down her tensed cheeks. She grabs something small - but hard. This time her energy drains into a clenched, bulging fist…It is 6:00pm.

The Bamboo Master
Bernard Sinai

"I can feel it." Kon seemed to squeal and hiss at the same time. "Em stap klostu stret," he said, breathing heavily as the bamboo in his hand shook and seemed to miraculously turn toward the East. "We shall find it soon," he continued as he started walking. Behind him a group of heavily armed men followed closely.

Thirty young warriors stood behind Kon, slowly digesting every vile word vomited from his mouth. They had marked themselves for battle with paint, armed themselves with machetes and axes, and looked furious and fearless like their ancestors who had fought off enemies to protect their family and lands. But this time they were hunting for a predator far more dangerous – they were battling an unseen enemy.

"It's close!" he hissed through his teeth as he started to up his pace. He started running and the bamboo compass he had in his possession started to shake violently. The warriors kept his pace, eager to do battle and vanquish this evil that had somehow come upon them.

It had started a month ago. The illness, the deaths and all the suffering seemed to sprout out of the ground. First, old Doe Ti fell ill and died. Then his daughters – all three of them and finally his wife succumbed to the same illness. They died a week apart from each other. However, it did not stop there.

A fortnight after Doe's wife met the Grim Ripper, their neighbor Hap Sens fell ill. Somehow death was not satisfied and wanted more. Fear started to grow in the small village of Krankitingting.

The people, being a superstitious lot started blaming evil spirits and a curse. As a measure to appease the people and end the fears, the village chief, Idi Ot, decided to hire Kon Mantu, a local witch hunter. This would eventually lead to where they were now.

Kon ran across the small creek and headed right up the hill. "It's up here!" he shouted, beckoning the warriors to follow. They all rushed up the hill and surrounded the hamlet. Inside smoke was coming out and they could hear singing. "It's inside," he said as he moved aside, making way for them to do their business.

He turned and walked away from the hamlet. He would let the warriors come to do what they had to do. He had done his part. He walked toward the chief who was standing behind the army of men. "I have done my part, now it's your turn."

"Are you sure?" The chief asked hesitantly.

"Yes!" Kon retorted. "I'm absolutely sure. The bamboo never lies."

"Okay then, we must get rid this evil before it consumes us all," the chief said and motioned the men to take up positions.

Kon turned away from the chief and started walking toward his house. Behind him he could hear the men slowly surrounding the hamlet in strategic locations. He knew what would happen – he chuckled under his breath – and an evil smirk formed on his lips.

He had everything he wanted. Power, prestige and now he would own the land of poor old Vikki Tim who lived on the hill. It would be part his payment for the service he provided.

He smiled, thinking how easy it was to convince the people that she had been the cause of their suffering. They were like puppets attached to his magical bamboo and no one dared to question the 'bamboo master', the master magician – the master of illusion.

Suddenly, he heard a female voice screaming and begging for mercy. Then, everything went silent, and soon thick smoke rose from the hill behind him.

He started whistling and continued his way home.

The Dilemma
Bernard Sinai

Simon took another deep breath and scratched his head. This was his first time ever to be in such a situation – such a dilemma. What should he say? What should he do? These questions pounded in his head like a preacher screaming, raising his voice for God to hear. The questions seemed to be amplified by the tight space of his small office.

His office was approximately a 3 by 3 metre box. It had a cheap 'L' shaped desk that faced the doorway. On it was a new HP computer that the department had recently purchased from Daltron.

He mainly used it for typing his reports and emailing. Although most of his emails were not office related it was an important part of his routine. On the other side of his beloved desk was Mr James Le, an expatriate businessman trying to buy some land in the city – and the cause of his dilemma.

Le pushed a plump brown envelope over to him, gave him a 'let's be friends' smile and said, "I'm sure all the paper work is in order."

He took another look at the papers and frowned. The land title that Le had applied for was already under someone else's name. How was he going to handle this? He thought of telling the man off, that the land was not for sale but he decided against it. Subtlety was the way to handle clients. Rrr! Rrr! Rrr! His chain of thoughts was suddenly interrupted by the vibration of his mobile phone.

The caller ID showed his wife's name. His wife never called unless it was an emergency. "Excuse me, sir. I have to take this. It will only be a moment," he said as he held the phone to his left ear. "Hello."

His wife sounded distraught. "Timmy has been suspended from school…," she managed between sobs, "because of his school fees."

His first born son Timothy, or as everyone called him, Timmy, was 9 years old and the apple of his eye. There was nothing he wouldn't do for his son; like the time when Timmy was 4 and had developed a rather mild case of the flu. He rushed the boy to the emergency ward and began demanding ER doctors to take a look at his son. He even went to the extent of threatening them.

He took a deep sigh, pressure started to build up in his chest and he found it hard to breath. He loosened his tie and took a drink from a bottle of Nature's Own he had bought that morning. "Don't worry dear, I'll take care of it", he lied as he hung up.

The truth was that he barely had enough money to buy food for the house. He had debts, bills, rent and so many other expenses that his government salary would not last a week let alone pay his son's school fees. His family made it through each fortnight thanks to his wife selling *buai* beside the house gate. However, due to the tense political situation in the city, she opted to stop until things cleared out. Now, he was their only source of income.

"Are you alright?" Le asked, sounding concerned. He had been watching, studying Simon like a hawk, waiting for the opportune moment to strike. It had arrived.

"Listen, I can see you are troubled. Is it financial? Maybe I can help?" Le blurted without waiting for an answer. He knew he had to strike while the iron was hot.

"Inside this envelope is K10, 000," he said pushing the brown package closer to Simon. "This will solve your financial worries," he said as a matter of half-fact. "It's a gift, a token of my appreciation for what you are going to do for me."

Simon's mind was in turmoil. He knew it was wrong. He could not take money. He thought of the money and the implications, and the complications it would have on his job, his family, his life. He could even get fired if someone knew…but he could also accomplish a lot with that amount of money.

He could pay little Timmy's school fees right up till college, he could even buy a car or make down payment for a house. His meagre government salary was always stretched with bills, fees and other pressing concerns. This was his chance to get ahead of the game.

He peered around his small office as if someone was watching as he slowly placed his right hand on the envelope and moved it to the edge of his desk, right into the open drawer. His immediate needs had been taken care of – now to return the favour.

"No worries," he said as he reached out his right hand to Le, "come tomorrow. I should have the paperwork sorted by then."

Le smiled like an old friend as he firmly grasped Simon's hand, "I'll see you tomorrow."

The Fan
C. V. Vada

The ceiling fan hung dangerously low, wheezing and choking on the thick wet period 8 air. Exposed wires in its mounting device made it look as if it had succumbed to the merciless tropical heat. On the blackboard, quadratic equations rolled out from the red piece of chalk in Mr Kavivi's hand like mishandled sausages at a drunken Christmas barbeque.

Normally, algebra would have added insult to injurious weather like this, but today was the third Wednesday of the State of Origin series, and no amount of required maths curriculum could curb the excitement of the class. Of course no one was more excited than Mr Kavivi himself who, much to the annoyance of his students had been using red chalk since Origin 1 as a mark of loyalty to his team (none of the multi-coloured chalk boxes he bought contained a maroon chalk so he decided to go with the closest shade of red he could find).

Max anxiously pressed a random button on his mobile phone to see the time. It was 15:30 PM. He looked over to Jerry with both hands spread out, indicating to his desk-mate that only 10 minutes remained until the study period bell would force Mr Kavivi out of their classroom and – as this was a government fortnight –probably out of the school altogether and into the nearest pub with a flat screen.

Just then, Max felt his phone vibrate as it received a text message from the Class Captain. He opened up the message; it read: 'K5 / Thurston / 1st TRY. Na upla?'

'Ah..em lonlon ah? K5 em bigpla tumas' remarked Jerry, who had also received the same message on his phone.

That remaining 10 minutes stretched on for ages. When the siren finally did sound Mr Kavivi responded hypnotically, quietly packing with a hazy, frozen smile on his face that reminded Max of an illustration of little mice from the Pied Piper storybook he had read as a child.

"Oh, my goodness me, I almost forgot,' chimed the educator whilst walking backwards toward the door to let himself out, 'for homework: do exercises from Chapter 11.2 and Chapter 11.3."

Loud sighs of horror masked inaudible multilingual grumbles. The frozen smile thawed out into a grin from ear to ear.

'Aiyo, Mr K. yu laik murderim ol man ah?' plead the Class Captain. After a quick glance through the textbook – he was one of the few to truly appreciate the magnitude of the assignment.

'Relax kids! I'm just pulling your legs! Oh children of Papua New Guinea, what kind of man would I be if I gave you homework on the day of the big game?! Especially if it's Daren Lockyer's last game?!'

Loud cheers of joy were echoed by collective sighs of relief.

'But,' he continued, 'but, if Maroons lose tonight... you have a topic test tomorrow!' The class erupted in earnest laughter at their predicament. 'After all, what kind of teacher would I be if I didn't push my students?'

'Ol lain o, noken wari - em nogat samtin. Maroons ba dustim Blues wan said-ya!' remarked Max.

'Yess-yah! Na why ba nogat?' And with that forced enunciation of what he understood to be the current slang phrase, Mr Kavivi dismissed himself with a military-style salute – and dashed out the door. The class exercised restraint for the entire 30 seconds it took their maths teacher to strut down the steel stairs, flounce along the footpath and leap across the loose-gravel quadrangle.

'Okay boys and girls, I think you all know what time it is,' the Class Captain said, 'I declare the bet shop open – '

Before another word was uttered, Jerry stood up on his feet and declared, 'Minichello!' before proceeding to stick up posters of the two teams on the blackboard.

The class of 47 with the exception of about 14 students who did not take part (by virtue of being either virtuous, broke or absent), spent the rest of the study period placing their K5 bets for the first try, with a few of them placing bets jointly. Max recorded all the information on a sheet of paper, which was then sighted by everyone and signed by the Class Captain. At the final siren, the students hurriedly made their way home.

That night Jerry walked down along the deserted street over to Max's house to watch the game. In a similar fashion during the previous games, their neighbourhood had split itself into two and each respective group had huddled itself around the biggest television set available, a safe distance away from one another. As tempting as it was to participate in the revelry, Jerry preferred to watch the final game quietly at Max's house.

Over his and Max's years of friendship, they had established their own 'Origin' tradition. Every year the pair would watch the third game from either of their houses. This year it was Max's turn to play host.

'Goodnight family!' said Jerry as he let himself through the door and into Max's living room. Max's mother and sisters (twins Vavine and Viola) greeted their visitor with a bowl full of betel nut and mustard. Jerry said thank you and grabbed a handful. He looked at the couch and noticed Max sitting alone in front of the television. 'Na Papz ol?'

'Papz and Tau are watching the game at Uncle Max's place' replied his friend, 'they're about to play the national anthem – you're just in time, bro! ' Jerry sat next to Max on the couch grinning, and as they had done each year since they were old enough to speak, both boys started singing along to 'Advance Australia Fair', making up the words as they went along.

Max's mother rolled her eyes and shouted, 'nogat sem blo yupla – em wanem? 'Greatest hits' blon tumbuna blo yupla, ah?!' The twins giggled.

As the Maroons kicked off, Viola set dinner (pizza and hot chips) on the coffee table. Jerry's eyes widened with happiness. It didn't get any better than this – watching rugby while eating junk food; now if only the Blues would rise to the occasion. His smug contentment lasted 16 minutes into the game, when Greg Inglis scored the first try, dashing any hopes of collecting the cash winnings in class the next day. To add insult to injury, Max, his mother and the Maroons faction gathered two houses away exploded in applause, jumping and screaming like they were in the grand stand of Suncorp Stadium. When they had calmed down, Jerry was quick to ask, 'Husait putim K5 lo Inglis?'

'Angela,' replied Max looking at the sheet of paper he had used to record the betting information.

'Angie? Ah, em sista ya... tumoro mi ba go grisim em lo baim lunch blo mi.'

The Maroons then continued to dominate the first half of the game scoring three more times, each successive try making Jerry more miserable and seeking comfort in an extra slice of Hawaiian pizza, while Max in contrast became more animated with excitement and left his share of Meat Lover's largely untouched. Then, in a display of athleticism similar to that which had won them the second game of the series, the Blues scored two tries in 5 minutes, bringing the score to 24-10 at the 40-minute whistle.

Jerry shot to his feet and started dancing like a Rastafarian. The twins cheered him on. Max cleared his throat and reminded them what the score line was. 'Let's not get too carried away... you guys are three tries behind,'

During the half time, Max sent his sisters to buy betel nut and mustard supplies which were now running low. 'Girls baim wanpla Spear blo mi tu,' demanded Max's mother as the twins made their way out of the house. When they returned, the second half of the game was underway. Max asked them why they had taken such a long time and Vavine pointed out that the market had been very busy.

'Undasten, ol man wachim game tu kisim haf taim blon ol,' remarked Jerry.

'Em nau, way blo em,' added Max's mother, puffing on her fresh stick of tobacco.

In the second half of the game the Maroons scored two tries. With a little less than 8 minutes of play left, when the Blues did score again but Jerry had conceded defeat, Max stood in front of the T.V where he proceeded to imitate the Rastafarian dance that Jerry had performed earlier and his mother and sisters were in stitches. Max carried on like this for a while and Jerry started to get annoyed. He picked up the wooden bowl and began pelting Max with the betel nut and mustard it contained. This only encouraged Max and when the betel nut and mustard ran out, Jerry threw the bowl.

He missed Max and got the TV instead, which slipped off the wall unit and smashed on to the ceramic tiled floor. Max switched it off quickly and looked up at Jerry with his mouth agape. Not knowing what to say or do, Jerry bolted for the door and disappeared into the night, leaving max and his family to pick up the pieces of their father and husband's beloved TV.

At school the next day an awkward silence gripped the two desk-mates. During the double period of English, Max made one attempt to speak to Jerry, but the latter didn't utter a single word.

Afterwards at the chemistry lab, Jerry avoided speaking altogether, even when Max politely asked to use his bottle of potassium permanganate, all he did was nod mechanically while staring sternly like lunatic at the Bunsen Burner in front of him.

When recess was over, Mr Kavivi, in spite of the intense heat and humidity, showed up in the classroom wearing a red long-sleeved dress shirt with a matching silk neck tie. As he entered the room he switched on the ceiling fan which clicked and hissed. 'Well class, my team has spared you a topic test today, so you should all stand up and give the Maroons a big round of app-' and before he could finish his sentence, the ceiling fan started to screech loudly, shaking from side to side.

Students shrieked in horror as the screeching got louder and louder and the entire fan completely fell of its mounting device and hung by its wires. Mr Kavivi ran toward the switch to turn it off but it was too late. The weight and momentum of the fan pulled the wires down causing the edge of the ceiling's old masonite sheets to crack. The fan came plunging down, blades still in motion and were just about to crash on top of Max when Jerry suddenly leaned forward to cover him. The fan blades hit Jerry in the head and knocked him out cold.

When Jerry woke up he found himself in the emergency room of a private hospital, surrounded by four fuzzy, familiar faces belonging to Mr Kavivi, the Class Captain, Max and Max's father Dr Loi. 'What happened?'

'You were in an accident,' answered Mr Kavivi, 'but you're okay now. You just need to rest until you feel better.'

Suddenly remembering what happened, Jerry sat upright and looked straight at Dr Loi, 'I'm sorry Dr- I didn't mean to smash your TV. It was an accident.'

'Son, it's okay. I couldn't hold anything against you after what you did today. You are very brave. Stupid, but brave. You suffered a nasty head injury and if Mr Kavivi hadn't switched off the fan when he did, it could have been much worse.'

'That's right, you could have been hit in the head and had your brain fried as well,' jabbed Max. To this they all laughed. Jerry felt relieved that the tension between them had dissolved.

After the two men had left, the Class Captain handed over an envelope to Jerry. 'Em wanem?'

'It's the money from the bets. After you were... evacuated, we had a meeting and the class thought you should have this, olsem lon givim liklik halivim lo said blo baim marasin na disla kain,'

Jerry then enquired about Angie and the Class Captain advised that the gesture had been her idea before wishing him a speedy recovery and heading home. 'Max, you have this.'

'No!' Max refused to take the envelope. Jerry persisted in trying to convince him, saying that he could use the money to buy a new TV, to which Max laughed, pointing out that TVs were quite expensive. 'Besides, Papz tok pinis ya – nogat samtin,'

'Well I guess there's only one thing left to do with this money then.'

'What?'

'I'll just have to buy a new fan for the classroom.'

"Norah Jones"
Nou Vada

For Sharon. Not exactly the story of us but still, I'll miss you, girl. With Love from Papua New Guinea

"Don't Know Why," was playing on my mobile's music player that day. Out of the mobile's modest speaker came out the song, in a modest volume, but as I remember it seemed so rich and occupying like the ocean. The tired and dirty Forum Square was now empty and the evening was gently setting in. It was truly peaceful. I was waiting for Rosemary. We decided we would spend every afternoon together, as confused lovers and sure friends, as free spirits. Maybe it was the season, maybe it was the economics and the politics, maybe it was that everyone finally grew up in third year of university, maybe it was that I finally grew up in my third year of university, but I was comfortable being seen in public with a girl I liked. She was beautiful; one of those neutral beauties that wasn't beautiful in the eye of one beholder and not so in the eye of another. She was pretty. She was plain. She was a neutral beauty.

We had made this peculiar pact one night up at Lover's Lane where we kissed for a minute. I remember we had gone down to the trade-store down at the Security Depot known simply as Sigi-base, before walking into the darkness of Lover's Lane, to get a couple of packets of gum. We were chewing the gum and joking about outside Sigi-base, and it was one of those moments where you laugh too hard than the joke warrants, and the howling laughter is followed by silence, and the silence is so unacceptable that the things kept in your conscious mind's back alleys and gutters leaps out of your mouth. "Let's go up there…" I said it out. The impulse won the night. "Ok," she said. Then and there I may have figured out she was my soul mate. An impulse response to an impulse question isn't the most scientific way of finding your soul mate, but then again there is no science of soul mates as far as I know.

We half-giggled up to a secluded spot in the dark. Lover's Lane, I thought…where many a baby was conceived. I half-giggled a bit louder at that thought, but also because I was nervous at what the possibilities of our visit to UPNG's most notorious stretch of lawn could turn out to be. We sat down on the grass and did just that for a while; sit. "I've never seen UPNG from up here – I mean like at night," she said. "I'm cold," she added. "Should we like get out from here or something," I said out of some strange feeling in my chest. I couldn't quite get my head around what this strange feeling was as I spoke, "I mean if you're not comfortable with stuff..." she quickly interrupted my minced up words, "No, no it's quite alright." And without speaking she moved closer to me. We kissed; the taste of spearmint bubble-gum on her lips. I realised what the strange feeling was. I was extremely nervous, but my heart was so calm; it wasn't beating and booming; it wasn't racing; proof perhaps of my theory about science and soul mates.

The pact we made was that every afternoon we'd sit together at Forum Square and watch the night set in, listening to Norah Jones on our mp3 players. What a beautiful song "Don't know why" is to listen to as Waigani Campus, ever desolate and ever vibrant, winds down to dusk.

We'd just sit there on any random day, holding hands, away from the cacophony of the mess line and the low and high hums from beyond the savannah plains of Morata's dirty mountains. One afternoon she told me a story. It was an interesting story that I now, for some reason, cannot remember. But at the end of the story she lead in a question, "If you did not make it back to uni, would you wait for me? Tell me boy, would you wait for me?" I smiled calmly, trying to conceal an uneasiness in me. "I would. I want you to know that I would," I told her. I remember the sun that day as it went down on Waigani. I remember how it was bright and glaring but not hot; her face in my view and the sun behind her. Her face in an overcast revealed her beauty, her brown eyes and accented lashes and her nose and her tight lips. Her hair was black and lazily bunned and streaks of the last-light shined through rogue strands unconformed to the order. "You're beautiful," I told her. She smiled and smiled into a blush. I wanted to ask her the same question. Besides the need to know, it is Papua New Guinean dating custom to ask a reciprocal question. Maybe it was because I felt like what we had was more than dating and I didn't want what I thought was a meaningful conversation to be drowned out by another sumatin courtship cliché. So I didn't ask her. I didn't ask her if she'd do the same for me. She would've given a clichéd answer to the question anyway.

We both didn't like public scrutiny from our peers into our personal lives. But our hook-up was respected by the UPNG crowd. We were like old souls. We were both just 21. Her friends were nice to me. My rabid group of mates were nice to her as well. People didn't give us second looks when we were in public places together. Maybe we had both, through our own lives on campus before we met, defeated the cynicism of the UPNG social critics and commentators.

The first time I took her up to my room to spend the night with me, the security guard posted to my dorm was so gracious to us, and let her in with me without objection, telling us that he wouldn't give others the privilege. I remember his actual words clearly enough. He said something like, "Mi no save, uncles – but yu tupla gat wanpla *gravity* lo frensip blo yupla". There is a peculiar way about how things are described by people at UPNG; a rarefied form of linguistic recklessness. If I, back then, read this now I'd probably say *"Wai bai nogat?"*

I get random memories so vivid of those nights I would take her to my room; but not about the romances. For some reason the obvious memories of sex feel like anecdotes; the things that linger on are visual residues of moments of deep thought and contemplation triggered by that physical proximity we both shared in those nights; memories etched in my mind that anchored strange epiphanies and anti-epiphanies; moments I miss. The most vivid one is of staring at a mosquito coil glow in the darkness of the room, with its familiar aroma, being invisibly twirled by the ceiling fan on the highest speed possible. It was about 3 am in the morning. She was already asleep, and for some reason I myself couldn't; so I just stared at the ember glow of the coil. There was something so mysterious and beautiful about it. I found the words of a prayer unfurling gently. And so I prayed to God. I had never prayed that sincerely in my life and have never since. It wasn't really a thanksgiving prayer, but was more a plea for direction. I was the most humanly happy as I could ever be, lying in bed with her, but I realised lying right there then and I believe it still now, that contrary to popular belief, the happiest times in a man's life is the time when he needs direction the most. It was heavy life philosophy for someone who was just a year or two out of his teens, but it makes perfect sense to me, even today. I prayed for the good part of three minutes, the longest I've prayed. I said 'Amen' and felt a sense of easiness and an equally potent feeling of sleepiness come over me. And as I drifted into sleep, the embers fading from sight of heavy eyes, I felt her snuggle against me. I felt the warmth of her skin, a strong feeling of happiness came over me.

She never came back to do her final year. We wondered often in confused courting dialogue whether the politics and economics of Papua New Guinea could get in the way of our love. And we'd always summarily dismiss the thought. Her parents couldn't afford tuition, and so she went to work at a law firm as a secretary. I came back and finished my degree. It was a sad year. Me without her and she without me.

Today I sit down at Forum Square again, where we used to sit. I am doing my second degree, a law degree, and I see young lovers passing by me, all happy and warm and I think about those confused dialogues about Politics and Economics. I think about the Namorong essay about the political economy of 'Everything that's wrong with PNG'. I'd like to be bitter and disillusioned about it all. I'd blame the economics and the politics and the status quo for her not being able to come back to uni and me somehow coming back. Today I know it would be a fruitless exercise in bitterness. The truth is, after the sadness, after her sadness and mine, we both moved on. That is the only real epiphany in the developing world. We get cheated and we move on, and make do with what we're left with. You can only hate the system so much, afterwards you learn to work with it; a warped form of the Stockholm Syndrome.

But after all is said and done with my story, I still listen to "Don't Know Why" on random afternoons just sitting at the Forum Square. I don't know why.

Happily Ever After
Alma Warokra

This story was inspired by and is dedicated to all the victims and those lives that were touched by the Rabaul Shipping disaster. May God guide you and give you peace.

'Yes, I will!' she laughed heartily as he leapt off his knee onto his feet and enveloped her in his fierce hug. They clung to each other happily, laughing gaily as he slipped the jewel-encrusted gold band onto her petite finger. It was a joyous occasion; a celebration between these two souls, now vowing to embark on their lifetime as one. Both families already knew that he would be proposing this night; just the night before he had gone to her father to ask for his daughter's hand in marriage.

Tears of joy shimmered in the couple's eyes as they shared their quiet dinner together; laughter followed them along the journey home. In but a few months, they would be husband and wife, and yes, what a wedding it would be…mingling the traditional and modern, involving this community they both grew up in. In a few months, all their dreams would be made a reality. Yes, only a few months away.

But tomorrow, he had yet to embark on a journey of a different kind. He was a perfectionist, and more than anything, sentimentalism coursed through his veins. He needed his whole family there for his wedding, and that meant travelling by ship to his mother's village and bringing her back. It would take no more than ten days at the most.

He rose early that morning, the wind howled noisily against the louver blades and whistled through the frangipani lining the house. He dressed hastily and made his way down. She was up and making their breakfast, both said nothing but went about with their normal duties; grave that they had to be apart, even only for a little while. After their simple breakfast, he shouldered his meagre possessions and they made their way down to the wharf.

She fingered the ring she had just received, toying with it unconsciously as if willing him to stay here with her. Worry gnawed away in the pit of her stomach, yet she said nothing because she loved him, and she knew this was something he must do. Now at the wharf, she somehow wished she could go as well. The tears welled up and she blinked profusely to keep them at bay. 'No tears today' was her repeated mantra for this day.

Time ticked away too fast for both their liking. Before they knew it, it was time to board the ship. He pulled her against him, and she buried her head in his chest. Why was she feeling this inner turmoil? He had travelled so often before, this was no different. He pulled away, but she hugged him closer. He looked down into her eyes searchingly.

'Don't go today. You have a week off… stay with me for a bit, and then you can go.' She knew it was silly of her, but she tried anyway.

'Don't worry, I'll be fine.' He said in his usual carefree way. 'I'll be back before you know it…and you'll see Mum again.'

'Promise you'll come home to me soon,' the forbidden tears now ran freely down her face.

'I promise I'll come back to you, and we'll have our wedding, our babies, and our happily ever after.' He smiled his characteristic smile as he wiped away her tears.

They said their farewells. He made his way to the gate, paused and looked back searching the crowd for the familiar face and figure, waved and then disappeared into the ship.

The clouds above grew dark and luminous, heavy-laden and waiting. Thunderclaps rendered the air. She stood there watching the love of her life going, feeling as dull as the weather. She wondered why it didn't just rain already. She watched helplessly; 'bye', she whispered as the ship pulled out into the roaring blue ocean. Her phone jingled; peering down through tears she read his message; 'I love you. I'll see you soon'.

Out on the open ocean, his thoughts lay only with one person. He sat in the cabin, people all around him yet feeling as if he was alone. He had seen the heartache in her eyes; he should not have left her. He lay in his bunk, thinking. Against the odds, he fell into a restless sleep in the early hours of the morning, tossing and turning as the ship lurched forward at an incessantly slow pace. The relentless rocking unsettled many of the passengers; but he was an old hand at this voyage; he had travelled it many times.

The rains came as suddenly as the night did; creeping in silently in the dark as if a thief to steal. They did not stop. The waves began to rise; as if angered by the mere presence of the vessel upon its back. They rolled continuously and dangerously; a tiny ship against menacing giants as a back-drop. Wind howled; the air was electric as lightning pierced and stabbed, lighting up the blood red sky; thunder clapped as if the gods were unappeased. Deep within the depths of the ship's crowded passenger cabin, he and the others slept soundlessly; unaware of the turn of events facing them above.

By the next morning the situation had worsened, if that were at all possible. Waves towered over the ship and tossed it about like a play-thing on the roaring ocean. The crowded vessel screamed in complaint; braving on against all odds. Finally, its little heart could not take it any further. The first wave slammed against the ship's flank, water poured over the rails and onto the deck.

He was shocked back into consciousness and thrown against the room floor as the ship tilted at a dangerous angle against the surging waters. Within a second the next giant wave hit, and water had already reached him down in the cabin. All the other passengers were scrambling to get up onto the deck; many were mothers and children who were still asleep in the early morning. The thick water was deathly cold against his ankles, calves, knees, thighs; and rising every second.

He knew he did not have long but knew also that there were still many trapped. He opened as many windows as he could on his way up, so that others could make their way out as well. As he made his way up onto the deck the third and final wave hit. He was thrown out into open water as the ship sank rapidly. With no life jacket, the rescue boats an eternity away, his heart sank…he knew that this would be it; this would be the way he would leave this life.

Tears mingled with the salty water as his life flashed before his eyes…resting finally on the image of his lovely fiancé awaiting his return. She would probably still be asleep at this hour, she wouldn't have a clue, he thought to himself. He gasped his final words, a prayer just for her, and then relinquished his life into the angry waves.

Back at home, she awoke with a sudden sickness in her stomach. She raced to the bathroom, knowing something was terribly wrong. Wave after nauseous wave enveloped her tiny frame as she bent limply over the bathroom basin, she knew something was amiss. She had felt it, why didn't she stop him from going…all sorts of thoughts ricocheted through her troubled mind. She already missed him with a vengeance.

The moment she turned on the radio, her worst nightmares were confirmed. His ship had gone down just a few hours ago; rescue efforts were under way and people were still being pulled out of the ocean. Tears streamed down her face, worry muddled her thoughts. How could this happen? It was as if it were a bad dream. And in that moment, she knew the fate of her fiancé. He was gone; there would be no happy reunion, no wedding. Liar, he wasn't coming back. He had left her. She clutched at her stomach, doubled over and collapsed onto the floor.

She awoke to the bright lights and sterility of a hospital room. Peering around she found her mother's teary face; her own hand enveloped in the warmness of her mothers. They sat in silence for a while, each trying to grasp the truth that nobody wanted to admit out loud. It was as if saying it would make it reality. Their reverie was interrupted by the doctor who walked into the room with greetings.

'Hello there,' he said empathically. 'Well I don't know what all the long faces are for but maybe I can cheer you up. It seems I'm playing the bearer of good news today.' He peered down to his charts to double-check that he had the right bed. 'Congratulations Miss, you're going to be a mummy!'

Tears, sadness, mourning, but through it all a bright ray of hope, bittersweet happiness…at least he was not gone altogether.

#Second
Alma Warokra

I loved him with every fibre of my being. I loved him with a fierce love. I loved him as a protective mother loves her child. How can such a love be insufficient, inadequate… unsatisfactory? What more is there? What more can there possibly be left to give? I gave him my life, my love. He took me from my father's home; we shared a home, a bed, the most intimate moments. He became everything to me… this man whom I no longer recognize…

All around me the delightful squeals of newborns sounded; it was a clinging enveloping sensation and hung heavy laden in the air. On either side of my bed, little girls dressed in pink and red. On the opposing bed, a young mother sat cooing softly into a blue ball of fluff nestled snugly against her chest. Yes, the air was thick, almost suffocating. I was finding it difficult to breathe. I needed air.

I got off the bed and edged my way slowly toward the ward door. I was going to the court yard to wander around a bit, regardless of the sharp stabbing pains from the neat scalpel blade scar across my abdomen that made its presence known uncomfortably. The pain in my heart far outweighed anything physical. I didn't understand why my baby had to die; why he didn't have a heartbeat. They cut me to get him out; but no matter what they did, they still couldn't save him.

This was supposed to be different. I carried him to term, unlike the prior miscarriages. Hot tears trickled from the corners of my eyes. I had done my crying; there were no tears left to fall. I was alone this time. My husband had not joined me as he did the first few times. After a while you get tired, he claimed. He told me he had important business to attend to, he puts the bread and butter on the table and what did I know of making money to complain.

I was going it alone this time. Lately he had been distant. I look into his eyes and I do not see the man I married; the man who smiled down at me as he took me away from the bride price ceremony. Today I see a stranger.

When he did come eventually, it was to pick me and my measly belongings up and take me home after everything was over. I told him it was a boy. He told me the funeral arrangements had already been taken care of. And that was the end of that discussion.

Two weeks later he called me to the table, I sat across from him.

'I've come to a decision,' he said simply as if discussing any normal topic of conversation. 'I am taking on a new wife'. My world as I knew it crumbled down around me. I was dumbfounded, and struggled for the right words, if any.

'How is this possible? What about me? Who is she, who is this home-wrecker?' All these questions resonated in my numbed mind yet could not find their way out. I sat there, still, silent, not sure what to do next.

'Did you hear me woman? I am taking on a second wife. I have a child to be born. I have her settled in a house at the other side of town. You may stay here, but I will be spending most of my time there'.

'Why?'…it was all I could manage to ask; so much more left unspoken.

'I have no children with you. It's your fault you cannot have any. You cannot force me to stay here with you, childless.'

And with that, he was up and out the door; gone again, like the setting sun. My anguish was of no concern to him.

So here I stay. I have nowhere to go. My family's hands have been tied. I have no way to sustain myself; I was so young when I married. I am doomed to live this life of misery; visited every other week by a man who no longer loves me; even the joy of motherhood taken from me. This is the life I live; the life since the second.

The Knocks
Brigette Wase

Overcrowding is one serious issue that is affecting most of the working class people in most urban areas of Papua New Guinea due to high rental accommodation rates. This story hopes to highlight some of the issues that further result when extended families are forced to live together to save costs.

"Knock, knock, knock"
"Knock, knock."
It sounded again, more insistent this time. "Oi, nau tasol mi kam insait. Yu laikim wanem na pairap lo doa stap?"

My cousin Annie gave an exasperated sigh, "Please let me in, I need to use the loo!" That's what they always say, every time they want to come into the only toilet that caters for us.

'Enough!' I command myself, 'and address the situation at hand,' I had just walked into the bathroom/toilet to have a shower. A minute had not even passed. In fact, I had not removed my clothes yet!

Why is it that people do not heed to the call of nature when it actually starts calling and wait until their bladder or anus is about to burst, before they make a move? I wondered to myself. In our house, you cannot have a shower or use the toilet in peace. There is always bound to be someone at the door, knocking. "Plis, nau tasol mi kam insait lo waswas, ino wanpela minit igo pas pinit na yu kam pairap lo doa stap."

Annie whimpered as if she was in pain, She probably was, I thought wickedly. "Please, I really, really need to use the loo. Otherwise, it's going to be another story," she cried out.

Great, now the neighbours have probably heard her. The toilet and shower room are located under the house in one room. For some unknown reason, sounds from this room are amplified, so our neighbours actually can hear everything. It takes a lot of effort to do things quietly.

I had no choice; I didn't want to be held responsible for her peeing all over the cement floor. I came out. She rushed in, not bothering to lock the door and I could hear her sigh of relief. "Idiot," I muttered darkly.

A queue was quickly forming outside the door. It was all part of the chaotic morning ritual, termed as the *rush-hour*. Besides those of us who were working and the school kids, we had the unemployed who had nothing better to do but clog up the queue. My aunt Irene walked down the stairs at the same time as my other aunt, Rose came to stand next to me. The audible sniffs weren't hard to miss. Uh-oh, here's trouble brewing, I thought as I edged away from Aunty Rose. Contempt was visible as both glared at each other. That moment, Annie came out. I slipped in before anyone could cut the line.

"And where are you trying to go this morning", Aunty Rose taunted Aunt Irene, "are you are an office lady, do you have a job?" She was spoiling for a fight, and she succeeded.

Aunty Irene promptly burst into tears. "I'm going to my brother. He'll buy my new plates. You think you're the only one who has family working, huh" she said between tears.

"Ha-hae!" Aunty Rose laughed contemptuously. In the bathroom, I continued with my morning rituals and listened at the same time.

They suddenly began shouting in tokples. Unfortunately for me, I couldn't understand a word as I didn't know how to speak tokples. A real city slicker I was. But I knew when bad words were spoken, that was not hard to translate. I grinned stupidly.

They had fought last night, not physically but verbally. Whoever, came up with the saying, sticks and stones may hurt my bones but words will never hurt me, hadn't met my aunts. The argument had half the household in tears. And it started over plates!

Unfortunately, both aunts had the same sets of plates. Some of the plates got broken and one aunt started accusing the other of doing it. Pretty stupid, if you ask me. So it went on with hidden secrets being revealed, complaints of bride price and customary land and so forth. Marriage, it seems didn't just involve a man and a woman, it involved everyone and everything.

My aunt Irene's married to my uncle, Aunty Rose's brother. The house belongs to him. Well, more like three houses in one yard that housed forty-four individuals from eleven different families that were related one way or another. We had every relation you can think of except great-grandchildren! My uncle was a kind man to allow all of us to live there. I was the niece, daughter of their second cousin.

The moment I turned on the water, they got physical. I could hear them spitting and scratching and clumsily swinging their fists in a semblance of knock-out punches. Kids were crying, teenagers were complaining of the embarrassment and the older people trying to prise them apart. "Wwwssshhh, go nambaut, nambaut yah, yupela maski pait lo hia," I contributed my share. Loud thuds emanated from the wall as bodies connected with it. I could already imagine the curious neighbours craning their necks over the flowers or worse, gathered in the yard, as our yard had no fence. I washed as quickly as I could and moved to where my towel hung. I was rushing to get ready for work but wanted to see a bit of the fight as well. Apparently I wasn't quick enough.

Those next moments will be forever etched in my memory. Without warning, the door burst open, Aunty Irene falling flat on her back followed by Aunty Rose on top of her. My uncles and cousin brothers rushed in and stopped in shocked silence. The only sounds coming were from the two struggling women. I had never been as horrified in my life as I was then, standing there with nothing but quick-reflex, strategically placed hands. Venus, eat your heart out, I thought ironically. A second or two passed before my male relations sprang into action, I ran to where my towel hung and covered myself. I couldn't even raise my head. My aunts were still oblivious to what had transpired when they burst through the door.

They managed to drag the kicking and screaming women apart and didn't even look in my direction and one of them closed the door. I slowly walked to the door and locked it again as best as I could and just stood there. I thought of going and standing under a full blast of the shower to cool the heat of the embarrassment but decided to forego it. The screaming and cursing continued until I heard a sharp slap and the start of a wail. One of my uncles had decided to shut his wife's mouth,

When I could trust myself to walk and a quiet of sort had descended outside, I slowly opened the door. Only to come face to face with the one person in the street, I didn't want to see just then. It was Eric, my colleague and the person I secretly admired. Neighbours had gathered outside sure enough which included the man of my dreams. I was in a complete state of mortification. He gave me a pitying smile then asked unnecessarily, "Are you alright?" Before I squeaked an unintelligible sound, his face lit up in the direction somewhere above my head. I turned, and saw my cousin Annie give a million watts smile back at him.

If the earth opened up that moment, I would have gladly jumped in. Coupled with my sheer embarrassment was anger and jealousy. I felt like slugging Annie and wiping that smile of Eric's face. It was because of her, I got caught out', I thought bitterly. If only she didn't want to use the loo the moment I had initially gone in. If only I didn't heed her knocks. I rushed up the stairs to my room.

There would be a family mediation. I couldn't care less. I wanted to make myself scarce as soon as possible. That's it, when I go to the office, I will start enquiring for a place to rent, I thought furiously. Living with my extended family was driving me crazy. But if only the rental prices were a bit low, I continued my train of thought. The crowd was dispersing. I walked out of the yard eagerly looking forward to work as I had never done before.

Oi, nau tasol mi kam insait. Yu laikim wanem na pairap lo doa stap?
Oi, I just got in, what do you want and why are you banging on the door?

Plis, nau tasol mi kam insait lo waswas, ino wanpela minit igo pas pinit na yu kam pairap lo doa stap.
Please, I just came in to have my shower, a minute has not yet passed and you're already banging the door.

Wwwssshhh, go nambaut, nambaut yah, yupela maski pait lo hia"
Wwwssshhh, go someplace and else and stop fighting outside the bathroom.

The Mountain
Brigette Wase

The air around me was freezing even as the midday sun blazed down on my head. I listened to the river gurgle merrily over the grey stones. The never-ending cacophony of birds and insects tried to outdo each. Yet it was the sound of peace and tranquility. Leaves stirred as the gentle breeze blew through them. I shivered even more.

Green - nothing but green as far as the eye could see until you saw the mountain. A physical mass with the blue sky beyond. The mountain, where she had just come from. I watched the woman wash the sweet potatoes that she had dug up this morning from the garden up on the mountain.

This should last us for two days, she was thinking. Funny, I could hear her thoughts as if she'd spoken aloud. Every now and then, she would stop and wipe away a tear that had managed to escape her eyes, trying to quell the sobs that threatened to erupt and the bile that rose too, leaving a bitter taste in her mouth. To stop the memory of last night - all the memories.

Images exploded before my mind's eye. The memory of last night, her memories. She couldn't stop them. They ran amok. She pushed a fist into her mouth and bit hard. Probably the pain would stop them.

I heard the rustle in the bushes. I turned and watched as he crept up behind her. The creeping of a skilled hunter towards his prey. I saw the two shade tree branches in his hands. Realization slowly dawned on me. I began to shout.

Then, a myriad of emotions overwhelmed me, threatening to drown out my shouting. Emotions emanating from the woman who sat beside the river and the man creeping up behind her. The raging anger, the bitter jealousy, the deep sadness, the encompassing loneliness and the love. Yes, love. Love for her children, love for him - though a little flame now, about to be extinguished.

She was now so lost in her painful reminiscence. I was beside myself with shouting. I became lost with her.

She had gathered the children around her near the fire. They had asked for a story. It had been awhile since she sat with her children. She cherished the moment. She picked up where she left off, towards the end, "Then the mother told her son in the dream, you will find my body in the garden. You must bury me and return to the garden the next day. The little boy woke up crying"

She paused, looking at each of the children's faces - all captivated by her story. Committing their faces to memory as if she would not see them ever again. Ivo, her first born daughter. Her mother's strength. She was born after the beatings started. Her mother was still amazed that she had survived to be born. Hanaina, a year younger than her sister. She brought happiness to her mother even if only for moments out of time. She wondered sadly if her children would ever know true happiness. But then, did she ever know true happiness?

"Mother, keep going," her son Keiembo piped up, the youngest, the talkative one, the only boy. She smiled, glad to shake off the feeling of doom.

"He did as his mother bid and buried her. The next day, he returned to the garden and was surprised to find shoots growing out from where he knew his mother's breasts to be. He planted sticks around these strange new shoots. Each day, in the garden he tended these plants, and beheld with wonder as it grew. One day, he was surprised to see fruit, the shape of a woman's breast. He poked it and drew back in fear when he saw sap, like milk run from it. That night he dreamt again of his mother. She said, my son, don't be afraid of the fruit. Wait until the fruit becomes yellow or orange then you can eat it. It will bring you nourishment, just as my breast milk gave you nourishment."

"Eh, Aia, what fruit is it? Tell me," her daughter Keriakaribe demanded. The pretty one and third amongst her three daughters. She was also impatient. The older girls shushed her.

"He listened to his mother and when the fruit was ripe he took one. He cut it and saw orange flesh filled with many black seeds. When he ate it was so sweet. And that was how the pawpaw came to be."

"Eeeaahh, it's only the pawpaw. And he didn't even know how to eat it. He probably ate the seeds too", said Keiembo. They all laughed.

They didn't hear him come up the steps. "What's going on here?" "Why are you all laughing?" he shouted at them. They quailed before his angry eyes. "Go to your rooms."

As she ushered her children into their room, he reached out and grabbed her hair and yanked. "Where'd you think you're going?" She fell to her knees. "Where were you today?" he demanded as he yanked harder. "I told you we were going to church, then to the garden."

"The children were with me everywhere I went," she gasped as the pain took over. He slapped her then, so hard that her head hit the wall. She thought she heard her children crying. He accused her then, telling her that she was lying, that she had gone to another man. He told her the whole village was talking about her. He continued to hit her.

Ivo screamed at him that what her mother said was true. That the villagers were lying. Or was it him who was lying? Always lying. He only hit her harder. Each blow, each kick as merciless as the one before. Then he raped her, as he had done yesterday, as he had done for as long as she could remember. The final humiliation.

Through eyes that were swelling fast shut, she saw him go into the children's room. She could hear him hit them. She tried to sit up. Her body wouldn't listen. It probably decided that it had enough of the violence. 'Rise,' she told herself, 'your children need your protection.' She dragged herself up and hobbled to door. That moment, he yanked the door open. She looked past his shoulder, she could see the Hanaina and Keriakaribe, both bleeding, leaning over Ivo. She'd been knocked unconscious after speaking back to him. Keiembo whimpered in the corner. That was the last image she saw of her children before she collapsed.

She felt the nudge on her side. The pain woke her in an instant. "Get up," he said. We must go to the garden. I don't want people seeing how ugly you are." She got up; barely seeing, but instinctively knowing what to do, where to go. She had no time to check her children. She gathered her bilum and followed him. The sharp, cold morning air woke her more causing the pain to cascade like waves through her. The sun peeked over the mountain range as she followed him on the track that led to the garden up in the mountain.

"Pamone, turn around. He's behind you!" I shouted hoarsely. Funny, I thought, I know her name. I shouted the more, but it was as if she couldn't hear me.

Something of my fear must have touched her because she looked my way. But it was as if she couldn't see me. My fear turned to sheer horror when I stared at her face. How could I warn her? How could I warn this woman who could not see or hear me? How could I warn this woman who was me!

The first blow struck across the back of her head, she pitched forward into the shallow river. She didn't even have time to cry out. The shock of the cold water and the pain blinded her. The sticks rained down on her. Not once did she utter a sound. By now, I could only croak, my voice long gone from the shouting. I watched helplessly. He hit her until she looked like pulp. For one moment, an image flashed across her mind, across my mind, the faces of her children. My children. She opened her barely-there eyes once more. She saw me. She was, I am Pamone. Then she closed her eyes.

I watched him drag my body down to the rapids. I knew he would let me go for the river to take me. He should've buried me so I'd become a pawpaw, I thought. I shivered. I turned after a moment to look one last time. The river gurgling over the grey stones. The never-ending cacophony of birds and insects sounding eerily, heralding my passing. There was no gentle breeze, just the cold. Grey. Nothing but grey as far as the eye could see until you saw the mountain. I slowly made my way to the mountain and the physical mass of the light beyond.

God's Blessing in Every Step of the Way
Elizabeth Wawaga

It was a bright and sunny morning; the sky was blue with clear clouds floating just below the shining sun. Stacey could smell the freshly cut grass still wet in the morning dew as she turned her head on her pillow not wanting to open her eyes but fully aware of that morning scent. Although it was her big day she seemed little interested in what lay ahead and her parents made no effort to wake her from her slumber. It was the day she had long waited for and one she had always dreamt of since her first year of university.

For the past four years Stacey had dreamt of this day, imagining how she would walk up to the podium and receive her degree in Business Management, but today it felt like any other day. For the last five months Stacey's life had been a battle between taking her own life and living for the sake of another. She had woken up that morning with mixed feelings; a proud feeling of finally graduating and the fear of what the future held for the growing foetus inside her.

As she tried to enjoy her tasteless breakfast of tea and biscuits, her mother called out to her while walking out the door; "Hey Stacey we won't make it to your graduation but we can party afterwards"

"Sure, I'm not planning to stay long there anyway." Stacey replied bluntly. This had been the relationship she had with her parents for the last six months and their absence at her graduation did not come as a surprise at all.

That morning Stacey slipped into a plain blue dress that she had picked up at the second hand store for two kina and slippers that looked almost like shoes but with small heels. She did not have any make up on but combed her hair after pleating it the night before. Her eye brows were naturally trimmed and did not need plucking. She had no perfume but a nice scented lotion, a gift given by her dad the year before. Her cousin had offered her graduation gown and she felt fortunate she did not have to worry about hiring one. As she slipped into it, she smiled at the feeling of the heavy cotton on her shoulder.

She walked out of the gate and caught a late bus to the university. As she sat on the bus, she was greeted with smiles and admiration from fellow passengers who had a fair idea she was dressed for an occasion. Her heart was racing and she felt heavier as she dragged herself off the bus at the university gate. Her feet felt like rocks as she walked to the hall to join the procession. Although she tried to smile, her smile vanished as she felt kicks from the little life inside of her.

She was smart and was graduating with good grades in her department but to her parents this meant nothing compared to the shame and disappointment brought on the family. For the past five months, she had borne nothing but shame and neglect. She had wanted none of this but she knew she could not undo the past. She had traded a few hours of fun for months of worry, nausea, weight gain and the pain of living with parents who hated her so much.

She looked around for her aunt but could not find her; she picked up the graduation program and sat down in its place fanning herself as she continued to search among the crowds for that familiar face. Her best friend who was sitting a few rows ahead, turned and smiled at her but the sadness was unmistaken as their eyes met. She dismissed it muttering back that she was hot.

For Stacey life had ended the moment she saw those two blue bars and she had given up hating herself, her boyfriend and her friends for that fateful day five months ago, all she wanted was for the day to end quickly. When her turn came she walked quickly up to the podium and shook the presenter's hand while giving her best fake smile and thanking him. She was relieved to hear the next person's name and walked quickly down the other side of the podium.

As she walked back to her seat, a lady from nowhere walked up to her and gave her a hug while whispering into her ear and saying; "This is from Aunty Nelly". Stacey burst into tears as she grabbed onto the lady she hardly knew. She wept bitterly for a couple of minutes then abruptly letting go and walking back to her seat. She could not hold back her tears and kept sobbing as she sat down. This was all she needed that whole morning; for someone to simply say they were proud of her even if they weren't the exact words; at least it sounded like it. She sat down and pulled herself together and wiping the last tear off her face and embracing the new strength she had just been given. As the day ended, everything else was a blur; a small gathering with relatives she hardly knew followed by a drinking spree for her father's friends.

That night as she curled up in her bed she said a word of prayer, thanking God for the day's achievement and repenting for her transgressions. She begged for a job and pleaded for a good life for the child she was bearing and cried herself to sleep.

The next few months were tough, Stacey sold cigarettes at the family home gate and in the nights she typed out application letters to be sent the next day at the nearest post office. She did not care anymore if the jobs required her qualifications, all she needed was a job and she needed it fast. Months went by and not a single response to any of her letters. Despite this she became more encouraged to keep applying; she felt it kept her sane while in such a situation. Soon life began to slowly turn around for her. She was slowly beginning to see God's hand as each day unfolded for her.

Street markets were closing down and her customers began to multiply. She began making twice her profits and by her ninth month, the street boys were helping out and buying her stocks from the main market. At this time she had also saved over K2500. She was overwhelmed and knew she was going to be alright and that the future was beginning to look brighter for her and her unborn child.

On a Sunday morning while she setting up stall at the roadside the unspeakable happened; her water broke and realising this she called out to her street friends for help. Mothers that were at the scene called for a taxi and she was quickly rushed to the hospital. She was terrified of what was about to happen, but with the mothers accompanying her she felt safer than at home. All she had was a small bag of baby clothes but nothing of her own.

By 5pm news had travelled throughout the street and everyone rushed to the hospital with warm clothes for Stacey. Stacey could not fight back the tears as she saw everyone waiting on her while she was in labour. The pain did not matter anymore; she had the support of every young lad on her street. After four hours of labour she welcomed the most beautiful thing she had never seen, a baby boy with tiny fingers and toes and she wasn't the only one rejoicing at the ward.

The next day Stacey was out of the hospital and with her son wrapped in white linen, she walked smiling and leaving behind the pain of her past life. She was overjoyed to see her parents with open arms as she walked through her gate. Nothing else mattered, she was where she need to be; finally at home.

Five months later, Stacey finally got a call from one of the most prestigious mining companies in the country for an interview. Despite the new experience; it was her son and God's hand that kept her on the right track. She made a good impression and with a quote that left the panel no choice but to hire her. She said "You are going to regret not recruiting me because wherever I go God's hands follow".

Today Stacey is one of the most respected senior female officers in the mining industry and earns over K400 000 per annum with privileges and working in a 56 days on and 14 days off roster. She is still single and currently supports baby Justin and her family. Whenever she is on her break she spends time with her son and supports the local rugby boys from her street. The people in her street love her and often many say if you look closely you can still see God's hand at work in her life.

My Name is Sandy
Imelda Yabara

She sat shivering. Constantly checking whether her skirt was covering her breasts, pulling it with trembling hands up again and again. Silently she mouthed a prayer thanking God that she had worn a long skirt that day.

Outside the sun shone but no sunlight shone through the window. It was blocked by the people staring in.

She closed her eyes trying to shut out the eyes.

"You okay?" he snapped in Pidgin, Papua New Guinea's second language, before slapping the file down on the table between them. She looked up at him. He threw down a black t-shirt and motioned for her to put it on before he pulled back a chair and plonked down. She pulled the t-shirt over her head. Then reached under it and carefully worked her skirt back down until she felt the waistband back around her waist. Once again she wrapped her arms around her body.

"You're lucky, they only hit you, cut you and ripped your clothes off. Other women have been in far worse situations," he said while looking at the people staring in. "What were you doing walking alone in the first place? You should know better. What did you expect when you put yourself in that sort of position?" he asked.

"I ... was walking to work," she explained.

"Well next time go with someone," he retorted. "How many?" he asked tapping his pen against the table as he looked at the 'Domestic Violence is a Crime' poster on the light blue cement wall.

"Three," she said quietly while reaching to her back. She pulled out the shirt stop it sticking to her back.

"What, speak up, what is wrong with you?" he snapped.

"Three," she tried again this time louder.

"What weapons did they have?" he asked.

"A rifle, bush knife and a kitchen knife," she told him closing her eyes feeling faint. "They ca ... me out from the overgrown grass on the vacant plot on the other side of the highway and.... called me to wait for them, so I ran across the umm .. highway to get to the other side," she carried on, not stopping.

"That's why they hit you and cut you, you should have listened to them," he scolded her.

"I thought……that. If … if I got to the other side of the .. the road then I could follow the iron fence and try to make it to the residential…housing area which is just before the warehouse where I worked but … they reached me before I got there.." she looked at him, bending up and down trying to make eye contact.

He kept shaking his head.

"Is there someone you want to call to pick you up or do you want us to drop you off at the hospital to get those cuts look at?" he asked looking at her for the second time since he walked through the door.

"I want to call …" she said.

"Use the phone on the table," he said while pushing out the chair to stand up.

She gulped before saying, "ex … excuse me sir."

He turned and glared. "Yesssss," he ground slowly out.

"Did…. ummmm…did you get them and don … don't you want to hear the rest of the story?," she asked steeling herself not to look away.

"No vehicle, besides they probably already ran away…and you should be thankful nothing bad happened, did they rape you?" he growled.

She shook her head. He turned and left.

She sat staring at the doorway after he left, before turning and looking at the people staring in. Only three remained.

"Shame, shame on you," she spat out. Two left, one stayed put, a grin spreading on his face. They stared at each other until he turned his head.

"Bitch," he mumbled as he walked away.

Minutes later she heard Rose's voice asking where she was. Rose burst in the room. She came to a dead stop.

"Let's just go home," she said, struggling to keep her voice in check.

Rose nodded, "Oh my god you're cut, your arms are cut," she said blinking rapidly trying to stop the tears from escaping.

"Rose, pleassse…," she pleaded.

Nodding again Rose helped her up and they made their way out the door and down the corridor to the front desk where her interviewer sat talking to another officer who glanced at them.

"Are you okay?," the officer asked coming out and attempting to take her other arm before realizing it had blood soaked strips of cloth tied around them.

"Sandy," she blurted out.

"What?" Rose asked her confused.

"My name is Sandy," she said again, louder almost screeching. "My name is Sandy, you didn't even ask my name to put on your report," Sandy said. "So I am telling you … it's Sandy and I'll get my husband to follow up to see if there is any progress," she screeched at the interviewer whose lip curled and twitched as he stared at her.

Then Sandy saw her husband tearing in, his face scrunched in anger, and the tears she had held back so long fell free.

"I'll be back," her husband told the officer, who was now asking the interviewer for Sandy's file, before gently steering her to the car.

"Thankful, he said, I should be thankful," Rose heard Sandy say over and over again as she tried to hold Sandy trying to stop her shivering. Sandy jerked back. Rose pulled her arm away then realized her inner arm was covered with blood.

"My arms, legs and my back hurt," Sandy moaned as her husband maneuvered the car out of the police station car park. At the end of the driveway, he stopped.

"Hospital?" he asked no one in particular, staring at his wife's black eyes, split swollen lips and bruised cheeks through the rear view mirror.

"Quickly," Rose said watching her sister-in-law talking to herself.

POETRY

Circle of Tears
Agnes Are

I know you can never understand the way I feel for you
It's harder for me to forget the times we shared
The way you find so easy to do.

Logically it's wrong to lie without a doubt but this feeling
within my heart can never be denied even though you've
locked me out.
To you, I'm just a friend but that's what I've led you to believe
and nothing more.

I know that if to love you were a crime, I'd have broken every
law. Maybe I'm misguided or just unwise but I find
something special when I look into your eyes.
something that tells me that you too hide behind the curtain
of lies.

I've witnessed as you gave your heart away to a different person
It hurts so much to know that you care for someone else the
way I care for you but I know it's just a symbol to prove
we're through.

Sometimes, I'm certain you do like me no matter what you say
But your love is just an image
I cannot find the key, like a wild animal you were born to be free.

Even though I may be walking against the wind
the price so far from my reach, I'm not willing to give in
If you think your friendship brings less pain than for your
sake I'll carry on the game though you make me hide from
the truth, I know the charade is not in van.

I know you have friends you wish to keep
I don't want to take them away from you.
I only want to be a part of your life.
Is that too much to ask, am I prying too deep?
I don't want to worry,
I've hurt so much trying to deny I care
I just want you to know that I still love you
If you ever need someone, I'll always be there for you.

Maybe things could be better
Maybe as time goes by you'll see
Maybe the circle of tears will end and you'll understand how
Special we could be.

Sonnet 3: I met a pig farmer the other day
Michael Dom

At the foot of Mount Giluwe we met
A place where they say ice falls from the sky
We spoke of pork and the lack of good vets
As we toil'd in his village piggery
Each planning how his stock would reach market
Did we both share a wish that pigs could fly?

Agriculture is our backbone we say
(Rhetorical ruse on farmers always)
From the highlands to the coastal islands
The struggle to feed ourselves never ends
Yet in our grand plans for development
We have forgotten what that really meant

If you met those who's unheard voices cry
You too would join me in questioning, why?

Beauty is in da water
Michael Dom

My Unkol tol mi dat
Water is beautyfall
Coz beauty is in da water
It is da life giver an keeper

Dat is da why we washes in da water
Coz we wants da beauty to be on our skins

An afta we washes in da water
We looks into da mirra
Coz we wants to see da beauty
on our own skins

But beauty it's only in da water, not on our skins
So our skins is gonna nids to wash again an again

My Unkol tol mi dat
We pipols always tinkin
About our own beauty skin
Not givin or keepin life

Dat is wat da water do for all us pipol
It flows an it gives us, an it keeps all of us in da life, free

Only da water is mirra of da sky
Nite and dae, always lookin back up
Showin da sky is beautyfall too
But da sky it's not givin life, it's only blue

Beauty is like da mirra of water dat shows bigga tings abav
Like da sky, an da sta-lite in da nite dat makes more beautyfall

An dat is da why it rains
Because da water its beauty must fall back daun
Fall from da sky to da graun
Coz only dat's where da life can be

We call it rainfall, when da water, its beauty falls from da sky
An it gives lifes to taro, banana, kumu an kaukau to grow

My Unkol tol mi dat
Dat is da why he likes waterfalls
Because it is da most beautyfall
Free falling water, powerfull of life but peacefull

An us pipols still got plenty to learn from waterfalls…

Ples we mitupela i bin stap wantaim*
Michael Dom

Ol kokonas diwai i bin sanap, mi tingim yet
Fopela, i save mekim mi ron igo long dua
Taim pairap bilong pundaun i toksave olsem ol i kam
Mi grisim kaikai wantaim kokonas
Na mitupela inapim laik stret

Strongpela win i bin kam long nait, em soim piksa
Bikpela laikim wantaim pait i stap namel long graun na solwara
Na mitupela ino bin save olsem
Dispela taim bai pinis klostu
Mitupela stori long diwai-wine em i no karim kaikai
Na putim iau tasol
Long ol toktok i nogat nek

Dispela ples nau em stap long tingting tasol
Swit bilong em i save bagarapim mi
Na pairap bilong ol kokonas i save givim bel hevi
Na gris bilong ol ino bikpela tumas
Olsem ples we mitupela i bin stap wantaim.

Where we lived

There were coconut trees, I remember
Four, which would have me at the door
With the sounds of their arrival
I creamed them for us
And we did not want more.

There was the wind that night, a sign
Tempestuous love affair of earth and sea
And we did not know that
That time would soon be at an end
We talked of the barren grapevine
And listened in silence
To words left unsaid.

Now where we lived is a memory
Unpleasantly sweet it clings to me
And the fall of every nut is a misery
And the cream is not as rich
As where we lived.

So near, so far – a sonnet to transience
Michael Dom

Why do you have to be a shooting star?
To come so near, yet fall so far.
For all to see but none to feel
Your blazing flame that was so surreal
The Silent Sky with cold black glare
Did see, did feel your hasty flare
He does not speak and ne'er will tell
Your tale he keeps with those who fell

The fiery path that was your light
Is as silent and black as the Old Night

No tracing scar to show your burning
No memory of your bright journeying
Why do you have to be a shooting star?
To come so near, yet fall so far.

As I bask in her afterglow
Michael Dom

If it is her love that awakens
Sunrise's subliminal song
I would bask in her afterglow anon
Drowsy headaches, muffled yawns
Odors of Arabica will remedy these
Ruby's surreal melody stirs easily
And breakfast is best in bed with Isi

Golden day invades our lair
And we laze in his envious glare
Like lizards in limbo
Intertwined in our dreaming
Knowing every waking moment
Enters an unknown destiny, where
Only time offers hope or meaning

Reservations for two
At our secluded café? Rather, today,
Meet me at Quartermain Hall
In your Puma's and blues
Together we'll walk a mile a way's
Another sunrise awaits your say.

A candlelight market in Port Moresby
Michael Dom

A distant glimmer welcomes neighbouring denizens
To a casual communion among masticating friends
As moths purge themselves upon your candle-flames
Bonfires of electricity blaze over parched n' blackened hills
And the threat of morning is carried by a west-wind chill
Yet nowhere else would we find such cordial respite
From domestic ennui at these hours south of midnight

Your softly flickering tabletops set in neat divisions
Are spread galore for creditors, with familiar provisions
And we are wont to stray on our nightly excursions
To your promise of camaraderie in lite-conversations
When we idly meander from our suburban asylums
Bathe us once again in your charmed candlelit glory
Be our one vestige of hope in this city of opportunity

And what tales do we have of each other to enlighten
Of politics and science, of economics and religion
The mundane amusements of plebeianism
How Nukie-boy betrayed his culpable wife
How she chased him waving her Tramontina-knife
And how the whole community followed after
To the station, to the courthouse and the market thereafter

Johnny got wan nu muruk insait his banis
Michael Dom

Johnny is my naybah. Johnny is my wantok's bestie.
Johnny got wan nu muruk insait his banis
an it's fiding on my trabolled brainses!

Johnny em tok olsem, we sud behave; us. Like he does, eh laka?
Sez we nid to be obedient citizenry
an try to work aroun eni un-pleasantry
But it's hard to be-have wen we don't have, Johnny.
Dose Have's, let dem be-have. We Have-nots, be-have not!

We not gonna follo rules dat alreadi sum bosses dem broken!

Johnny he sed like dat 'we behave and be civil'. Aahh?
Civil little servants, set de precedence
Dem evil little bastards juss fuck up de kantri mahn!

Must be hard to be wan obedient little civil servant
wen so many Big Men leaders dem so disobedient, eh laka?
An me to be-have?! Am I yor smallboi, or?! Am I yor longlong?!
Tokim MP be-have, becoz he already have, Johnny!
He have your money and mine, Johnny!

My nada wantok sez, many of us is laik 'neo-tribal'
Planti man meri raun lus nating, planti sidaun lo banis
Lukluk tasol, stap-stap. Longlong!
Nogat tingting, nogat toktok
na luk olsem nogat man blo wok!

But dat wan nu muruk yu got insait yor banis, Johnny,
it got wan crafty style.
Wan blary ugly bird but style yah!
Poor bugger got no wings to fly,
but good long legs to run wan strong resis, ah Johnny?

We not gonna follo rules dat alreadi sum bosses dem broken!

Sampla kisim nupela tingting, sampla autim gutpela tok
Mekim niupela rules, nau yet, nau yet!
Mekim ol lidamahn bihainim lo!
Tingting gut. Toktok gut. Mekim gut.

This is My Place
Michael Dom

This prose poem is a story about creativity and unity from the perspective of a young child.

I want to stay in this place.
It's beautiful here and it's so …peaceful, and … free!
But even though I can come and go as I please, I know I can't stay for as long as I'd like to.
(Not yet anyway.)
I have to go back out into The Real World and be with everyone else, together – Suffering.
I wish I could bring my friends with me, when I come here
But it's hard to fit them all into my head, and maybe they have their own places to go to.
That makes me sad about being there, in The Real World.
My friends and I, and everyone else as well, we all go into our own-little-worlds.
So we live together separately.
And going into our own-little-worlds is nothing at all like coming to this place.
All of The Real World is crowded with billions of different own-little-worlds
With only one thing the same: Isolation.
And coming here is like an escape from my own-little-world to a better place.
So I wish my friends had a place like this to go to.
But I don't know if those places would be quite the same as here.
Although I don't think they could ever be too different.
I heard that Different and Same once lived together in one-big-room, called The Unreal World.
Then Somebody decided to build a great-big-wall called Isolation.
And make two-small-rooms and give them the name The Real World.

One of the two-small-rooms was called The Different Real World.
The other one of the two-small-rooms was called The Same Real World.
Nobody knows how everyone got split up into those two-small-rooms or why it happened.
Then Everybody kept dividing up the two-small-rooms into smaller and smaller rooms
So that Somebody could see that Everybody was in total control.
Somebody said the great-big-wall of Isolation made The Unreal World become The Real World
Because the great-big-wall could be seen and touched and there was no escape from it.
Not like in The Unreal World where there were wide-open-spaces stretching until Forever.
Now everyone could be kept under control and not wander around everywhere
Or cause trouble or get lost or be hiding away so that Somebody didn't know where they were.
And that's how we ended up in our own-little-worlds.
Billions of smaller rooms with our own-little-worlds were invented for all the billions of people.
That made it much easier for Everybody to watch and learn and report back to Somebody
What people were doing or saying or even thinking.
That's what I heard, but Nobody knows how everything really happened.
Nobody told Anybody why Somebody made everyone live inside their own-little-worlds.
How to believe in only those horrible two-small-rooms we each separately call The Real World.
Nobody knows how Everybody joined more walls onto the great-big-wall called Isolation.
(And the really scary part is it's still happening today!)
Anybody could tell that Somebody was evil and that Everybody was a villain.
But it wasn't Anybody's business.
I don't know if it really matters if Anybody or Nobody cares about us,
Because we're still stuck with Everybody building walls and Somebody is still the boss.
We're all together in The Real World with all those walls that Everybody builds
Keeping us separate in own-little-worlds – Suffering.
The Real World is nothing like The Unreal World used to be; beautiful and peaceful and free.

In The Real World the great big wall of Isolation divides the two Places,
Different and Same.
It's not fair on anyone because we aren't able to share anything anymore.
And I think that's a nice thing to do – to share stuff that's either mine or
yours.
I'd like to get everyone else to do that too – share stuff
Like candy and toys or games and secrets or even adventures.
If we could do that now, with respect, then with trust, then as friends –
share stuff
Then that stuff becomes ours together and we've seen right through the
great-big-wall Isolation.
I also think it's important, because of what I heard once, for everyone's
sense of reason.
I heard someone crying and crying, in pain like dying, to know if there
was anyone out there
Who could help her or knew and shared what she was going through –
you know, Suffering.
(But I kept that a secret because she didn't know I was behind the other
wall listening.)
I think sharing can help overcome Isolation.
And sharing stuff as friends eases Suffering.
It would be really nice if I could share this place with everyone else.
If I could tell people about this place, My Place,
May be other people would tell me about Their Place.
What things would be like Different and what would be like Same?
And how could we share those Places and bring them back together
again?
May be in stories with words and pictures?
Like in a book or a magazine, but not as expensive.
Something simple and easy to pass on to someone else,
(Contagious even, like the flu!)
But there could be billions of everyone's stories about Their Place.
It might get too heavy to carry them all in our heads or hands.
So we should stick them all on one great big storyboard.
Then sharing them would be much easier.
(Like on Facebook, but without the digital graffiti!)
We can use that wall called Isolation as our storyboard – Our Place.
(Yes! That should teach Somebody and Everybody a lesson or two or
billions!)
Maybe for a short time we could stay there together, in Our Place.
Maybe for a short time it would be like Places are like in The Unreal
World.

We could leave Suffering behind and wander off into Forever and share adventures
Where it's beautiful and peaceful and free.
If I tell a story about My Place it might be about Different or about Same.
Maybe other people would like this story.
They might like my idea of Different and not like my idea of Same.
Maybe they'd be interested in knowing more about My Place anyway.
(Which liberated me from my own-little-world and taught me all about Different and Same.)
Maybe they'd like to visit me and hear Tales from My Place.
That would be very nice, but I mightn't want them all to stay for too long.
Just to visit.
Yes, visiting would be alright.
After all, this is My Place and I want to share it with someone who likes Different and Same too.

Haiku written about night time at a village along the Papua coast
Michael Dom

the house is silent
fighting geckos wake the dog
…enters lahara

sleepless rambling dreams
drugged by the tropical night:
flee the verandah!

neighbours offer tea –
no security lamps here
only buai palms

bubus fire is lit:
shadows playing with torches
their voices pass by

far off sparks flicker
'twixt dark skies and black waters:
children are laughing

the floorboard nails squeak –
with bellies full of sago
and smoked magani

a bone dry palm frond
crashes to the ground nearby –
another dog barks

warm, ghostly sleek sand
slides softly between bare toes –
somewhere a pig grunts

glowing graveyard path:
beyond the coconut grove
the bursting seabed (there awaits the sea)

smooth liquid embrace
soaking and soothing, at once
fish skim the surface

murky reflections
have robbed me of my laughter:
stars and eyes glisten

seas hold no quarter:
an irresistible draw
to moonless vigils

*According to wikiHow a **literary haiku** should have 'a 5-7-5 syllable pattern…' and adhere to the use of season words, a two-part juxtapositional structure,* *and primarily objective sensory imagery'. Please count the syllables, a friend tells me I've mistaken them before, but some rules can be bent and others broken. A critical point is the splitting of the poem into two parts, where, the **bold font** is the **fragment** and the black font is the **phrase**. If this haiku keeps working, then it might turn out to become a **renga**.*

Today another good man passed
Michael Dom

This poem contains two Haiku

Today another good man passed
Into the never.
There will never be a sufficient sum of sorrowful tears.
Will the air be filled with the wailing fears?
Of those presented with
The written
And
The unwritten
Account
Of his triumphs
Meaning
Of his dreams
Remnants
Of what was
Revelations
Of what might have been
What we were offered
What we were denied
That glimmer of light
We followed
(We) Blindly
Extinguished.

A nameless poet –

Emptied of his shining words
Enters the never

What we had seen
Was
An image
A perfect reflection
In our imperfect world
But
We did not know that
We knew
We saw
Only what was apparent
Only what we had been told
And were inspired by
What we read in stories
In books
And blogs
What we dreamed
In our souls
Were
Seeds planted
By words
That we had either
Misunderstood
Or
Understood incompletely
We have never seen
What may yet be
We know only
We see only
What was
What is
In our
Own
Version

Of reality.

As a poet dreams;
A bright, clear vision guides us
Through the darkest hours

But we can never go with him
Nor can we imagine
Where he walks
Into the never
Before us
Before we
Ever knew
He had
Dreamed
Then
And now
That is unknowable for us
What we cannot speak of
What we have never heard
What we have never seen
Nor our bravest dreams ever attained
In the darkness
(It was) It is our own wailing that fills our ears
We do not (want to) listen
For the resonance
Of his words
Of his life
In ours.

Hearing rain approach while reading in bed at night; Morobe Province
Michael Dom

I heard an ensemble stir and strain,
rising over crowded mountains and valleys
in palpable waves through the shadow of night;
aimed inland by Solomon's regal baton.

Those errant winds refreshed their compositions
at that heavenly percussionists outpouring,
every tree, every shrub waving leaves in applause;
even my roof provided a thunderous encore.

Set adrift on my bed in the magnificent flood,
amid nocturnal choruses of crickets, katydids and toads,
behind each sublime sonata, a simpler melody flows;
a symphony of paradise restores me once more.

i got sex on my mind –in the club!
Michael Dom

drowning in this
opium of city nights –
lights, liquor, ladies

i got sex on my mind, always
sex.

all the nightclub waitresses are actresses
in my pornographic vision
they bring more poison; desirable, drinkable;

and another bottle
brown, wet, frothing at the top end
wrap your lips around that babe!

i got sex on my mind, always
sex.

warm hands closing aground that
hard slick liquid length
lips sucking deeply at the tip of that fag,
rubbing-up on the floor
bump and grind
babe give me more!

i got sex on my mind, always
sex.

somehow, amidst the haze of cigarette smoke,
beyond the urinal fumes and alcoholic vomit,
i find myself, between one kind of relief
and another
a stranger in the mirror asks,
'who are you fucking tonight babe?'

i got sex on my mind, always
sex.

she's pointing at me beneath that tank top,
bouncing, in tight pants and bling-blings,
those gyrating hips – seduced by disco lights,
spinning balls and brains and all
and i'm thinking it's got a sign says,
    "take me drunk babe, i'm home!"

i got sex on my mind, always
sex.

tray loads later i ask her again,
'what's your name babe?'
she makes some squeal that's drowned
by the dj's pumping system
and right now i'm picturing a bushy little grotto

damp with sweat and other sticky fluids…

i got sex on my mind, always
sex.

diving in i seem to forget something
about a poster i read in a hallway
which someone said was good advice
but it doesn't make a difference anyway
they got some retired politician instead of that doctor
and i never liked rubber gloves either.

i'm drowning somewhere between this dream
some ladies panties and the last drink.

State of the Public Service
Michael Dom

Fourteen lines with seven syllables then dashed to three syllables, to make ten syllables in each line.

The public service we do - is not known.
The public we do service, - once a month.
The service we do public, - for the boss.
We do the public service. - They pay us.
We service. The public do. - No one cares.
We, the public, do service. - It's all good.
We service. Do the public? - Does anyone?
Do we service the public? - Yes we do!
Do we, the public, service? - Yes, sometimes.
Service the public, do we? - Not today.
Service we do the public - is secret.
Welcome to bureaucracy. - Out for lunch, (back at four).
If you have good ideas, - like I did, (long ago),
When you enter, please leave them - at the door.

Sonnet 1: Parallel Lanes to Nowhere
Michael Dom

Travelling roads that wind over mountains
Where trees and high *Imperata* are blinds
Traffic passing by on parallel lanes:
Converse directions with dividing lines

On prehistoric treks of time and chance
Each step chosen for a safe arrival
Hand-made stories, legends in chants and dance:
Ancestral maps were means of survival

But now we drive along broad thoroughfares
Disregarding those places where we step
Doing whatever we want, unawares:
Destinations aren't just names on a map

Nomads and seafarers found their somewhere
Their kin cruise parallel lanes to nowhere.

Lucky little lizard
Michael Dom

Tak! Tak! Tak-tak, tak-tak, tak-tak, tak-tak! …
Small mercies fall upon a tin roof
Glad tidings whistle through rafters
A pleasant evening between here and there
And a song to share with musing geckos
Eating silly bugs bedazzled
By luminous glows.

Tchk! Tchk-tchk, tchk-tchk, tchk-tchk! …
Staccato feeling at a flick of tail
Defying laws that hold me

Neither over nor under
Neutrally buoyant or rather
Drowning in suspended animation
Better a ceiling clinging critter.

Tshhh! Tshhh-tshhh, tshhh! tshh, tssshhhhh!
Simmering rice on a hot gas stove
Is habit not hunger driven
Mouthful of moth
He scurries off
Like some freak reflection
Of me entering the kitchen.

Wibbly-wobbly, dribbly-gobbly, bibbly-bobbly, blur!
Glaring, defiant, lizard to giant
In retort to my musing, at a meager moth,
He snaps once then twice –it's gone!
In a quick lick n' a wink: 'Urrrp!'
Then them-there glazed eyes
Lucky little lizard.

A pendulum plays a well-known rhythm
Michael Dom

Movements between a left and a right swing
A pendulum plays a well-known rhythm
Moments between the ticking and tocking
An empty park-bench on a quiet lawn
A lonely figure bracing in the storm
Movements between a left and a right swing
Out at large, on and on the world races
Sometimes life is spent in little spaces
Moments between the ticking and tocking

Hearing bright laughter thru the gloomy fog
The distant baying of a hunting dog
Movements between a left and a right swing
Like a long lost memory towards dawn
In the absence of a shadow once known
Moments between the ticking and tocking
Life, long or short, finds a nominal sum
At the door to an unknown room knocking
Movements between a left and a right swing
Moments between the ticking and tocking

Return to Mambon Nil
Michael Dom

This poem was penned in 2006, when I first returned to my father's lands, as an adult. It has been edited after six years and transformed from verse into this prosaic form. Although the story is a personal experience it echoes the situation of many young Papua New Guinean men today. Many of us are at least fortunate enough to return to our roots with welcoming. This poem is dedicated to my late father Kuri Dom, on the 25th anniversary of his passing on 17 January 1987, ten thousand miles from home, to my mother Ruth Ulgan Maldoa Dom, who brought us back ten thousand miles, my sister Sola Gracia Dom, and my brother Stanley Saint Paul Dom, who eventually led me home to Mambon Nil.

Daylight breaks on Yoba Kogul's eastern face.
A highland wind gusts: sharp and fresh.
It cuts, sutures and saturates our bodies with each unconscious breath.

A pallid sun crowned in yellow-white halo shimmers over crests of green swathed hills as we wade through glistening wet kunai.
The morning mist hangs like a sleek blanket swaddled around the breast of a sleeping child.

Yar trees grow proudly here, straight and strong on the undulating slopes.

Yet they fall in obedience to the swing of Sinke's axe.

A hausman must be prepared.

It has been a long time coming, but today two sons have returned home, to Mombon Nil.

Wara Nepilpil runs in the valley and the river where a father bathed is now used by his sons.

Across the dividing valleys we hear an ululating call.

Clear in the crisp air, its message is well known to all.

We must attend a gathering.

The grandsons of Dom Oganpewa must become who they were meant to be.

The elders are fading and we must be ready to stand in rank.

Will others also heed this calling?

Our brothers are now scattered far and wide.

Yet the distances are not so great if our hearts are united in one cause.

Are we not Bulagau, Tabare Sine, returned now to Mambon Nil and reborn in the chill water?

Who then will question us when we stand on the cliffs edge and survey our heritage?

Yoba Kogul's rugged walls have stood witness to all that was and now watches over all that will be.

Our grandfather has passed and his long separated sons now walk with him once again.

Our time has come to receive their blessing.

Will we be deserving of our heritage?

Will our ancestors call us to their Hausman with pride?

What lies in the palms of our hands today must be used for those who come after.

As generations of fathers gave to their sons, we are now guardians of their future.

Our blood sings in our veins when we stand upon the red-brown earth of these rolling hills.

Let us gather here like the tributaries of Nepilpil, gurgling in the forested valleys.

Here our fathers have lived and fought and farmed for untold generations past.

Here our mothers have raised their children with dignity and pride.

Here our battle cries have frozen hearts and spears have shattered shields.

Here our homesteads now still stand, waiting, welcoming.

The warmth and security of our communal fireplace is a pleasure we all know well.

Where evening meals are shared with family and stories heartily regaled late at night.

Will we joke together once again of adventures we have had apart?

It would be good to do so, for this has ever been the way of our people.

Already I hear our laughter and look forward to seeing the light in your eyes.

We are the future of our people.
We are entrusted with their hopes and dreams.
Let us honour their convictions and preserve their worthy ideals.
Let us be their best representation to the world of tomorrow.
Let us laugh and walk hand in hand as brothers do.

Yoba Kogul remains a bulwark of our homeland.
Nepilpil will revive us as once it did our fathers.
And when we stand at Mambon Nil our ancestors will know us.
We are Bulagau, Tabare Sine.

Mama
Jimmy Drekore

Dedicated to the DWU students who lost their parents in the plane crash

You told me
you were coming
I didn't eat
I didn't sleep

I arrived

before the rest
looking into the skies
waiting in my best
with joy in my eyes

I waited, waited and waited

My heart became empty
Like the skies ahead
My eyes became blurry
With no signs ahead

Tears slowly descended

When I heard you went down
In a ball of flame
I wanted to drown
Just the same

I refused

To hear
It must not be you
My biggest fear
Came true

You told me
You were coming

Yes mummy
You did

But I didn't know
You would come in the wind

Seasonal Seducers
Jimmy Drekore

The season has come
They will come
They are seasonal seducers
Coming in flashy cruisers
Escorted by disciples
With deceiving principles
They smile
That royal smile
They wave
That majestic wave
They take the stand
The grand stand
They tell you
They'll fight for you
They tell you
They'll bring service for you
They tell you
They'll build this for you
Build this...
Build that...
Bla bla blaaa
How can they fight?
When flying like a kite
How can they bring service?
When buying votes is their service
Look at the sole of your feet
It is all written in it

Don't listen to these seducers
Coming in tinted cruisers
They don't walk
They only talk
So don't be fooled

A Poet's Quest
Jeffrey Mane Febi

If humans were formed from dust, & poetry is human's meager attempt to reveal the beautiful or sublime; the beauty of this dust from which we originated from is unsurpassed

Once a man in his quest to be poetic,
Twisted and mingled words to find
Subtle beauty in meager arrangements.

At birth of day;
When the day was ripe;
At death of day;
Even when the night's eye
Was sleeping, he searched

His dreams. Reaped them apart;
Turned them upside down and
Scribbled their charms on memory.

Only to find hosts of
Re-arranged clichés.
Exhausted, out loud he cried.

'Give me a drink of thesaurus, and
Cigars rolled in pages of a dictionary.
I'd be drunk with beautiful metaphors,
And be high with unusual rhymes that

Sing and dance. I'd sing along and
Sprightly dance that our voices may
Reach over vales and hills
Till my mind's ink is drawn.

Yes! O yes, an echo on shelf
Lonely and dusty continues to sing.
On platforms or from behind silent corners,
I'd care not because, time …;
Would've dealt with me".

Dreams of a place
Jeffrey Mane Febi

Our political leaders fight for power while the little people continue to suffer. Our suffering seems endless but certainly our dreams have not expired and will give us the strength to walk on. How we get to where we want to go and what kind of PNG we want to see then is in our dreams and no one can steal it. So don't give up! Tireless hand (Time) continues and it is up to us to become agents for change, even if it means to suffer as we make our way slowly to that destination – a PNG we would like to have.

Did the play of mighty tongues,
Harass your wretched heart once,
Twice, then more than many times;

Then your dream haunts,
While, away tireless hand chimes?

Did the play of mighty tongues,
Your dream on a journey forces,
When the storms were unkind;
Then send it on unplanned courses,
On many a different wind?

I too have a heart broken,
With a dream restless and old;
That yearns to journey to a place,
Gentle whispers, us have told
Is full of wondrous grace.

Will you join me on a journey to this
Noble place without a name;
A name you and I would give,
While we play our own game
And live and let live?

But I can't promise a smooth trip;
Our dreams, our wrath will keep,
And our hearts will find a way.
We may all the way creep,
But surely we will not stray.

Let the rhythm of our hearts,
And song of a place without name,
Deliver us strength to sweat.
Getting there is our noble aim
And this we will not regret.

Hey, did I see a flicker in your heart,
Through holes in the wretched one?
The flicker in my heart dance,
And though there'll be no sun,
We surely will make our advance.

A place without name we seek;
We must not be meek;
A place without name we seek;
We must not be weak?
A place without name we seek.

The Bougainville Crisis
Sophie Garana

Creeping quietly out of my thatched roof hut
I make sure not a single noise is made
To avoid being heard by the enemy faction

Ears as sharp as a donkey
I snatch an empty basket and a knife
As blunt as a rough stone
Quickly I make my way
To the garden for the day's portion of food.

Every movement is made with caution
For the enemy faction is ready to kill
For reasons unknown
Quickly I harvest what crop is ready
And get ready to make my way back to my hut.

As I'm loading my basket
Behind my stooped back a figure moves
Swiftly as a black crow
Among the trees and shrubs nearby.

My heart starts to beat faster than normal
And I ponder about all these happenings
Thoughts of my children
Left behind in the hut trouble me
Questions come my way
Is this the last day of my life?
Am I one of the targets?
And why?

Bang! The sound of a gun is heard nearby
Quickly I throw the basket down

Making a noise as loud as a falling dry coconut
And stumble away to the nearby bushes
Breathing even faster than usual
I try not to be heard by anyone.

As I try to comfort myself and peep amongst
The bushes in the direction of the gun fire
I feel prickles on my legs
Looking down to see what it is
I'm startled to see hundreds of ants
As many as an army of soldiers
I cannot shout though the pain
On my legs is getting worse
I have disturbed these ants
And I deserve to be bitten.

I try to move a few steps
Away from these ants
At the same time rubbing them
Off my legs but to no avail
More seem to be coming and no ending
To these insects.

In the act of doing that
I feel a hand on my
Left shoulder from the back
I cry out with great fright and run
Out to the open garden
The hand still felt on my shoulder

I cry the loudest with all my might
The cry is heard by women in the neighbouring garden
Anxious to know what it is
All run to the commotion site.

I hate to turn back and see who it is

Quickly he shouts out my name
Panno ....!
At that instant I turn around
To see who it is
My young uncle with a gun.

The frightening cry turns into a
Cry of joy joined by the women
Who ran to my shouting.

The laughter continues till the tear ducts
Can give no more tears.

Legal Joke
David Gonol

As far as four-year-old Marapa was concerned, it was a major crime. Someone had stolen his chocolate so he called 000 and summoned Boroko Police to his home at Waigani, near the Parliament House. "Marapa was most distraught," Inspector Wambul Glaulga said. "He named two prime suspects – his two-year-old brother and one-year-old Sister." The Boroko Police arrested the two prime suspects and subsequently charged them with stealing under section 372 of the Criminal Code. On trial at the Boroko District Court, the two accused pleaded guilty. So the first accused said, "I saw Marapa had a chocolate in his lunch bag, so I started forming the idea of stealing it in my mind: that did not take long to actually happen. As soon as he left the room, I quickly executed what I had on my mind. I broke it in the middle and gave one half to my sister." At this the trial magistrate said: "You admitted you had mens rea which resulted in the actus rea. Thus you are liable to face the full consequence of the law." The trial magistrate therefore sentenced the first accused to three years imprisonment with hard labour under section 372(1) of the Criminal Code. The second accused (one-year-old sister), in her defence she said, "Excuse me Mr. Magistrate, to be honest with you and myself, I didn't know that stealing chocolate from our brother's bag was a criminal offence. Thus when he asked me as to who stole it, and I thought it was not a criminal offence, so I didn't say anything." At this the trial magistrate said, "Ignorantia juris non excusat," thereby finding her guilty of being an accessory after the fact under section 10 of Criminal Code. Accordingly, the trial magistrate sentenced her to two years imprisonment.

However, the two siblings appealed the decision of the Boroko District Court to the Waigani National Court on the ground that they were underage and that their acts and omissions could not constitute any criminal offence. The Waigani National Court of course upheld the appeal and quashed the decision of the Boroko District Court on the ground that the two siblings were under the age of seven and that under section 30 of the Criminal Code they could not be held criminally liable. The Waigani National Court further ordered that each party bear their own cost!

A Dog's Philosophy
Anthony Kippel

The Dogfather says: "don't bark unless you're barked at."
Meaning - don't look for trouble, let trouble look for you.
The Dogfather says: "don't beg for your food."
Meaning - patience is a virtue.
The Dogfather says: "don't piddle on the tyres."
Meaning – don't bite the hand that feeds you.
The Dogfather says: "don't lick elsewhere, but your master's feet."
Meaning – humble yourself.
The Dogfather says: "don't chase the neighbour's cat."
Meaning – don't commit adultery.
The Dogfather says: "don't poo on the lawn."
Meaning – keep personal stuff to yourself.
The Dogfather says: "don't bring mud into the house."
Meaning – leave work at work.
The Dogfather says: "let one flea in and thousands will follow."

Meaning – beware of opportunists and parasites.
The Dogfather says: "don't wag your tail too much."
Meaning – be faithful to one partner.

I am sorry it has been so frustrating
Mary Koisen

This is something I wrote for my darling partner who is a consultant to this ever changing country. He has so much passion and tries so hard in his ability to impart as much as he can and direct decision making only for the betterment of this nation. Most times he comes home broken feeling deflated as most of what he endeavours to achieve comes tumbling down. Even though I don't understand much of what is happening as most issues are sensitive and thus he cannot impart these, I feel his pain. I dedicate this to all the expatriates and genuine people who have adopted this nation and would like to say we understand some of your frustrations and were thankful for all your endeavours. Never give up

I'm sorry it is and has been frustrating for you
I know there are shadows out there selling this nation right before your very eyes
I know as much as you fight to maintain this nation and its abundance
And try to "capacity build" this nation and its people
These shadows get in the way of things and breakdown the foundation on which you have invested much time and passion
I am sincerely sorry for the way things are going
Yet at the same time I cannot accept to be thrown down into the pits with all these shadowy recalcitrants and be branded with the same iron.
It pains me to hear you say these things
That all we will amount to is "nothing"
It tears into the heart of things and makes me see you differently
You cannot be this person I once knew.
No-more will I speak of the little joys I cherish about this changing nation
The mini developments I see this nation strives to achieve
No more sharing my deepest hurts and secret joys in regards to these
As in your eyes "we are not what we are but pretend to be what were

not"…
Enough
I am tired
And I am weary for this sort of talk
Therefore
Please
Enough

This Part of the World
Anita M. Konga

This part of the world
though a loose speck in the vast blue of the Pacific
is the home of a thousand tribes
It carries a countless rocky highlands
and a million more deep and unforgiving lowlands
It shines out the splendour of its beauty
under the gentle gaze of the tropical sun
breathing life through the richness of its coral atolls and varying sea
shores

This part of the world
Unaccustomed to industrialization
still bears the deeds of globalization
The forefathers had found,
valued and
depended on
cultivation for centuries.
Now many had been answers to the
misery of science
uncertain on keeping faith in their own beliefs
and adapting western culture.

This part of the world

abundant of wealth begrudged by races
has had its share of contribution
to the course of civilization
but is still a stranger to modernization
fire for a light;
vines for a bridge;
feet for a ride;
mishap to the perfection of
economy,
law and
humanity.

This part of the world
is new to Westminster Democracy
but politics has been its culture for ages
in a society of the most powerful kinsmen;
its clan knows its name
its tribe knows its name
-a tribe known for its wealth of beauty and fame
It knows its kind not by written law
but by blood and inheritance

This part of the world
known best for its vile deeds
of poverty and disorder
yet is blessed with mother land – a pride
She meets the unlimited needs of her children
She will watch them rise
leaving behind the garments of history
picking up their banner, raising it high against
the challenging winds of the
twenty first century
into a new dawn
determined to reach their destination as one.

Mama's Bilum
Erick Kowa

Dedicated to all mothers and sons of Papua New Guinea, a nation of many nations, a blessed land of great contrasts – God bless this great land.

A knit of natural fibres, finely woven with colours of rainbow,
A touch of pure mastery, you hold the mystery of legends
You hang here on these white walls, watching over me
As I lay in bliss, across a thousand seas in this faraway land
Slung across my shoulders, my silent companion
As I journey across many lands, of steel and stone and glass
You remain timeless, a story of my origins
My identity, my story, my mama's bilum

Weightless,
Yet a gentle bearer of all that I possess,
On my trail through destiny
Yielding,
Yet without complaint, you jam my material cravings
As I journey down the river of time
Impenetrable,
Yet a generous guardian of all that I possess,
Big and small, light and heavy
Unpretentious,
Yet you are all that I have, when fortunes of mortals desert me
When I wonder alone, praying for new beginnings
Masterpiece,
Yet a living legend, more than sheer work of a mother's gifted hands,
You evolve with time, in shape and size and colour
My only, loyal companion, my mama's *bilum*

Besides the night fire that never dies, when the world sleeps,
There she sits, humming a chant of the legends,

The song of her mother's mother, the ballad of her soul
Meticulous and dexterous, those worn gifted hands weave,
Crafting images of her emotions,
Soulful and angelic, her laments slice the still of night,
Consecrating her craft with prophesies from dreamtime,
Seasoned and ordained, her magic hands endure, in silence they twine,
Spinning trademarks of her imagination, the matrix of her totem,
Poised and flexed, on her old tattered mat, she weaves and laments
Chanting her native dialect, with pains of her longings
To the God unseen, for her children's destiny
Her psalms hang here, in this ageless story, on this white wall,
Watching over me, as I rest my head in peace, in this faraway land
My inspiration, my guardian, my mama's *bilum*

Her laments brought me here, to this foreign shore
This modest string bag, this timeless pouch,
A script of tribal origins, a womb of new beginnings
The archive of all I ever possessed, from moments in time
On foreign soil, alone on the edge of time,
Gazing into future, my timeless pouch, right by me
My prophesy, my genesis, my mama's *bilum*

Trails of the Yellow Man
Erick Kowa

Bipo bipo tru. In dream time. In the jungles of New Guinea. There lives a man. His sons. His daughters. His wives. His dogs... father and sons, back. From a day trip. Finds. Trails of the Yellow Man....in search for wood. And fire. For Light. That never dies. This is. Their story. This is. His story....

[Crickets creaking, waterfall crackles, the cover of dusk, as canopy mist befell the forest floor. There is no light on the forest floor. There never is...]

Shhhhhhhh! The Yellow Man....
There he comes... his strides, can you hear?

A conspiracy from within. Of darkness. From darkness.
Shhhhhhh! Listen now.
Look. Closer. His swagman, can you see?
The tattoos! On his forehead. On his back. Could he be. Your own?
Shhhhhhh! Don't move....
Wait. Quiet. Listen. Lest he hears, the sound of your bow strings.

[...Gentle whispers. From spirits within...]
Oh wild mortal, when will you learn, if ever you will?
The battle is within. In the hour of sweet sleep. In the recess of your mind
The battle is within. On the comforts of your bed. Where your head rests
The battle is within. At banquets of foreign kings. Where your tummy rumbles
Arise! Oh you mighty man. Awake now! You daughters of hope
Keep watch. Like your fathers did. In Days of Old
Hide the fire. Like your mothers did. When time began
Arise! Oh you sons of this land. Defend. Trails to your sanctuary
Lest you make love to morning- lose your soul, lose your head, lose your hand
Lest you slumber- a generation gone
Watch now, the sleeping child. Guard now, the virgin woman.

[The yellow man lays down his basket, takes out his dinner from his swag, and eats, looking innocent to eyes of the uninitiated. He takes out his bamboo flutes, and makes music to welcome the night. He then takes out; his last bundle of coconut fronds, and set it alight. For light on the forest floor. There is no light on the forest floor. There never is...Is this really, a gesture of friendship?...]

Shhhhhhh! Sniff..... Smell that?
The aroma from his basket.
Shhhhhhh! Listen.... Catch that?
The music from his drum
Shhhhhhh!... Pause. Take your time
Could be poison. A conspiracy. Of darkness. From darkness

Shhhhh! Hold yourself. Be calm now, lest your mouth water. Stay a bit longer
Watch. Listen. Wait. See. Hear. Judge. The Yellow Man

[...Gentle whispers. From spirits within...]
Oh hairy wild man, it's only a bowl of beans! Red beans!.
Your pedigree, needs food of a different kind.
The kind that comes in whispers; father to son, mother to daughter
Oh great warrior! Hear now and see today!
Oh, daughters of zion! Look out, lest you moan, for your babies
Sniff the air, and tell me what you smell. I don't smell meat anymore.
Search the sky, and show me what you see. The aves. Were here before
Climb the hills, where your fathers walked, and show me the kwilas.
The ancient of them, are distant memories
Fish the waters, where your mothers fished, show me the catch
I see baskets. Empty baskets. No fish. No clams. Empty shells. Dead corals.
Oh great warrior, endure now, this final hour
Don't you know? Can't you see? This is war! The yellow man. Is never your friend. Never was. Never is. Never will be. Your friend
I hear wailing. I smell blood. I hear a mother's moan. Defend. This Land!

[Morning birds sing, waterfall crackles, the cock crows, the sight of twilight, the smell of morning dew. A new day. Light has finally arrived. To the forest floor...]

This is. Their story. This is His story.

The Great Speech – A Bush Poet's Commentary
Erick Kowa

This is a bush poet's response to PNG Prime Minister Peter O'Neil's Speech in Kokopo - PNG. "PNG lacks Economic Independence" as published in The Post Courier, 18 November 2011

Papua New Guinea's challenge now is to be economically independent, says Prime Minister Peter O'Neill.

Yes Sir, this piece of music sounds familiar. Since primary school!!!!!!
This we recite, in our sleep!!!!!
Our ears ache. For melodies of substance. For rhymes of a different kind.
Our tummies ache. For fresh bread.
This stale pancake. From of your kitchen. Is killing us!

Speaking in Rabaul yesterday during the launching of the Mataure Rabaul Microfinance Limited (MRML), Mr O'Neill said the country has had political independence, among other things, but he questioned if that had changed the lives of the ordinary people, adding that only a few people had benefitted.

C'mon!!!...Sir???
"Ordinary people"? WHO? Show me the face!
WHERE? Show me the house!
HOW MANY? Give me a number!
STATISTIC?!
"few people", NUMBER?! LOCATION ?! ORIGINS?!

He said the 2012 National Election was far more important than previous elections as it should ensure that PNG had economic independence so that by 2014, the country would have enormous wealth.
"…..but if we continue to elect irresponsible governments or if we

continue to elect corrupt governments, we will miss that opportunity," he said.

Oh! So it's the election now eh?!, What about "the SYSTEM"?!
"Corrupt governments"? Weren't you courting one for quite a while now?!
SHOW ME ITS FACE! ENLIGHTEN ME! To recognize its face. To know its voice!
Lest I continue. Down trails of misery…

Mr O'Neill said that PNG must learn from previous projects in the country which included world class mines such as the Panguna mine in the Autonomous Region of Bougainville and the current Ok Tedi and Lihir mines.
"The revenues that we have got from these mines have been mismanaged as such that we don't even have any money now," he said.

Money Money Money Money Money Money Money Money Money Money Money Money Money!
World Class World Class World Class World Class World Class World Class World Class World Class!
Mine Mine Mine Mine Mine Mine Mine Mine Mine Mine Mine Mine Mine Mine Mine Mine Mine!
Mismanaged Mismanaged Mismanaged Mismanaged Mismanaged Mismanaged Mismanaged Mismanaged Mismanaged!
No Money No Money No Money No Money No Money No Money No Money No Money No Money No Money!

Ouch! That sour cream? Agggaaaaiiinnnn?!! No!
SOUR, that cream is …
ACIDIC, on my sago pancake
HORIBBLE tastes, your sour cream.
Something fresh, have you?
"SYSTEM" brand maybe? "POLICY" brand perhaps?

He said that was why the Government was trying to make sure the little resources that it got money from to make up the budget was distributed evenly around the country.

(Yawn), (Yawning), (Keep Yawning)…(arms raised over head and stretch…) (yawn some more…)
(((((((((SSSnnnnoooooozzzzz,,,,,zzzzzzzzz,,,,ssshhhhh!zzzzz,,,zzzzzzzzzz,,)))))

Mr O'Neill said PNG must learn from the mismanagement of revenues from resource projects over the years and the Government believed strongly that they must make sure that they put a law around the management of these funds.
The Prime Minister said the Government would be setting up a fund management law in the next session of Parliament.

BUZZZZZZZ!!!!!BUZZZZZZZ!!!!!!NPF REPORT PLEASE
(((((((((Mr Journalist)))))))!
BZZZZZ!!!!!BZZZZZ!!!!!!NPF REPORT PLEASE
(((((TRANSPARENCY INTERNATIONAL)))!
BZZZZZ!!!!!BZZZZZ!!!!!! OMBUDSMEN?
((((((Where aaarrreee yoouuu))))))!?
………………………………………………………………………………
……

He said it was important that PNG had to have a law to manage funds and reports could be made every three months.
Mr O'Neill told those who gathered at the launch yesterday that he had nominated former PM and Kokopo MP Sir Rabbie Namaliu to head the fund.

(Dial 000)… (((Krrrnnnggg Krrrnnnggg)))) (((Krrrrnnnggg Krrrnnnggg))))….
(No answer)
Somebody please!!!! HELP!!!!!
Ol famili ya olgeta kaikai kol bret blong aste na ol kisim bikpla sik pekpek wara ya!!!!!!
Please try! Dial again 000 on Digicel. See if the falcon jet ambulance shows up

She's a mother - That's how!
Lapieh Landu

How do I walk through this room with my head held high?
Without the guard across the door glancing at my bust
How do I walk through this room with my head held high?
Without the clerk at the desk sniffling at my musk
How do I walk through this room with my head held high?
Without the delivery boy starring at my loosened hair
How do I walk through this room with my head held high?
Without wondering what they all assume, if they dare!

How does she walk through this room with her head held high?
She slept with the boss; her bust was her ticket that's how!
How does she walk through this room with her head held high?
Isn't that the same musk he wears! That is it! That's how!
How does she walk through this room with her head held high?
Her hairs all loosened, it must have been a long night…..surely that's how!
How does she walk through this room with her head held high?
We all wonder why, we all wonder how!

How did she walk through the room with her head held high?
Didn't they know she just had a baby- a few pounds here and there!
How did she walk through the room with her head held high?
Two kids divorced and alone - putting on the right musk was the least of her worries!
How did she walk through the room with her head held high?
Another bad hair day, couldn't find the comb- not bothered!
How did she walk through the room with her head held high?
Don't judge she's a mother- - that's how!

For you I will….
Lapieh Landu

I'll put on my mask for you today; just so I can see you smile
I'll forget he kicked me around and ripped my blouse apart
Put it all behind me, for it's my duty and your right to be happy

I'll put on my mask for you today; just so I can see you smile
I'll put a bandage on the wound he gave me with the kitchen knife
Put it all behind me, for it's my duty and your right to be happy

I'll put on my mask for you today; just so I can see you smile
Fill in the holes he made, as he drove the shaft through my skin
Put it all behind me, for it's my duty and your right to be happy

I'll put on my mask for you today; just so you I can see you smile
Wear a scarf over my head; hide away to bruises he left me
Put it all behind me, for it's my duty and your right to be happy

I'll put on my mask for you today; just so I can see you smile
I'll swallow the pain, so my broken body won't bring you a tear
Put it all behind me, for its my duty and your right to be happy

I'll put on my mask for you today; just so I can see you smile
Ill force the food down my throat, so you can eat yours too
Put it all behind me, of it's my duty and your right to be happy

I'll put on my mask for you today; just so I can see you smile
Yes, I'll play with you today and Ill laugh out loud too
Put it all behind me, for it's my duty and your right to be happy

I'll put on my mask for you today, like I do every other day
I'll be your mother, your father and your friend
Put it all behind us, for we deserve to be happy.

Misconception
Lapieh Landu

Dedicated to Malcolm Gauthier- thank you, for the enlightenment to realise the importance of gender equity and justice. You inspire me....

I am a man, strong, fierce and ardent
I stand with pride, dignity and poise
I chose to have her as my companion
A lifetime of laughter, colours and noise

Friends, bikes and books
Our life was flowers rainbows and bliss
We were happy, undeniably happy
Endless hugs, discourse and a kiss

The maker was all too kind
He blessed us with something so divine
My eyes he had so exact
Her skin as rich as wine

Years tracked by and so did our youth
Blisters and bruises I earned
To make ends meet I sacrificed
The comfort of my unit in return

I am a man, strong fierce and ardent
I stand with pride, dignity and poise
But when the going gets tough
I too weep for I have no choice

I chose to have her as my confidant
I've elected this path for me
I try, I hurt, and I hold affirm
Legal imprisonment it can be

One day I come home from work
Tired, bruised and glitches
It's funny, I don't remember the rest
I woke up in brutal plain and stitches

My eyes scurry the room for her
Whilst my thoughts rushed in plight
It was hatred and misconception
That robbed us both that night

I am a man, strong, fierce and ardent
I stand with pride, dignity and poise
How do I comfort my weeping child?
No words but a shower of toys

Yesterday I was a loving husband
Doting father and loyal friend
Today I am but far from it all
Names so cruel; My God! It just won't end!

I told her I'd never hurt her
For God sake- not even a fly!
I fell in love with her from the start
And I'd love her till I die

For I am a man, strong, fierce and ardent
I stand with pride, dignity and poise
I'd give everything to make her understand
That she'd always been my choice

What happened back then!
Lapieh Landu

This poem expresses the issue of racial segregation in our country, what happened back then...something that my generation can't seem to understand and accept with ease today...the fact that despite our rightfulness and national sovereignty, we were once deprived...

I cannot understand what happened back then!
The factions of superior and periphery
Why her heels graced the footpath
And my feet, the rigid soil
I cannot understand what happened back then!
The hatred and indifference
Why his grog consumed in class
And I, sculled mine in the streets
I cannot understand what happened back then!
The revulsion and animosity
Why his house sailed our hills
And mine loiter the outskirts
I cannot understand what happened back then!
The delusion and coldness
Why his illness healed with ease
And my child died without
I cannot understand what happened back then!
The injustice and wrongness
Why he retained his title as boss
And I not nearly his subordinate
I cannot understand what happened back then!
The vulnerability of my leaders
Why they have the preference
And I settled for anything I receive
I cannot understand what happened back then!
The openness to influence

The reception of standards
The concession of culture and
The enslavement of oneself
I just cannot understand what happened back then!

Struggling between two cultures
Patricia Martin

Young, wild and free
I grew to believe that the tapa and grass-skirt is for the villager
I chose to wear jeans and shirts
Accusations and assault appalled me

Aren't I a Papua New Guinean growing up between two cultures?
I disposed the thought to relieve myself of shame
For not knowing my peoples' ways
Bored and bothered, I bungled the bridge of my cultural identity

Logic started whispering tormenting scads of loss
From what?
Haughty hugged me tight
And gave me sobriquet

On a fast lane, fast food and falling frenzy
I heard voices chanting
Goon… Goon… Goon… Goon
Have you forgotten?

That being a Papua New Guinean
You have cultural roots
Your ancestors wore tapa and grass-skirt
Simplicity was the order in the village

And oh, yes there is a place called village

Where the father and brother of your father live
Where your father's brother can also be called dad
Where your grandmother cooks food in a clay pot

Where dinner is served in wooden bowls
Where you sit on a sago leaf woven mat and eat
Where you sleep in a bush material house
This is shelter and home to your people

I blush yet baffled
What has become of me?
To live that life is difficult
To adapt is unthinkable

Pride rests in the deepest part of my inner being
To know who I really am
The comfort of what I am experiencing now
Inhibits me from confronting the truth

I hear an unpleasant continuous music
Beckoning me to sing
I choose instead to listen
Intently will I listen

The dark cloud hovering over me will be diffused
Then I will embrace reality
And be liberated
To accept growing up between two distinct cultures

Road to Seclusion
Hinuvi Onafimo

One, two …six lazy steps
And two blue chairs away,
An Asian beauty
Consciously steps out of herself,
But cautiously took my hand – a black hand
And walked slowly.
O Sayako my dear,
I remember
How our knees bend
on the raw tatami and
Your long black hair
Flew into my eyes.

That beautiful night,
When we both ran
To reach our somehow same goal,
You reach the line
Before I came home.
O Sayako my dear
I remember
On the road to seclusion
How our eyes burnt with love
And our steady legs
Hurried off into the hungry night.

Tatami – Japanese mat

Nervous Poet
Hinuvi Onafimo

A nervous poet
Stood on trembling legs
And cast a nervous glance
To the hungry eyes
That had gathered before him
To feed from his harvest.

His time has finally arrived.
Before the feast began
He must empty the truth – the ultimate truth.

This will be his first,
People will feed from his lips
Product of his literary harvest
Collected cracking raw brain cells.

A Poet's Chant
Hinuvi Onafimo

A dusty road
Upswept by the grand wind
Reaches a door
Of a far reaching realm;
A poet's singing mouth.

Yesterday's chants
With poetic look,
Now courts with a bird
On a dry branch

In the naked sky

Echoes that cry,
Journeyed with marching men,
On a ruined plain,
Reaches a door,
To the old poet.

Old Sibuta
Hinuvi Onafimo

The old country road
When I asked my old mama
She could not remember
How many times
She had walked through.

Down the road,
I will not forget
The old sibuta
Where hanging like a bat
I would slumber peacefully in
And with the cold mountain wind
Like other branches
I would sway back and forth.

And the old road
That leads to mama's door
Every afternoon, from the field,
She would follow home
With the old sibuta
Hanging against her back.

If only I could pause now,

How it was then,
I shall remember…
The old sibuta

*Sibuta – big hand woven bilum (bag) used for carrying large quantities of food.
It is also used to ferry infant babies.*

A Journey to My Womb
Hinuvi Onafimo

The sun over Nipinaga ridge
When I watch from Kigimu
Invites me home
To the womb of my mothers.

Listen
Children of Nipinaga
The wombs of our mothers are rejoicing.
As days grow near
The chants from their lips
Praises our arrival

The tears that flow every night
Falls like Damaguta Waterfall
Down their faces.

Sons & daughters of Nipinaga,
When the journey is over,
Remember to offer a pray
To the old wombs.

Paddle Me Back
Gelab Piak

Paddle me back to my village,
Back to the days of my childhood,
Paddle me through calm waters,
Far from evil and danger,
As I pass the first old villages,
My memories race ahead of me,

Paddle me back to my home,
Where time is calm and comforting,
Paddle me back, while I hold my breath,
And close my eyes,
As we come pass Gide creek,
I can feel my nerves kicking,
As my legs shiver,

Paddle me back to my village,
While I'm young and eager and willing,
Paddle me back, dear, whoever you are,
I don't know where I'm leaving for,
Spread my wings and I shall sail,
I can see the canoe place inching closer,
My lips are so dry, I'm thirsty,
And dying for a taste of the ground.

Christianity
Leonard Fong Roka

Christ, Christ
You Lord of the sky; the moon and the sun.
The rain and wind pay you homage,
O master of the universe.

Christ, Christ
Why you no eat my food with me?
Mama brings you the best of our garden
Every Sunday, but I see the padre gobbling it all.
Why he no wait for you?

Christ, Christ
My gods, the Kama-kiki and Koma-rara
Eat a lot. Grandma and pa feed them; they
Love fresh or smoked fish.

Christ, Christ
When Koma-kiki and Koma-rara
Get furious with we,
The mighty Laluai floods; the winds destroy
And the Solomon sea
Roars to our fear.

Christ, Christ
Why do you no answer me,
You sick or just tired?

Dance to the beautiful sea
Leonard Fong Roka

There are days where I sit and wonder
why the sun raises o'er Pokpok isle
and fade to sleep behind Pava'ire mountain village
without sparing a moment in Araba for a dance.
Time and seasons come and go
and still, she passes above me without heed.
Should she be my mama denying me
a hectic dance chit-chat?
No! No! My Kongara love bird, Dong'kiring-kiring,
the sun is the goddess, Barama-birama
from Boi'ra, they say swims to Tausi'na isle
and shoots to the fountains of Kavarong River
for inspiration.
She'd says: I've given you the Bovong,
the Kaperia, the Tumpu'kasi
and the Taraka brawling waters
for your wisdom dance; dance to the estuary.
There is dance of joy…
Dance of joy!
The sun dances in the blue sky.
You dance from the peaks to the sea.
Dance! Dance!
Dance to the beautiful sea.

The Magic of Kunu'nava
Leonard Fong Roka

Nem'makaa[1]…
the magic little boy
loves blowing his *kovi*[2]
high in the black hills.
Lusts listening erect
those sinking, rocking sacred echo go
rolling
bumping
crushing pellucid quake!
through the deepest valleys to the *kunu'nava*[3]
that legend house heat
of mystic chastity
scaring away the owl spells
like clouds fading dying
due to no adoration dogma,
but just chatting o
laughing away'd his trespasses.

O magic.
The magic…the magic little boy
who blows across ranges
tunes of strangeness…
anew
mysterious
tempos that retrieve
the blood of virgos;
o chaste magic little girls
from the initiation of *kunu'nava*.

Amazed.
Shocked in disbelief

and inclined to the verses
of joy sweating, burning and glowing they sing:
'o magic…
the magic little boy
come…o come…
come you magician
of a hundred rivers and slopes.
Come kiss this cone
sharp breasts and
caress them to fire
and fetch your share of dreams
and power.

Come… o come…
come disqualify my holiness.
Smear my lips
with that spell of mystic oils—
the surge of your pride—
that pride…o…pride.

O magic…
magic …the magic little boy.
Come…*o'ii bakaa^t nem'makaa*,
the heir of my menstruation genesis…
oh boy, o.
Boy of my happiness and heritage.
Come!
O come…by
the taboos of your forefathers
pay your homage
to the night owners—
o killer of souls—
who keep the door of the *kunu'nava*
as owls of death.

Death. O death…

In the dark canopies, it's death.

Death it is, my magician
Of a hundred rivers and slopes.
O magician,
homage the spells over and over
with the magic flutes
from the blackest hills and peaks of fog.'

To the verses, the boy yodels: 'o owl spells,
care for my womanhood, I am the boy…and
she owes me the powers.
Pleasures.
Joyful dances
and wisdom potions of rain making –
seasons and life—and prolonged love making nights.

Secure my life,
my good servants of the *kunu'nava*,
she's the cuddle of my loins…
fattened by the first produce
of the land and seasons.

She is the pride of me, the foreigner.
O magician of a hundred rivers and slopes.

She was, o gods
hidden from the eyes of moons and suns…
those broth spillagers.

O, owls
in the canopies of death,
caress my spirit amidst those virgins
initiating to the mysteries
of womanhood and
child bearing pains

after naked sleeping of joy.

O owl spells,
spirited clouds and fireflies,
care for my joy in the *kunu'nava*.
The artery of my testimony.'

O magic,
the magic little boy
of a hundred rivers and slopes.

The magic,
the magic little boy…
He blows
the melodies of dance
to the nights and spirits til dawn.
Sweating erotic hearting
and lust pains blowing to the great land—
peoples of experience—of women
and smeared thighs,
you'd had it all before the *kunu'nava*.

The bright sun is over the sea
coming to rage my heart,
dry to emptiness.
My tender of dreams
and moisture of pride, oh impatient
magic little boy.
Company the magic,
to the house of *kunu'nava*.
Have me sink and lost
between the lost thighs
and bring forth womanhood of big buttocks.

O womenfolk,
of skill and endurance

bring
to the fall of spirited nights
o'er the majestic kunu'nava
and her fountain of life…
that erotic life so long.

Dance in joyful moaning…
o magic, the magic little boy…
Shout and scream and roll…
and cry:
'o mother earth
dance with me to the gate
of magic and wonders of miracles and gods.
Mother,
mother earth
dance with me to the gate of magic and wonders
of miracles and gods.
Mother…o
mother earth
blow your flute to the *kunu'nava*,
sleeping like skull
under the azure sky.

Burn…crackling
must be your superstitious torches…
Quaking beds are beds
to warm the fingers of power
and caress those cone breasts and sweet lips.
O mother earth's boy!
The magic,
the magic little boy.
He dances and dances for the gods and spirits
under the magic of *kunu'nava*.

Nem'makaa- a teenage boy, Kovi- bamboo flute used for singsing kaur, Kunu'nava- initiation huts for girls at menarche, O'ü baka- oh (in pleasure)

A Journey Far Away
Marie-Rose Sau

Far away yet again
To the land of the misty mountains
And never ending rough roads
Where the clouds descend to
Kiss the treetops
In the wake of the morning

The land of the famous Nokondi
Apo land now as it is known
A land masked with beautiful flowers
Home of the aromatic Kongo Kofi
And Asaro Mudman
The gateway the great Highlands regions

Yet on you must journey
The winding roads dare not stop you
A mission to complete
One that is dangerous
Yet a must
That you will endure

Daulo you must pass
To a place I miss dearly
Home of the bugas
Of my angras and my ambais
My paradise that dwells
At the feet of the Mt. Wilhelm

Sadly that is not where
Your story ends
The road is long and tiring

Your aches and tire
I pray they be soothed
By my bidding that you be safe

Another stop to make
Where people stand proud
Strong tribal loyalties
And complicated clan affiliations
Surrounded by magnificent mountains
And home to the prosperous Wahgi Valley

Where Nambawan Tea is brought to life
And yet it is but another pause
For you are yet to get there
Far away from where I write today
Where the air is stained cold
Yet there the Hulis dance

Flamboyant and with spirit
Yes, far away yet again
To the land of the misty mountains
And never ending rough roads
Where the clouds descend to
Kiss the treetops

In the wake of the morning....

Timeless Attitudes
Peter Sevara

Far from the freeway, near my house
of used materials and twenty people.
A toilet and shower fed by buckets of water
Firewood for the makeshift kitchen.
Son is celled-up crying mama;
Daughter happily rides an oiled-up sugar papa.
Mama plays Queen twenty four seven,
Papa stands King at the bar of every tavern.
Eda Ranu doesn't give a piss
PNG Pawa is a rain scared miss.

Far from my house, near my street
Footpath-less tracks and non-existent lights…
Carjacking, pick-pocketing and street fights…
Betelnut splashed roads, corrugated high barbwire fences
Rubbish-clogged, open-air, sewerage-drains
Any day drink-ups and unauthorized traffic officers
Government officers boozing and blasting his car stereo.
Bitch full drunk, snorting in the back seat.
Police come panel beat…questions asked later…
Emergency room is waiting room
You wait until you're an emergency

Far from my street, near the freeway
Four people cram the door, balance like a yachter
Anywhere's a bus-stop; everywhere's a cushion-less seat
Incomplete routes, police and transport road block
Officer walks by taxi, slyly picks up his tip and says 'ok go'
Splayed on the canvassed roof, sing your forefathers memories
Smooch the yellow-top mama; fling her up in the air
Let her glitter on the pothole ridden coal-tar.

Give the driver his beer!
Piss drunk, he's a seer…
Freeway ah?
Free…no challenges, no threats, no holdbacks;
Ways…roads, access, actions….
There are no challenges on this road, no threats to this access, no holding back of any action.
You are permitted entry and exit anytime, you have easy access to anything and everything. Do whatever action you want…do not hold back...'
A freeway…built far from the squatters, illiterate, and inaccessible
Fuck if you think I'm too drunk to drive! This is the real me!

Trupla Man*
Bernard Sinai

Trupla man, paitim meri blong yu long side blong rot
Yu paitim bros, bikmaus na tok yu tasol
Yu no bisi olsem ol bai kisim yu go long kot
Tasol pasin yu mekim em i blong ol raskol
Trupla man, yu holim diwai na yu ting yu man
Singaut na bikmaus olsem yu papa graun
Tasol taim yu han nating bai yu run
Yu save yu sanap bai yu pundaun long graun
Trupla man i no save paitim meri
Trupla man i save lukautim meri
Trupla man i no man blong pait
Tasol trupla man i save long pait
Yu no trupla man, yu mas giaman man ya

***Real man**
Real man, you beat your wife at the roadside
Then you beat your chest, and brag and boast

You don't understand they'll take you to court
You're behaving just like a troublemaker
Real man, you hold a club and think you're a man
You shout and swagger like you own the land
But when you're unarmed, you flee
You know you will not stand firm then
Real men don't beat their wives
Real men know how to protect their wives
Real men are not troublemakers
But real men know how to fight
You're not a real man; you're a fraud

Twenty Two Women
Loujaya Toni

Twenty two women
Sitting ducks
Shot at
Mercilessly
By trigger happy mouths;

A
Nameless, faceless number
Posing
Threatening shadows
Women in waiting
Wanna-be politicians
Hopeful governors;

Unknown but significant
Twenty two women
All wanting
In on parliament;

They are daunting shadows

Reaching in
To the men's haus
Haunting his wildest political dreams
Forcing a hand in his schemes
Being
A very present number
At all
His deliberations
Seen and heard more
Than a mere apparition;
Twenty two women
Waiting their dues.

Once Upon a Prime Time
Loujaya Toni

Once upon a prime time television
In a faraway fixed location
CNN and ABC couldn't miss it
No world government could dis-it
PNG
Paradise of Non-Geniuses who could take your best efforts apart
And
Present you with what you never intended;

A day in the life of the Unexpected
We support blood
We respect sweat
We acknowledge tears;

We live on a rural-urban divide
We practice cutting edge
We are the reality show the ratings commission warned you about
We moved out of PGR into AO
There are no splices or edits

We are a one take
Action people
Box offices cannot hold us
We are bigger than HOLLYWOOD

Everyone knows where we are
But
No one in their right mind should come here!

She Lied
Loujaya Toni

1

After several years of marriage
She could tell
When the body came home sometimes
The mind chose to dwell where the body had been;

That's when the motions were
Mechanical
The spirit was not in it
She knew
And
He knew
But
They faked it
No one spake it
Not until …

11

She lied
She laced her lies
It was convenient for her to do so
It was easy
He believed her

That
Was good enough for now
If he asked her tomorrow
She was forced
To remember what she had said today
So her story could stick
She was quick about her business
There were no attachments
No love lost
Just a cash in enterprise
Then
The bread began to rise
Forcing its presence thru the under-clothes
Layer of lying layer couldn't hide the protrusion
The confusion
The result of fusion
She lied down
Covered in lace
It was convenient for her to do so
It came easy
She died so her story could stick;

111

She was the conscience that troubled his guilt
She rocked his boat
She wouldn't let sleeping dogs lie
She got under his skin
His patience wore thin
He discarded it
Left it hanging at half mast
After a few drinks
He was having a blast
Now that he got his thoughts together
He was ready to tell her
The sooner the better;

A grand entry with a boot thru the door
And a fist to the jaw
She had long been dead
Only now it looked as if he killed her
She lied
Even in death
Only now he got what he deserved.

To Whom it May Concern
Loujaya Toni

To whom it may concern
The interested
The one who wants to know
The curious
The one who is going to do something about it
About the knowledge
Of the contents
Herein and herewith
Who will read it
And respond to it
Copy and file it
Make a recommendation
Write a response
Offer a correspondence
Notify the author
Supply the details
Enclose a copy
Sign the signature
End the dictate
Check the notate
Seal the deal
Post the script
Offer a hand
See that it lands

In the hands of the author
A finished piece of attention to
From you know who
The one concerned
The dear sir/madam
The yours faithfully
And yours truly;

To whom it may concern
I may not have arrived
But I have written something
For your eyes and your ears
For your heart and your tears
I have no fears
It has been years
Like yesterday in a bottle
I send it to you
Who may be concerned!

The Making of Me
Emma Wakpi

I am who I am
Because my Grandfather
Swathed in feathers and lard
Fought for his land
With bows and arrows
Toiled in his garden
Alongside his bride
Loved his family
With strength and pride

I am who I am
Because my Grandmother

Swathed in grass skirts and lard
Fought for her land
Alongside her husband
Toiled in her garden
Ancient wisdom her guide
Loved her family
With fierceness and pride

I am who I am
Because my Father
Swathed in pig grease and grass
Struggled with school
With pen and paper
Adapted to change
With shirt and trouser
Ancient, recent,
Meshing, creating the future

I am who I am
An Ancient People
A Modern World
Primordial Customs
Scholastic Pursuits
Cultural Strongholds
Technological Breakthroughs
Developing a Nation
Making History
Making me…Me

I am who I am
Because my Grandfathers
Clothed with shirts and long pants
Came to this land
Proclaiming Christ
Toiled in the sun
To show their love

To a people so foreign
Yet so beloved

I am who I am
Because my Grandmothers
Clothed with shirts and long skirts
Came to this land
Proclaiming Christ
Braving the wilderness
Relinquishing the known
To prove their love
For the yet unknown

I am who I am
Because my Mother
Shrouded in birth and blood
Struggled to live
In a world of heartache and love
With quiet resolve
Accepted her lot
And modelled a life
Of hope, peace and love

I am who I am
A Foreign People
A Brand New Message
Health and School
Mission Minded
Christ and His Love
Bible Grounded
Developing a Nation
Making History
Making me…Me

In bed with Me #2
Imelda Yabara

In my bed
we lie,
all three of we,

a clone,
a ghost
and me,

pain roars for battle,
against
my unseen enemy,

to inflict,
the same,
as was
dealt to me,

my spirit prances,
eager for a war,
lost,
before it begins.

against an apparition,
for a clone,
I do not know,

we dine,
my bond,
his shackles,
next to me,

across from me,
beside the moon and stars,
he sits,

a mannequin,
blood red,
painted on grin,

I touch,
but do not feel,

I speak,
He grins,

here we lie,
a clone,
lying beside,
a ghost,
who lies,
next to me

Way out of reach
Imelda Yabara

On a street a father sits,
Heart refusing defeat,

Next to him his daughter sleeps,
Tears running down her cheeks,

He's called everyone,
who will listen to his pleas,
to help him pay,
his child's school fees,

He knows he must give,
his child the opportunity,
to be educated and maybe get a degree,

He wonders how education
has been so expensive,
that it has become a luxury,

So tomorrow he will meet with her teacher's,
to beg for another week,

To give him time to find the money,
so she can be free.

ESSAYS

Untighten Your Fist
Lorraine Basse

Violence against women has become the norm in many parts of the country and is one of the many issues affecting our country today. There are many factors that are involved in domestic violence but the three that are most common are (1) private matters, (2) payment of bride price and (3) the mentality of 'a male dominated society'. Most men regard women as objects and therefore, blame their wives for every little thing that they find fault in. For instance bearing a female child when they want a male, work pressure, family obligations, forgetting to clean the house or wash the dishes, children crying, food not cooked to his liking, does not like the way she is dressing, no respect, not enough food in the house and talking to a male stranger to name a few. This in turn leads to quarrels, arguments, disunity and to domestic violence within and among families creating a tension in the village, community, the society and the country as a whole.

Domestic violence is seen in most pars as a private matter. Therefore, whenever a man hits his wife, most people; neighbours and the authorities concerned pretend that they cannot see what is going on and turn a deaf ear. Only some are brave enough or man enough to stand up for the victims. Since most communities view domestic violence as a private matter, only some of the victims press charges, and prosecutions are rare; most of those affected by it, think it is normal. Moreover, growing up in a culturally oriented society makes many women think that it is their duty to make their husbands happy and therefore, have no right to refuse sex with their husbands. They obligingly give in to their husbands wishes even though they do not like it. This in turn leads to many problems and tensions in the family, the community and the society as a whole. These people who are affected by violence sometimes do not know they can get help, are too scared or are too ashamed to come forward.

Another matter viewed as private and a form of violence is rape. Rape in the past was regarded as a war strategy in most parts of Papua New Guinea and was therefore not seen as an issue. There was no concept of rape in marriage either. Rape or sexual assault is 'an assault by a person involving sexual intercourse with or without sexual penetration of another person without that person's consent.' Men have the mentality that: 'My wife is my wife and whatever we do in the vicinity of our dwelling is our private business.'

The rapists when reported or apprehended sometimes do not face trials and walk freely around, especially if he or she was someone important in the community; sometimes they break out of jail. Even though 'rape is punishable by imprisonment and sentences were imposed on convicted assailants, few rapists were apprehended. The willingness of some communities to settle incidents of rape through material compensation rather than criminal prosecution makes the crime difficult to combat.' Rape whether you like it or not, is a crime and should be dealt with accordingly and not something to be shunned or viewed as a private matter.

Wife beating too is seen as a private matter in almost all parts of the country. Reports show that some of the highest rates of violence and abuse of women in the world occur in Papua New Guinea. However, in 1986 the Law Reform Commission of Papua New Guinea decided to take a stand and began its campaign against wife-beating. And now PNG is one of the few developing countries to embark on a 'nationwide program of legal, social and educational measures'. The immense public-campaign was carried out to try and change the attitudes and the norm of wife-beating. As a result of the campaign, some of the policies were changed and the constabulary 'began treating wife-beating like any other form of assault and were arresting and prosecuting offenders.'

The other factor that mitigates domestic violence is the payment of bride price. Whenever men pay for their wives, they have a propensity to believe that they are their possessions. In some parts of the country, especially in the highlands provinces, this type of practice is common. Men tend to view women as objects when they are being paid for. This gives them the mentality that they own women and they can do anything they want. Men do not care about women's feelings if they had paid their bride price. Some clans also give the men full responsibility and authority to do whatever he wants with his wife. Thus, paying a bride price tends to reinforce the view that women are property.

In 1987, a government minister said in a statement that 'we pay for our wives, so we own them and can belt them any time we like'. Now this type of mentality has been instilled in the mindset of some men in PNG. We can say that our culture says to beat wives if she is in the wrong but who gave you the right to hit someone? It is also against the law, and if caught then tougher penalties should be ensured to make the offender pay for his actions. In addition, 'in the villages, a husband's right to chastise his wife physically was accepted, with some tribes even recognizing this by presenting a stick to the bridegroom in return for the payment of bride price.'

There is no law that limits the full participation of women in all aspects of life, but the deeply rooted patriarchal culture sometimes stops women from fully participating in any development. PNG as a male-dominated country gives few opportunities to women in communal life. Moreover, development itself can be a link to violence. There is also the rise of a new culture of boyfriends hitting their girlfriends at the secondary and tertiary level of education.

Rapid social change sweeps away centuries of old ways of doing things creating stress and insecurity. However, this has greatly changed in the last couple of years giving women equal participation in all walks of life.

Today, women are doctors, lawyers, managers, directors and officers to name a few. Women tend to jump in the race to show their counterparts that if you can do it I can do it. Whereas in the past they just sat on the fence and observed. Women can now get higher positions and achieve their aims and dreams; they can aspire and become successful. They fully know their rights and therefore, they do not get abused or misled quickly, unlike in the past. And now there is current pushing of the Bill for 22 reserved seats for women, which was originally included in the constitution but never passed into effect.

To conclude, the most damaging effect women face as a result of domestic violence and which they are forced to endure is the humiliation and pain of violence. As a result of violence women see themselves as weak, vulnerable, helpless, inadequate and helpless. Domestic violence can surely be erased if both parties understand and do not abuse each other's rights. They must understand that it has drastic effects on the victim. Children too are affected by what they see in their families and there is a possibility that they can repeat what they observe in later life. Therefore, men should understand that women are created to be their partners and not something to be regarded as under him; as the famous saying goes; "woman was created from the rib of man, not from his head to be above him, nor his feet to be walked upon, but from his side to be equal, near his arm to be protected and close to his heart to be loved."

There is an urgent need for the government of the day to see and ensure that wife-beating is a serious problem affecting and affected by development.

The government needs to provide resources to deal with it because simple campaigns and awareness programs cannot solely eradicate the issue.

There should be a 'Domestic Violence Act' introduced to deal with such cases.

The churches should work in partnership to promote equality among their congregation.

The education department should set in place curriculums to deal with this issue in the schooling system from prep to university. It should start at the prep or elementary level because a child's first years of growth will surely affect his or her life later.

There should be awareness within the family that violence is not an answer to a problem. "Family is the social unit of a society and the country as a whole."

Outreach activities should be provided by the organizations and institutions concerned to raise awareness in the communities because sometimes people do not know they can get help or are too scared or ashamed to come forward.

Is Sex Education Compatible in Primary Schools in PNG?
Werner Cohill

I can remember some years back, when there used to be an advertisement on EMTV about the awareness of condoms. A medical doctor appeared during commercial breaks and spoke explicitly about safe sex through the use of condoms. While watching the popular 'CHM Making Music' program every Thursday evening or the Friday night football, the commercial breaks were switched off by many people to avoid viewing this advertisement.

Quite recently, it was reported in one of daily newspaper that a student from a named primary school in the Nation's Capital was suspended from classes. He was caught by his teacher watching porn during class time on his mobile phone.

These two cases exemplify how important sex education ought to be defined and understood for our young people. It is imperative for these young people to receive such education disseminated to them. In the long run this lack is not good for their health and physical well-being.

As for the former, there was huge public resentment towards this particular advertisement. Concerned parents and adult alike were in total disagreement with the advertisement as they thought it was morally and religiously wrong for it to be viewed by children. The newspapers and the local radio stations became the venting forums for people to express their frustrations and make known their views and state the immediate effects this advertisement would have on the young people. Fortunately for the medical doctor he was not harmed but the gossiping world disliked him. The medical doctor proved critics wrong by later representing PNG in international engagements, notably in Timor Leste and becoming PNG's Top Health Administrator – the Health Secretary. I admire him to this day.

However, as for the latter there were no public commentaries or resentment towards the general conduct of our young people in terms of accessing pornography. What now will be the outcome or the end results of this report? Is it worth reading such stories and is it now time to address sex education seriously by taking the bull by its horns?

The debate on whether it is worth having sex education taught in primary schools has never been discussed at length. Obviously the age factor has limited the advocacy for such education to be furthered in its course. This essay intends to discuss the importance of sex education in Papua New Guinea. More specifically, it aims to discuss the compatibility of sex education at the primary level of education. The argument here is not to seek to teach students about sex alone, but rather broaden their mind sets about the dangers, what they need to know, how to deal with issues relating to sexual health and the reproductive system.

When the topic of sex education pops up in a discussion on the streets, at school and among peers, the obvious topic is about sexual pleasures or encounters. There is more to the definition than our shallow and immature understanding of the topic however. The definition of sex education simply refers to teachings about the different sexes, the types of relationships between opposite sexes, the importance of sex and its doings, the reproductive system and related issues or challenges developing from this topic. In science, sex education is a broad term used to describe education about human sexual anatomy, sexual reproduction, sexual intercourse and other aspects of the human sexual behaviour.

According to Dr. Babatunde Osotimehin, the Executive Director of the United Nations Population Fund (UNFPA), and the UN under-Secretary-General, sex education is like teaching people how to drive by telling them in detail what is under the bonnet, how the bits work, how to maintain them safely to avoid accidents, what the controls do and when to go on the road. It is all about the mechanics.

Sex education is fast becoming part and parcel of young people's educational upbringing in many western countries, including Australia. This was evident during an 'Insight Program' on SBS Television' recently, where an audience of mostly teenagers were asked about how influential pornography was and is in their lives. Some of them admitted watching porn as early as eleven years old. They claimed to have received more information from such stuff than being taught by their parents or at school. More interesting was the case where elementary schools students are given lessons on sex education.

Having been brought up in societies where the traditional beliefs and value systems have a strong influence on our growth and development, sex and its entire doings are a tabu for us, especially the young ones. Coupled with this, is the strong inclination of our different religious beliefs and church practices. These are the principle challenges from day one, forbidding us as parents to providing a profound understanding about sex to the young ones. To a larger extent, the Education Department and its line agencies have based their arguments on the age of young people allowed to receive such education.

As the world is changing through innovations in information technologies and communications, peoples' behaviour and conception of sex is changing. A wave of pornography is hitting our shores and pushing the societal and biblical walls of relationships and marriages, the essence of love and respect far wider open. Thus pornography is becoming readily available in the country where five years ago it was restricted to those that ventured abroad.

More so, the social mores and behaviour cycles of young people have greatly changed. The spread of pandemic diseases, like HIV and Aids, and issues like prostitution and human smuggling and drug trafficking tops the list of the social underpinning concerning and involving young people. The young people are the targets of the ever growing gap between the developed and the developing world.

This raises serious issues about the incompatibility of no sex education in primary schools. The challenges that were alluded to as the yardstick for sex education to be taught are negligent of the outcome that the young people will suffer from. More specifically social problems, like unwanted pregnancies and prostitution, is rife among our young people. Cases of incest and under-age sex are also rife among them.

These issues have be carefully analysed to see how influential they are or how persuasive they are in arguing for the compatibility of sex education at the primary level of education. The following two issues provide reasons to justify the compatibility of sex education at the primary level of education.

First are the issues of internet accessibility and the dissemination of sex information. Having access to the internet has shifted from internet cafes to the palms of our hands. The mobile phone has made the surfing of the internet more convenient and it takes less time. You have access to it where you are – as is where is. With little or no control over which sites are restricted and which are not, young people find themselves having access to the restricted ones. The males will be accessing sites about females and the females doing the opposite. The sites that are most frequently visited are porn sites and the lust for it becomes a secret mission for these young people. The story I alluded to earlier clearly demonstrates this point and sure enough this is rampant in most schools throughout the country. Only time will tell when more such stories will be reported and how effective those in authority will respond to mitigate the consequences.

Second is the issue of the development of mind-sets and the behaviour of young people. The children of this generation are more open-minded about both material and non-material stuff. Let's put it this way, the ability of a thirteen year old to grasp onto ideas today may be much different from someone his age some ten years ago.

Money can be a classic example of the material stuff that young people can always look forward to from their parents. Most children expect nothing more than money from their parents. The knowledge about money can be obtained, on average, by children at around the age of two or three.

In the same way, non-material stuff like romance and love, relationship and marriage, and sex may seem less important to us as adults but they form priority agendas for the young people. The young people of this generation frankly take for granted relationships, marriages and sex. However, they lack the basic information about the essentials and core of this stuff. Sadly for them, the consequences are often beyond their reach, especially young girls who do not seem to foresee their future after pregnancy. Teenage pregnancies or the 'teen mum' dilemma is becoming more a developmental issue than a family problem.

The argument about the incompatibility of sex education in primary schools should be a thing of the past now. Sex education should now be understood as an important part of a child's growth and development. The UN Secretary General had to state this during a recent high level meeting on young people in New York, "We cannot ignore the facts, many young people are sexually active, and because of this, they may face risks to their health, including sexual violence". Therefore, all governments need to make available comprehensive sexual education as well as confidential sexual and reproductive health services that will help young people to make responsible choices regarding their sexuality.

On this note, the relevant government departments and agencies should seriously consider introducing sex education at the primary level of education.

Robust Force or Rogue Cops: The future of the Royal Papua New Guinea Constabulary
Werner Cohill

The performance and actions of our police force (the Royal PNG Constabulary) in recent times have not been good. Our fellow countrymen in blue are not seen to be enforcing and upholding the rule of law as they are constitutionally tasked to do. The police are responsible to making sure every citizens dwells within the confines of the National Constitution. In the same way, they are tasked to uphold the rule of law by making sure any citizen disobeying the laws of the land are prosecuted and punished.

Despite being a disciplinary force, the actions and performance of the force as well as individual cops have come under scrutiny on many occasions. These poor actions and performances of the police force are often beyond their code of conduct. The growing public perception is that, though it is a disciplinary force, it very much lacks discipline. It appears obvious that within our communities the people are more scared of the police than the criminals.

This essay explores the performance of the Royal Papua New Guinea Constabulary in recent times, in terms of enforcing the rule of law and the general upkeep of law and order in our communities. Their performances are viewed against the 'cop setback', issues that often make headlines in our print media and on television. These 'cop setbacks' committed by our police force are criminal in nature, yet very little is done to bring justice to the victims.

Now what are these setbacks?

One of the major setbacks is that the State has over the years paid huge sums of money as compensation as a result of the actions of the police. Throughout the years, the State has had to settle compensation claims from people and communities for disturbances and destruction committed by the police force. Cases of police raids, houses set on fire, properties ransacked and destroyed, and even deaths all lead to compensation.

In most cases, the operations of the police force are commended by their superiors. However, excessive force and destruction in the process is the main underlying reason for the State having to settle compensation demands. At other times, it is the police force's own doing at their own will which has ended with the State taking the responsibility.

Engaging in illegal activities contrary to their duties and responsibilities is a serious setback found among our police force. A growing practice nowadays is the unauthorised escorts or security provided by the force to certain individuals, both in the public and private sphere. At other times it is the unauthorised traffic roadblocks or related minor traffic offences which do not warrant traffic reprimands. Yet the commuters or the public are punished or their personnel belongings searched. These actions performed or exercised are illegal and whatever course of action taken automatically warrants justice.

It is often claimed that quite a few serious armed robberies worth thousands of kina, may be linked to police personnel involvement. The series of BSP Bank robberies a few years back by William Kapris is a classic example. It was alleged that policemen were directly involved in all these robberies, but all the glory was given to the key man William Kapris.

Instances of misusing logistical support and equipment, like vehicles for personal use is a bigger problem. On a larger scale is the use of state issued firearms and uniforms for criminal activities which is utterly wrong.

Unlawful custody of people in police lock-ups is another one of the setbacks; a tactic used by duty officers to entice those behind bars for social pleasures. It is common sense that any person found to have committed an offence must be charge or otherwise and not locked-up unnecessarily.

The consumption of alcohol during working hours is an insane approach in enforcing the rule of law and is another setback. We are all aware what sort of actions drunken officers can do. Drinking and driving is an offence yet the very people responsible for exercising this law are breaching it. At the same time it is beyond their code of conduct to be on duty under the influence of alcohol.

Another simmering setback that has recently come to light has been domestic violence. Our policemen have become prime actors in domestic violence. The police force is supposed to be built on character and discipline and this must be maintained at all times, both during working and off duty hours.

As reported in our dailies newspapers, a wife of a cop came out telling about the agony she has been experiencing from her husband. The ordeal had been going on for some time until she could not take it anymore and had to come out in public. There were other similar stories that run in the headlines in our print media. The trust and confidence in our police to handle issues relating to domestic violence cannot be upheld anymore. It is sickening trying to seek justice from an authority which is supposed to provide justice for domestic violence victims yet its own actions speaks a different language.

The events emanating from the political impasse mid last year (2011) hit the Royal Papua New Guinea Constabulary the hardest. The force was divided into two factions. One faction was with the regime elected by parliament and the other was with the judiciary appointed regime.

What transpired at Government House following the Supreme Court ruling in August last year was totally disturbing. If only a single bullet had been fired then the situation would have ended up in bloodshed. Thank heavens nothing of the sort eventuated.

Even more appalling was the manner in which the Members of Parliament from the O'Neill-Namah regime were treated by the police personnel loyal to the Somare Regime at Government House in Konedobu. This really brought the demise of the reputation of the Royal PNG Constabulary. Indeed, this bad impression was televised across the region and to the world. Political turmoil was taking shape but disappeared into the foot of Burns Peak.

From all these setbacks and other simmering issues, the question we have to ask ourselves now is where is the Royal PNG Constabulary heading in the future? Are we seeing a once robust force that will now be manipulated by rogue officers?

Was it a robust force, vested with the authority to ensure that the internal security of the country is maintained at all times on a bipartisan basis failing? Was it the doing of rogue cops, year in year out, who only want to bring the force into disrepute and tarnish its good name? Whatever the case the reputation of the Royal Papua New Guinea Constabulary has been tarnished big time. It has devalued the force and defamed the character of the many who have with great respect and honour served in whatever capacity with dignity and loyalty.

The onus now is on the National Government to seriously consider arresting these developments by resourcing the Royal PNG Constabulary. The challenges facing the police force in performing their duties and responsibilities have risen because successive governments have failed to fully address them. The problem with our so-called bureaucrats is that though they have eyes they cannot see.

The assurance and commitments made by the O'Neill-Namah regime in Parliament since taking office to re-build the police force must be brought to fruition. The boom in the population growth of the country is challenging the provision of basic services to our communities, and law and order is no exception. At the same time, it is a moral obligation that discipline to be upheld and exercised by the police force. Their code of conduct must not be seen as another hand-out but should become a tiger with real teeth and claws. This means that rogue cops must be dealt with accordingly and punished.

More so, future governments must not compromise the politics of the day using the police force. The experiences of the last nine months since last August have challenged our politics, the National Constitution and our national security. This precedence which has been set must not be used as an excuse in the future.

Should there be need for outside assistance, it is recommended that the policing aspect of the Enhanced Cooperation Programme (ECP) be brought back into the country. This time we must not let the concept of sovereignty drive patriotism too much so that we forget that there is a serious law and order situation in the country.

The Royal PNG Constabulary has come a long way in the history of our country. It was initially a two-partied organisation, the Royal Papuan Constabulary established by the Australian Colonial Administration and the New Guinea Police Force established by the German Colonial Administration. Both became a unified force when the administrations of Papua and New Guinea were combined. The remnants of colonialism like the famous police brass band and the establishment of Police Motu as a language will always be a beacon of hope for the police force.

Let's not mince words about buai bisnis
Michael Dom

Buai bisnis is a real but either maligned or ignored agenda in PNG, apart from somewhat ad hoc attempts to try and minimise the associated health impacts and ascetic concerns of city markets, streets and public places. But if so many people are affected by buai bisnis shouldn't it be a central concern to us Papua New Guineans getting our collective acts together?

There are two separate issues to address: (1) regulating the betel nut industry for health and environmental concerns in urban areas and (2) facilitating for the betel nut trade to continue its function of transferring money equitably to rural people through those involved in the informal sector.

On the first issue, despite numerous attempts, particularly in urban areas, to literally clean up our act regarding PNG's favourite mouth-watering appetizers, because of the resulting discharge which creates unsightly red stains, there seems little success in curbing the onslaught on our municipalities.

Even the Health Department warnings of the disastrous results of chewing this addictive, alkaloid drenched nut, masticated with mustard fruit and blended with lime, are ignored!

Health warnings are all very well intentioned and if the authorities wanted to go that far they should ban betel nut sales altogether. That appears to be an impractical option. (Methinks though that next to a shortage of rice that action may create concerns about rioting!) On the other hand health warnings should be supported, because they provide a means of awareness (deterrence of over doing it) and advocacy to take better care of our own oral health as well as community health and hygiene.

There is no doubt that the health warnings are well justified, the ascetic appeal and environmental hygiene is a real public health concern and that the habit of chewing in public places (particularly PMV's) can be a disgusting habit of some individuals. But let's face the uncomfortable truth, people love chewing buai, most of our suburban communities revolve around betel nut markets, segments of the community rely (some almost entirely) on betel nut sales to meet their daily needs for sustenance and 'the money goes back home'. Buai is part of our PNG lifestyle and not just about livelihoods.

Therefore, if we were to acknowledge the fact that a vast majority of people want to chew buai, and are unlikely to quit their habit in the near future, then we may be more mentally prepared to start finding more workable and enforceable solutions. And these solutions may not need to be costly or cumbersome in effecting.

On the second issue, regardless of the purely economic perspective that 'betel nut does not introduce any new money' into the system, it is recognized that the betel nut trade is not only an active and popular business venture but an entire industry of its own. Moreover, buai bisnis is a means of gainful employment where people feel self-empowered to be doing something to earn their own income, no matter how big or large the financial returns.

Many anecdotal reports from different areas tell of Highland buai traders chartering airplane flights to Sepik during times when there was short supply. That aside, even the daily transport of buai along the Highlands highway is phenomenal.

Economists should consider mapping the supply chain of this trade. I think it would be quite impressive. (In fact such a study was undertaken by an Australian PhD student, Tim Sharp, around about 2007-2008, if I recall correctly).

In another posting David Kitchnoge made a point about encouraging rural people to grow commodity crops. But such a suggestion may fall on deaf ears partly because there are too many challenges to overcome with the production and marketing of the commodity crops which we are already familiar with: time to harvest, labour effort, financial investment, processing equipment and farm machinery needs, infrastructural needs such as reliable access to markets, transport and storage facilities.

In other words it's relatively easier growing betel nuts and there is more immediate financial return, without the need for major inputs or payments for services and the profits are tax free.

The great challenge is for us to improve the effectiveness and efficiency of producing agricultural commodities to make an industry as attractive as or more attractive than the betel nut trade. It may be necessary to package this primary production in a manner that provides avenue for other business development, such as storage (perhaps with local security provided) and transport or vehicle maintenance and similar small service businesses. In that manner whole 'corridors' may become available for people to take part in the economy. There are many government plans in place, and some hopefully, will be implemented to realise development at the rural level.

It may be true that betel nut trade does not, in the macroeconomic sense, 'bring in new money' to the country. But the betel trade today remains one of the major players in the micro economies of several interconnected provinces.

The livelihoods of many families are subsidised on small buai bisnis and importantly women and youths are able to take part in buai bisnis as well, which adds a social dimension that may not be well understood. We should take good account of these factors so that we can find the needed balance to improve on the conflicting agenda of buai marketing and chewing versus oral health and environmental concern, and rural versus urban livelihood options.

In addition betel nut trade demands mustard and lime production (to make the mix complete, eh laka?). The latter may be the cause of environmental concern, where sometime coral is used rather than sea shells, and this a potentially more harmful ingredient because of the caustic nature of lime (Calcium carbonate). Mustard fruit (daka) is also a very lucrative business for farming families in some areas where the fruit, being a spice crop, develops particular characteristics (for example 'olan' daka from Morobe).

There is a lot more to understand about how our local buai bisnis, a home-grown industry works. We should endeavour to understand it better if we are to make any improvements in the lives of both rural and urban people, formally or informally engaged, for health or for environmental reasons.

We should be asking ourselves how we can learn from the success of the betel nut trade so that we can improve other commodity crops. Doesn't that sound like using a home-grown solution, i.e. the PNG way?

What's *buai* got to do with it?
Michael Dom

It is unfortunately true that betel nut trade does not make any direct contribution to foreign exchange earnings for PNG. Well, neither does *brus* or *pinats* or *kumu* or *kaukau* or *tapoika* or: wait a minute, neither do most of the fresh fruit and vegetables we grow and sell in our local market places all over the country!

The question is posed; are there similarities between the *buai bisnis* agenda and any of the 'traditional PNG' crop and livestock produce?

How about this one: some wise guy (supposedly a research scientist) wrote that at last count there were at least 1.8 million native pigs being kept by village farmers across PNG. One of his colleagues then estimated that this pork meat production was 27 times more than the total output of commercial production in the country.

But that situation may change now that we've got the LNG blowing everything out of proportion. The commercial farms as well as the many rural farmers and farming organizations in PNG are now trying to capitalize on the market created by the LNG boom to start up livestock businesses and my guess is that there'll be a lot of interested potbellied politicians involved too; pigs of all kinds!

Anyway, back to our scientists, another one recently commented that a very conservative estimate of the gross value of traditional pig production (i.e. not charging typical PNG prices for pigs) was PGK 162 million or AUD 69 million. Not a bad bit of business, *eh laka*? But, if we were to stick to our economic explanation, this 'village production' doesn't bring in any foreign exchange either because it has not been tied into a 'formal production' system that has output into an overseas market. Simply put, we need to sell to someone not living in PNG to get some Aussie dollar.

So we can count this as another wasted opportunity because we haven't learned enough about the workings and potential of that existing traditional PNG pig production system in order to harness and control it for our collective economic betterment. Instead PNG is a net importer of meat and we can buy pig jowls from Australia for around PGK12 per kilo at a local butchery in Mt. Hagen. Go figure!

And that's only about pig production, if we were to talk about *kaukau* the same sorry tale would be repeated, even though those rural sweet potato farmers move container loads of bagged tubers from the highlands to Lae and on to Port Moresby, without government assistance! (Ask Consort and Bismark Shipping.) By the way, sweet potato is a delicacy in Australia and McDonalds sells a sweet potato chip specialty with its traditional Big Mac's.

So what does betel nut have to do with it?

The arguments for better facilitating the betel nut trade are similar; learning and control (and both together too!). That's one of the jobs of government (and that means us too!), to find out how things are working, if they can be improved for the betterment of one and all and, in a more philosophical sense as one friend on PNG Attitude has recently expounded, to balance the agenda of individualism and pluralism – persons and people.

If we wish to maintain our urban environments in a healthy, hygienic and aesthetically pleasing fashion while still enjoying our betel nut chewing habits then it's about time we learned and took better control of at least two things; (1) how *buai bisnis* works and (2) how the actors and their customers impact on the public areas, especially since it's the customers who create the *buai* stains.

The latter point may be a matter for psychologists, sociologists, social engineers and city commissions to figure out. I propose that it is possible that the needs of *buai bisnis* and city authorities are not in total conflict. After all the betel nut trade depends on the 'urban natives', its primary customers, in order to exist profitably. Furthermore, it is worth reiterating that the betel nut trade is probably one of the most effective means in which money is transferred from urban centres to rural villages.

The first issue however, is one that I've written about previously and which concerns the economy in PNG, where small-scale businesses and street vending has, according to conventional wisdom, negative macroeconomic repercussions in the loss of foreign exchange.

So what makes the betel nut trade work as a local industry that spreads around PNG currency? The easy answer is demand and supply. In PNG the demand is everywhere so the more interesting aspect is supply.

The betel nut trade is an important cash income earner for many rural and urban families. Furthermore, where the betel nut palm is grown it is readily inter-planted with other garden and cash crops affording an opportunistic source of income. In other words there is no conflict, at least among village farmers, about any competitive loss between betel nut and say, cocoa and copra production.

Anecdotally, it's cheaper to buy *buai* in Tambul WHP than in Tokarara NCD, but definitely more costly in Tabubil. But such an example is also indicative of the relative wealth of customers as well as the surfeit of supply along differing supply chains.

There are many other questions about the betel nut trade that should be raised too like:

What makes the betel nut supply chain so efficient and effective that betel nut has become a cash crop of convenience, and along with its accessory products mustard and lime, travel from the coast right up into the hinterlands of the country (sometimes illegally)?

Who are the actors in this trade and supply chain, what are their strengths, weaknesses and challenges and how have they used and overcome them without any external interventions?

What resources and services do they access and what avenues of financial capital are available to them?

These seem to me to be some pretty important questions for understanding the betel nut trade but there are likely to be more. If we don't know the answer to these questions then how do we expect to curb betel nut trade without coming to logger heads with a very large proportion of our people who either demand or are economically dependent on *buai bisnis*?

While it is pleasing to see that the NCD Commission is trying to clamp down on illegal markets and uncontrolled street vending in the capital city, it is likely that in the short and long term there will be continued resistance to such drastic enforced changes.

My impression of the NCD commission and thereby the government approach to betel nut trade is that with one hand we would crush our informal sector, while asking people to farm more cash crops to contribute to earning foreign exchange. Then with the other hand we give away millions of kina to a business run by an already wealthy business man to set up an airline that much less than one thousandth of the population can afford to use regularly if at all, despite the lower fares. And that's just one example.

This is the same crowd that delivered a National Agricultural Development Plan then somehow managed to lose track of spending on hundreds of millions of kina while simultaneously giving themselves a 100% pay rise (a motion which was unopposed by any MP in parliament). And we're not splitting too many hairs on that issue are we PNG?

While agricultural production is promoted by almost every single MP and government team, preaching the same weary rhetoric about our back bone, we are yet to see any significant and sustainable interventions for farming communities in PNG to be able to contribute meaningfully to earning foreign exchange.

What's *buai* got to do with it? Well, PNG put your money where your mouth is and try chewing on that!

Sir Koitaga Mano OBE and the House of Assembly
David Gonol

Our politicians today are very highly educated and they should be able to achieve great things for this country with their knowledge and vast experience.

However, this was not the case back in 1964 when the first group of politicians entered the House of Assembly for the first time after the first ever general elections in the country.

Sir Koitaga Mano was one of the first uneducated politicians to be elected to the House of Assembly representing the then Ialibu-Pangia Tambul-Nebilyer & Kandep Open Electorate.

According to Sir Koitaga, many of his fellow politicians from the highlands were also uneducated. They could not even read or write, and yet they were elected to the House of Assembly. Perhaps it was just because they understood Tok Pisin.

When they first came to Port Moresby soon after election, they were taken up to Sogeri National High School. There they were taught how to eat with knives and forks, make their own beds and dress in a professional manner. They were also taught how to conduct themselves in the House of Assembly during session times.

Of course these things sound simple today but back then they were necessary. How else could you expect these groups of uneducated village men to do things right and in a more professional manner?

I interviewed Sir Koitaga at length, especially concerning his House of Assembly days. He told me many things – some of which are rather funny whereas others are sad but those were the things they did with their limited knowledge while setting the foundations of this great nation.

The people see our politicians today simply as a 'Money Face', meaning they love money more than anything else. They love money so much that they commit public funds to their own use or award contracts to their relatives or cronies or park public moneys in secret overseas bank accounts or buy properties overseas using public funds.

However, the House of Assembly politicians were very simple and honest. Their discussions were also very simple. Their aim was to gain independence even though several Highlands politicians wanted to delay independence.

They talked about what kind of government system would be suitable for this country and how they would unite all the tribes in this country so as to live peacefully as one nation.

They didn't talk about money very often. They only talked about their vision of what the future of the country would be like. Of course they successfully achieved most of what they had always talked about. Among others, they gained independence in 1975, adopted for PNG the Westminster system of government, and brought into existence a powerful Constitution.

Even though they were lowly educated, they carefully planned and established the foundations of this democratic nation and so this great nation has stood the test of time, and received praises from other nations as one of the longest surviving democracies in the developing world – all thanks to the wisdom of our forefathers.

I also asked Sir Koitaga how much they were paid and what they did with their pay. He said they were only paid about $150 per fortnight. Of course that was big money back then, but they didn't know how to use it wisely. Every pay day, some of them would meet in an office at the back of the House of Assembly, bet money and gamble. Each of them would bet say $30 or $40 or $50. Some of them were state ministers.

I further asked him whether or not he took part, and if so how many times. He replied, 'Bubu, mi plai tupela taim na win wanpela taim tasol.' (Bubu, I played twice but won only once.') Well, others may see this as something silly they did given their stature at the time, but I believe it was a prophetic act.

These were the founders of this great nation who were talking about the future on the floor of the House of Assembly and were at the same time gambling behind the scenes. Was that not a prophetic act which is being fulfilled today?

I believe this prophetic act of our founding fathers is now coming to pass. Most of our leaders are talking about developing this nation and yet behind the scenes they are awarding contracts to their cronies or buying properties overseas or depositing millions of kina in secret bank accounts overseas, thereby gambling away the riches of this nation.

On one of his recent visits to Parliament House, Sir Koitaga went up to the door, held the two kundu handles and said, 'I proposed for a Kundu House but it was what Sir Michael and the late Sir Tei Abal proposed that got approved. Sir Michael proposed a Sepik Haus Tambran and Sir Tei Abal proposed a Highlands Roundhouse. So you see the front of the Parliament resembles a Haus Tambran and the back resembles a typical round houses in the Highlands.'

I further asked whether or not he had made any contributions at the national level, and he said, 'Of course I did. Before one term of parliament consisted of four years, but it was in one of the 1975 Parliamentary sessions that I moved a motion on a question without notice that one term should consist of five years. The Parliament agreed and that motion became law.'

'Another contribution was Somare's face on the fifty kina note. It was not Somare's idea that his face should appear on the fifty kina note, no. It was my idea. How I proposed the idea is that during a Parliamentary session, the parliamentarians were discussing the issue of designs on the fifty kina note and I just stood up and asked a question without notice, saying, Papua Niugini ol animal i lukautim or ol man i lukautim? Sapos ol man i lukautim orit putim pes bilong Prime Minister bilong yumi, Michael Somare, long dispela moni'. (Is PNG being looked after by animals or by men? If it is being looked after by men, then let the Prime Minister Michael Somare's face appear on the proposed note.)

Sir Koitaga is now 82 years old. After serving the country as a politician both at the national and local levels for 58 years he has now retreated to his village, Tamail, in the Tambul District, WHP.

During his active political days he served three terms altogether in both the House of Assembly and the PNG Parliament from 1964 until he finally lost in the 1977 general elections.

Apart from being a member for Tambul-Nebilyer, he had also been a ward councillor for his Komolgam tribe from 1964 until 2008 when he finally resigned.

In 2008 the Queen recognised his contribution towards this great nation and knighted him as an Officer of the British Empire (OBE) thereby making him Sir Koitaga Mano.

Before such great men as Sir Koitaga are immersed into eternity, we must capture and preserve their stories so that future generations can draw inspiration from their predecessors, who led simple, honest lives but achieved great things for our country.

Get the balance right between social and economic realities that underlie the development of professional sport in PNG
David Kitchnoge

Let me start by saying anything that brings close to 800 different tribes in our country together as a united nation is a good thing. Because of our diverse cultures, anything that causes us to find common ground is an important agent for national unity, a prerequisite for proper and harmonious nation building.

For a lot of nations, it took terrible and forceful human tragedy that required people to stand up in unison to fight a common enemy to foster the sense of nationalism and pride. It took adversity to define their nation's character. But in the absence of a major calamity, sport has emerged over the years as an important agent that can foster similar national pride and camaraderie. The combative nature of sports is the one major striking similarity it has to a physical warfare. It is the element that promotes feelings of oneness and the pursuit of a common goal of victory.

It is no wonder that stories about sporting rivalries are often written using militaristic vocabulary. Hence, sport has become the modern day substitute of physical warfare and adversity to bring people together for a common goal. From this perspective, it is not hard to see why every Papua New Guinean from all four corners of our country shares the one common passion when our national teams go into battle with other teams from other countries.

Rugby league appears to be the most supported sporting code as demonstrated by the raw passion we have for our national team, the Kumuls. I know I shouted my lungs dry for our team when they played in the last Rugby League World Cup, and so were everyone on my street at Waigani, Port Moresby and indeed throughout the nation. In the first game when we almost beat England, I was beaming with pride and tears freely rolled down my cheeks by default. I never forced the tears. They just came from nowhere. It was truly a rare feeling of adrenalin rush. I felt the same when Ryan Pini and Dika Toua competed at the Commonwealth Games and when Stanley Nandex head hunted his opponents with those powerful kicks.

Recognising the important uniting aspect of sports and Rugby League in particular, our government has committed to building a modern stadium in Port Moresby and has put together a team to bid for the right to enter a PNG team in Australia's National Rugby League competition. Such a move appears to make sense from a social perspective. But how does it sit in the overall scheme of things in respect of where our national priorities lie.

We are now talking professional sport and there is much more to it than simply building a nice modern sporting stadium and entering a team in the NRL. Sport has evolved over the years to become an industry in its own right where its traditional entertainment value has been monetised. It has become big business and, therefore, like every other business, the important precondition of a willing and able market must exist to sustain it. Without such a market, its imminent demise in the not too distant future is as sure as the going down of the rays.

I know a lot of people will come out swinging when they read this, but I am happy to play devil's advocate for the sake of providing balance in the thinking behind introducing professional sport in our country at this juncture. Even when I was completely overwhelmed by the emotions of seeing the Kumuls compete bravely to the end, I still refuse to listen to my heart when it comes to making a decision which would put an enormous strain on our nation's finances. This is because although we do have a very willing local market for the product, that market is largely handicapped financially.

Our sporting market in PNG simply does not possess the economic characteristics required to support professional sports, whether it be Rugby League, Soccer, Netball, Cricket or any one of the other codes. There are very few people in Port Moresby and PNG who can afford to constantly squeeze entertainment spending, including for sport, out of their disposable income over an extended period of time. For starters, we have not adequately developed our middle class, who are the backbone of any economy, before asking them to support professional sport in a practical way.

So in the absence of an appropriately affluent market to support it, professional sport in PNG, especially our proposed NRL team, would continue to look elsewhere for its sustenance once it has been established. Two other sources of funding spring to mind: big businesses and the government.

I cannot speak for big businesses because they will obviously be guided by commercial disciplines when committing their financial resources towards this course. But I would like to observe that the market must still absorb their costs and they will surely feel the heat at some stage when this fails. Businesses are responsible to their shareholders first and foremost and must earn an appropriate level of profits before engaging in activities such as sponsoring professional sport. Their support to professional sport will be an investment only to the extent that they can demonstrably recoup it with an appropriate margin from the market in a sustained manner. This clearly cannot happen in the PNG market under our current economic circumstances.

Those who think we can get big businesses in the extractive industry, or other businesses and individuals who rely on them, to support professional sport in our country are living in a fool's paradise. It is like walking merrily down to the gallows with full knowledge of your looming execution.

With support from the market and big businesses looking increasingly shaky, where does that leave us with the government? With all due respect to the government's intentions and support of our NRL bid, I think this is an ill-conceived move because it is sure to put significant pressure on the government's limited finances going forward. The market cannot support this mammoth economic liability we are about to create. So the government will have to bear most of the financial burden at the expense of other key priority development expenditures such as health care, human resource development and infrastructure. In fact the government is already struggling to fund these important areas without unnecessary commitments such as this.

I dare say the talk about fielding a PNG Rugby League team in the NRL is hardly a visionary decision and will only result in distorting government's spending priorities in the long term. This idea must be ditched and sports must be developed in a more sustainable way so as to not shift the government's focus away from its key priority areas. As a nation, we surely can do without sport but not without proper health care, an appropriate investment in human capital development and a continuous focus on building and maintaining our key infrastructure network.

I challenge the government to do everything within its powers to empower the great majority of our people who are crying out for basic services, instead of introducing things that have a real potential to distort its priorities in future.

We, the people, will rise up over time and build a more sustainable professional sporting industry in PNG when our socio economic situation improves. Now is not the time!

Are we ready 30 years on…..?
Lapieh Landu

As a child so fragile, frail and vulnerable, so is my country. Forcefully brought up into a foreign culture, still adapting to change and obliged to mature. Battered and bruised in the toil of animosity; indifference, segregation and racism in the midst of my own home land. Yet I am pushed aside and told to feed on the scraps . Oh, how my heart aches, hungry for equity I am pushed to question ones existence, one's morality. I question why I am the outcaste in my own land. Three decades on, yet, independence seems so farfetched; unrealistic and an implausible dream awaiting truth. Why have I accepted what has been given to me.

Why do I still give in to the so-called 'superior' clique and accept the label as 'periphery'? Are we the marginalized community – the locals in our own land? Is this trend one which will continue in the near future? Will my children always accept second best and have no courage to stand firm in the decisions that govern all? Will they make allowances for the expatriates that work among them or feel intimidated still that whatever found knowledge they contain will never measure up to that of theirs. It is an inclination that has developed in the time of the kiaps and since then, set a depraved humdrum which exists in all areas of life.

In all aspects of humanity, we are equal in every sense; physical, mental, social, spiritual psychological, we are equal. Indeed our territories, languages, cultural traditions and pigments may defer us slightly, we still are equal. We (the locals) are the superior faction for we own the land, we make up the majority, we set the laws – we have the power! Why then do we bow down to their knowledge, their skin, their wealth, their technology? What are we so afraid of? Is it the fear of losing their trust and cutting ropes to their so called friendly AID? In political science, we learn that there is no such thing as a free gift. In stating that, it brings to mind the brutal reality or concept that we have to give back.

Now, with a young and aspiring country endowed with so much resource and wealth it gives light to why the 'old dogs' would turn their noses our way. Our country in the last twenty years has become a breeding ground for foreign investment and a loophole for Asian counterfeits at the cost of greedy and selfish policy benders who give less thought or care for the direction and welfare of the development of the people- the paramount reason why they hold their seats. Where has all the integrity gone to? There is the notion that, with great power should come great responsibility, yet this is unlikely among many law and policy makers, upholders and generally, all Papua New Guineans. There is little or no sense of responsibility among the people in power. The focus of importance has diverted the greedy and the needy have become the neglected faction of society.

We cry for power among the indigenous, we urge to chase out the Asians, the Indians and the West, but are we able to carry on from where they left off? Are we mature enough in our outlook to sustain new life after them? We have for many years relied on their systems and ways of doing things like a disabled person on his crutches, are we strong enough to walk without that support? In the turning of tables, we see a collapse in this attempt. We have become more reliant, weaker and more vulnerable. We have sold customary land and when we cannot sell, we make laws around our customs so as to get things our way. We have bought every counterfeit item they've fed us. We have applauded the Informal Sector Act, I believe simply because we find that we can become independent? Or have we just become more accepting of the standards set for us and come to believe that that is where we stand in the community and this is as much as I, as a citizen, uneducated and jobless can do! Why haven't we looked beyond our limits and turned our hobbies into businesses or been innovative! That is exactly it; we lack motivation and drive to better ourselves. We sit on our behinds and wait while foreigners realize the potential of our land and make the best of it and then- we complain! Do we have to go behind correctional rehabilitation institutions like that of Beon Prison in Madang, to realize our real potential?

We have become like dogs feasting on our own land. It is now survival of the fittest. This is evident as the highlanders dominate the market and business sector of the economy, from the trading of betel nut to the boom in real estate and transport agencies giving minute room for the coastal people.

In the turn of time our government has also made drastic shifts. As we see the Somare Government since the release of independence takes us through a whirlwind of events from the independence of this nation, to the 'resource wars' in our islands; the revaluation of the Kina to privatization issues and the influx of foreign investors whilst the O'Neil government restores hope in the people with priority fixations, free education and an attempt to restoring dignity back into the PNG Government and the nation as a whole. Indeed many sought to question the self-integrity of the new government with its swift implementation violating our constitution in which it has the rightful duty to uphold. What have we become and where are we heading? Are we ready to walk without these crutches that we have long depended on? Do we have a vision, an aim, an objective that we wish to pursue? Or are we walking blindly into the dark. Indeed, we cannot turn back time; we cannot bring back our bush materials, our old way of life in which our forefathers have demonstrated for us. We cannot go back and fix our mistakes. We can only look forward, for what is to come and prepare for how we can best accommodate for it so that we all benefit fairly.

We cannot preserve our culture, but 'maintaining' it would be an appropriate terminology to describe it. We can uphold our belief systems without compromising them completely. We can maintain our languages by integrating them in our education curriculum, safeguard our land by practicing sustainable development and educating our people thoroughly of the importance of our land; we can reduce crime rates in our country by prioritizing education and providing an avenue for human development.

Our country is a land of abundance and beautiful people. When outsiders visit our land, they return to theirs not only with the thought of the vulnerability of our people and land but with the distinct memory of our *'pasin'*(personality). It is who we are to them and not what we are. It is what we give and not what we ask for. It is what we portray and not how we are perceived.

I am proud to say I am Papua New Guinean, I am proud of my cultural distinctiveness and my heritage. It is overwhelming to know that wealth floods us in every aspect of resource, culture and people. We have never suffered famine, we have never suffered drought, we are free, we are blessed; we are Papua New Guinea.

Nakan in Madang Town
Stanley Mark

Little Nakan hurried across the busy lane to pick the empty 500 ml Sprite container that was thrown into the buai stained rusty rubbish drum. His skinny left fingers held firmly a white plastic bag containing a couple of empty containers while his right fingers clung on to his buckle, pulling it up to his skinny waist every second, making sure not to let it fall and expose his undernourished legs below.

His sun-burnt forehead and cheeks overflowing with sweat showed that he has roamed the avenues of Madang town all day for empty containers. But he had no choice. He must collect containers in order to eat and survive.

Seven year old, Nakan Akus comes from Tambunum village in the East Sepik province. He lives with his mother and four brothers and sister at the Wagol settlement, a few blocks opposite Lae Building Contractor's headquarter in Madang. His father had left them for Lae "longpela taim" and they have never heard from him. The K50 that his father was paid working as a bus crew wasn't enough for both food and school fees, so Nakan had to leave Kusbau Primary School at Grade Two in 2006. However, as the first born in the family, he felt that he had the responsibility to take care of the family.

It all began on one Monday morning, when two of his pals from the settlement persuaded him to follow them to Madang town. He was bewildered to see them going from one rubbish bin to another picking empty 500 ml Coca Cola, Sprite and Fanta containers. He didn't trust his pals when they told him that the containers would make them a great fortune until at the end of the day, when they smilingly received a bunch of eight K2 notes from a buyer.

Nakan then decided that container-collection would help him and his mother, his three small sisters and his brother to have some food on their table every day.

Nakan says he goes to town at 12 noon every day and collects empty containers till 4 pm in the afternoon. He brings his containers especially to the ice block sellers and sells them for 30 toea each. Because there are many others like him doing the same thing, he receives K5.00 -K7.00 from the containers he collects. He takes his money to the Madang market or Balasigo market and buys a heap of kaukau, two-three bunches of raw Kalafua bananas and aibika, a dry coconut and spends the rest on peanuts for his sisters and bus fare home.

"Prais bilong kaikai long stoa i antap tumas na hat long baim rice, olsem na mi save kisim moni mi kisim long konteina i go long maket. Em bai orait sapos gavaman opis daunim prais (Prices of store goods are very high and it's hard for me to afford rice so I take the money I receive from containers to the market. It would be easy if the government office lower the prices)," he frowns with puckered brow.

Nakan hasn't had any visiting uncles, aunties and cousins or any other relatives as far as he can remember. His mother looks after his sisters and brother at home while he goes to town on his daily container-collection routine. And his mother does not discourage him from going.

He lowers his head and via parted lips, he whispers, "Mi save painim ol konteina long kisim kaikai blo ol sista na brata na mama bilong mi. Mi save sori long mama bilong mi (I look for container to get food for my sisters, brother and my mother. I feel sorry for my mother)".

Street children are a recently an emerging phenomenon. The population is very young, with more than 60 per cent under the age of 13. The major factors contributing to the increase in street children are domestic violence, divorce, parental unemployment, urban migration, political and economic instability, and peer influences. Moreover, natural disasters are affecting the daily lives of people, displacing families, and destroying crops and property and adding to this problem.

Disasters like the Manam volcanic eruption has made thousands of people homeless and has contributed to the increase in the number of children living on the streets in Madang and other urban centres for that matter. The children, like Nakan, are either collecting empty containers and tin cans or begging for a living in the cities' sidewalks.

Before the free education policy was introduced in 2011 into 2012, parents would spend thousands of kina for their children in schools. As of 2001, 69 percent of children who started primary school were likely to quit after grade five. And in rural areas, the lack of access to schools reportedly contributes to low enrolment.

A major challenge in Papua New Guinea is that there are no government policies directly addressing the situation of street children. Other major challenges include the lack of government support, lack of resources, and a lack of effective coordination and support between NGOs and government agencies.

Divine Word University Student Service Director, Steven Namosa says that Nakan is a hero to his family. However, from his tidy-looking office, he says that the father and mother have the responsibility to provide food for the family. The father should not run away from home if there is a problem between him and his wife or if he has no job. "Because of this, the innocent kids face the consequences and become the victims of the parents' problems," he says.

He also blames the elected leaders for not addressing the kind of situation Nakan is facing today.

He says though Nakan has a village where he could go back and live a good life, he needs enough money to pay for his transport home. "We should not say that's his problem. This is where a leader should intervene to stop Nakan collecting containers to earn a living," he said.

Nakan does not believe in miracles. As the DWU students, waiting for 9A bus with plastics of cosmetics and restaurant left-overs stood watching, he dashed past them with his plastic of empty containers and picked the empty Sprite container in the rubbish bin. He used his half-torn shirt and wiped the betel nut stains and carefully dropped it into his plastic bag. This will earn Nakan 30 toea coins. His sweaty cheeks widened with a beautiful smile and he dashed off to another bin nearby.

He has to get some more.

Does PNG really have an attitude problem?
Martyn Namorong

I asked some of my friends on a chat site to highlight some issues that were of concern to them about Papua New Guinea.

Those who responded mentioned issues such as lack of good governance, access to education, poor health indicators and an *attitude problem*. Many viewed a change in people's attitudes as a precondition for real change elsewhere.

What do people mean when they refer to the attitude problem? For Governor Powes Parkop of the nation's capital, it centres on littering and respect for public property. The Police think it's to do with crime and public nuisance. Teachers say juvenile delinquency and students think it's to do with schools being mismanaged or teachers not attending class.

Most people think it's the urban drifters who need to be prevented from leaving their villages by the Vagrancy Act. The urban drifters and anyone who isn't a politician thinks it's the corrupt, pot-bellied big shots who wear cowboy hats and drive in Toyota Landcruisers, as Jeffrey Febi once stated.

It seems everyone has an attitude problem, including me - and that's according to the woman who gave birth to me.

In describing the concept of the State, someone wrote that because the State belongs to everyone, it belongs to no-one. In applying this to the so called attitude problem, one can say that because everyone has an attitude problem, no-one has and attitude problem. Sounds counter-intuitive, doesn't it? Yet it makes sense. Because if everyone wears pink, no-one is out of order.

What if Governor Parkop didn't blame the general public for the mess and reflected on how inefficient the garbage collection mechanism was thus creating the eyesore. What if the teachers saw that they had enrolled more students than they could manage? What if the students reflected on the high demand on school resources that led to a lack of capacity?

What if the urban dwellers reflected on the push factors that forced people to move to the city, because decisions made by powerful city elite did not serve the interests of the rural majority?

I always thought street vendors were a public nuisance until I became one. Interestingly, my customers would think every other street vendor except me should be sent packing. I never knew how kind Goilala people could be until I met my *buai* mums – the women from whom I buy betel nut to resell.

The attitude problem is a façade. It is used a lot by influential people to distort the truth. Unfortunately, many of us have joined the bandwagon and are pointing the fingers at each other. It has become a term that is now synonymous with the fringe dwellers of the city – the poorly educated urban poor.

Because these people are of lower socio economic and educational background, they are unable to articulate their arguments the way their critics do. They do not put out media statements or appear on television to defend their dignity. Thus the one-sided prejudiced attacks are now seen by many uncritical minds as the gospel truth.

Every time there is a failure on the part of Police they are able to find a convenient excuse and blame the 'publics' attitude problem. Politicians who are poorly managing the affairs of the State cry foul over the public's *pasin* (attitude). *senisim pasin* (change of attitude) seems to be a favourite mantra, even amongst so called advocates of change.

So does PNG have an attitude problem? Yes it does, but it isn't what is being communicated in the mainstream media. The attitude problem is one of a failure to build a modern multicultural society and a sense of communal existence.

There are no modern communities in all towns and cities. What we have are enclaves of tribal or neo-tribal groupings. There is little person-to-person interaction outside of one's personally defined social zone. There is a failure to coexist in a modern society and so by default, people live as if they are still in their traditional tribal territories.

The task that no one is up to is social engineering- building communities and fusion points. Sport has an important role in building new fusion communities. Sadly, popular sports such as rugby league are perpetuating the status quo by having tribalistic province based clubs.

Schools also are places to develop new mindsets; however educators perpetuate the cultural baggage. Instead of deliberately encouraging cross-cultural interaction, students are tagged and boxed into traditional cultural groupings during so called cultural shows.

Imagine an Asaro mud men dance being performed by Sepik students. The Sepik students learn to appreciate the art, culture and mythology of the Asaro people and begin to empathise and identify common ground with their peers.

No one is building communities and defining a new modern society. We all are stuck in our social enclaves and hurling abuse at those outside. So the people you think have an attitude problem, also believe that you have an attitude problem.

What is Development?
Martyn Namorong

Greenpeace is delusional and Rimbunan Hijau is reckless. What's new? I did a lot of tree hugging in the past and it didn't get me anywhere. (Nou Vada, Law student).

When a young kid in law school posts such comments on Facebook, they need to be taken seriously. Nou Vada is the most intelligent and articulate young Papua New Guinean I've come across. I don't know he's reasoning behind the comments but they do express a perception and perhaps confusion amongst many Papua New Guineans that Green Groups are anti-development.

This perception arises from the reality that environmental activists have become synonymous with headline grabbing protest activities. Thus the impression that the public gets is that the *greenies* just want to stop all sorts of projects.

Indeed, resource exploiters regularly dog-whistle the public with 'anti-green' clichés such that many now subscribe to the view that all green groups or non-governmental organizations (NGOs) want to stop development..

I suppose in any case, both sides may have some merit to their arguments. Personally, I wish to visit the Constitution of Papua New Guinea to find out how it expresses Papua New Guinea's development agenda. And perhaps a law student like Nou may articulate it better than a *buai* seller like me.

Papua New Guinea's development agenda, regardless of what the Greens or the Capitalists say, is set out in its National Goals and Directive Principles as expressed in the Constitution.

In a film by Scott Waide, lawyer Ganjiki Wayne states that the writers of the Constitution weren't so much interested in physical/structural development as in the integral development of the individual. It was a somewhat spiritual rather that material development that the founders of this nation were interested in.

This concept of development is expressed in the First National Goal and

Directive Principles regarding Integral Human Development. The development model envisaged by the Founders of this nation is indeed found in Goal number Five - Papua New Guinean Ways. Goal number Five specifically calls for any activity whether social, political or economic, to be consistent with the ways of Papua New Guinean societies.

Thus, if any social, political or economic activity that impinges upon the Papua New Guinean way of life, it is against the Spirit of the Constitution. And since it is the Constitution that gives legal authority to the Nation State, the state of the nation should be consistent with the desires of the Constitution as expressed in the National Goals and Directive Principles.

Now the Constitution gets its legitimacy from the citizens of this nation. The Constitution is therefore an expression of the general will of the people of Papua New Guinea. The People, through their Constitution, have expressed their desire that any social, political or economic activity be consistent with Papua New Guinean Ways.

Why was it necessary to explicitly call for all development activity to be consistent with Papua New Guinean Ways? The answer is simple, for over 40 000 years before colonization indigenous Papua New Guineans were fully independent people. It was their Papua New Guinean Ways that made them totally independent.

It is this fullness of political and economic independence that the writers of the Constitution expressed in Goal Number Three of the National Goals and Directive Principles – National Sovereignty and Self Reliance. The communal ownership of land and sharing of resources and responsibilities that enabled equality and participation of all members of traditional societies is expressed by Goal Number Two – Equality and Participation. Goal Number Four on Natural Resources and Environment basically reflects the sustainable livelihood of traditional societies and their minimal impact on the environment.

I do not believe these Goals are a rejection of modernity by the writers of the Constitution. Rather, they express a desire to avoid the pitfalls of the greed of western capitalism as witnessed in the current context of global economic crisis. This fear is expressed in this prophetic statement by the Constitutional Planning Committee.

We see the darkness of neon lights.

*We see the despair and loneliness in the urban cities.
We see the alienation of (the people) that is the result of the
present machine orientated economy.*

*We see true social security and (the people's) happiness being
diminished in the name of economic progress.*

*We caution therefore that large-scale industries should be pursued only after very careful
and thorough consideration of the likely consequences upon the social and spiritual fabric
of our people…*

*There is overwhelming evidence to suggest that a significant number of people who live by
the fruits of multi-million dollar multi-national corporations live in misery, loneliness
and spiritual poverty.*

*We believe that since we are a rural people, our strength should be essentially in the land
and the use of our innate artistic talents.*
(Papua New Guinea Constitutional Planning Committee, 1975)

Fundamentally, the lowest common denominator between all societies in this multi-cultural nation is the relationships people have with their land. It is the land that defines a person. This is expressed in the first question two Papua New Guineans ask each other when they meet for the first time; "Where are you from?"

Any social, political or economic activity that displaces people from their land and prevents them from accessing and utilizing their ancestral land is contrary to the Papua New Guinean Way referred to in Goal Number Five. It is therefore not sufficient to just resettle people and pay compensation for the land they have been displaced from.

They will never be accepted by another tribe nor will they accept the new reality. The landlord will restrict their access to gardening and hunting grounds making the settlers feel very insecure. The settlers will also have lost their sacred sites and traditional resources that used to be acquired from their ancestral land. No amount of money can compensate for the loss of security, culture and identity that is associated with alienation from ancestral land.

What happens next happened on Bougainville on a larger scale but is already expressed in the form of various social problems and disruptions to economic activities. What it means to be Papua New Guinean is to have a connection with the land. That is what gives one an identity and a sense of social security.

Development within the context of Goal number Five must respect and safe-guard this intimate relationship between the land and its people. We don't own the land, it owns us. We are guardians of the land our forefathers fought to protect for our sake. There is no honour in not fighting to protect one's land.

Any activity that does not subscribe to these Five National Goals and Directive Principles is not development but *bagarapment*. That is why blood had to be spilt on Bougainville when people revolted against the destruction of the *Mekamui* – the sacred land, which is the source of everything.

How to break free from the vicious cycle of dinau*
Francis Nii

Living everyday life on borrowed money is a big problem for thousands of workers in Papua New Guinea today.

Approximately three quarters of the working population in the country are so enslaved by dinau that they find it extremely difficult to break free from its grip. 'Dinau kilim mi yia (Debts are killing me)' is a national sentiment among the workforce.

People who earn less than a thousand kina a fortnight and are single bread winners with large families are the most affected. Gamblers, alcohol users and cigarette and betel nut consumers are doomed without borrowed money.

The vicious circle of debts evolves from the squandering of take-home fortnightly income (after income tax, bank loans etc. have been deducted) on unbudgeted non-essentials like alcohol, cigarettes, betel nuts, customary and extended family obligations and gambling on the pokies, horse races, cards and the lottery.

Papua New Guineans know how to budget their income either mentally or in written form. However the problem is that they have a high tendency of not adhering to their budgets. They spend unscrupulously. As a result they run out of money for necessities like food, fuel, and bus fares etc. well before the next pay packet arrives.

To provide for these basic needs, they have to find money somehow. The easiest and fastest way to borrow cash is from the fast growing money lending business known as 'maket moni' at exorbitant fortnightly interest rates of 30, 40 and even 50 or 100 per cent. The usurers readily lend as long as the loan seekers agree to the interest charged and at the same time surrender their EFTPOS cards with the pin codes to the money lenders to collect their dues directly from the ATMs*.

The prevailing trend is that when the previous loan is repaid, new financial pressures bite into the family budget forcing the bread winner to borrow again. Each time consciously or unconsciously the loan increases until the total debt comprising the principal plus interest reaches an unmanageable proportion. Often the debt equals or exceeds the total take-home income of the bread winner-cum-debtor.

The vicious circle of debt comes into effect at this point. The money lender has the upper hand taking the entire take-home income of the borrower. The poor person then borrows again from the usurer to sustain his or her family's life and they go round and round like that payday after payday.

The consequences of the vicious circle of debts on the social and economic welfare of the workers and their families are diverse. None payment of children's school fees, disconnection of electricity and water supplies due to non-payment of bills, sale of household items like TV sets etc. and prostitution by female family members to supplement food for the home are some common consequences. The extremes are court proceedings and loss of jobs when the borrowers try to evade their loans by getting new EFTPOS cards with new pin codes or running away to new locations and new jobs.

How can people who have been enslaved by debt for many years break free from its grip? Before embracing any plan, it is of paramount importance that one must have the will power to break free. Having your heart and mind fully committed to breaking free is the foundation for any plan to be fruitful because most plans will involve self-discipline and personal sacrifices.

Once your mind and heart are fixed then you should list down all the possible means and ways and assess them one by one. Eventually you should come up with one best option to follow.

My recommendation would be lifestyle adjustment - making adjustments or changes to one's current style of living. There are two components to the lifestyle adjustment plan. First is cost saving through budget cuts. You must cut down your fortnightly spending on the non-essentials that have been mentioned above as well as other expenses. How much percentage is to be slashed on each item is up to individuals to decide. However I would recommend for 50 per cent cuts on alcohol, cigarettes, betel nuts and customary and extended family obligations. I strongly recommend 100 per cent cut on gambling, meaning a complete stop to any form of gambling. Reduce communication by 40 per cent.

Reduce electricity and water rates, fuel like kerosene and petrol or diesel for private motor vehicles by at least 25 per cent. If you are renting accommodation it is worth searching around for a cheaper home. The list is not exhaustive. You can add more to it.

The second component that directly complements the cost saving measures is a change of habits. You must avoid those people you used to drink, chew, smoke and gamble with as much as possible. Avoid entering into long conversations with them. Say hi, see you later and move on. If you don't do that the temptation of the old habits and peer pressure will drag you back to square one. You will get nowhere.

Do not go near your old favourite drinking and gambling dens especially on paydays and weekends. Take your family to the park, beach, river, sporting field or church fellowship.

You must boldly set boundaries to customary and extended family obligations and pressures and stand by your decision. You must have the guts to say no to their unnecessary demands.

You must stop calling or receiving calls from phone friends who have been flirtatiously enticing you into sending them credits and cash. Twenty kina can save your family one decent meal.

You must openly talk about your problems and your intentions with your relatives and friends including your old drinking, chewing and gambling mates. They must understand why you have changed your spending and social habits. Their understanding, respect and cooperation are important for the success of your plan.

Speed up your loan reduction by making additional repayments with 50 per cent of the money you have saved fortnightly from your cost saving measures.

If you strictly adhere to your break-free plan, you will find that your financial position and social habits have significantly improved. Your debts will have gone in six to twelve months. You will have surplus money in your account to meet your family needs before the next pay packet arrives. You can easily manage your children's school fee loans without jeopardizing your family's welfare.

Once you have broken free from the grip of the vicious circle of debts, it is important that you maintain it.

Be very careful of the temptations of the old habits because to many people they are as sweet as honey. They can't live without them. If you get back into the vicious circle again, you might never get out of it for the rest of your life.

Look for books and articles on money management and budget tips in the libraries, bookshops, magazines and newspapers and read them. They will help you to properly manage your finance because the debt problem stems from poor management of your hard earned cash.

A good piece of general advice to the current and future workforce is that you must budget your take-home fortnightly income scrupulously and strictly adhere to the budget until the next pay packet arrives. Live within your means and you will never get into debt.

loan

Wake up PNG!
Francis Nii

Why should Papua New Guinea continue to push for an HIV & AIDS policy that has been tested over a decade and has proven to be fruitless?

Despite millions of kina in aid money being poured into the war against the deadly virus HIV every year for more than a decade, HIV infections are still on the rise. The official HIV prevalence rate of 1.6 % as reported by the National AIDS Council is based on the registered cases and does not reflect the true picture of the endemic.

Experts believed that there are many healthy HIV carriers roaming around undetected. They believed that the true HIV prevalence rate should be within the range of 2 and 2.5%.

Papua New Guinea has a small population and already a significant number of its professionals as well as ordinary people have succumbed to AIDS. We cannot continue to be complacent and wishy washy in our war against HIV & AIDS and lose more people.

Apart from the band-aid dressing of massive public awareness and education programs on HIV & AIDS, the authorities should get down to the root of the problem and address it. The root of the problem is glaringly obvious before our eyes and the health authorities are very well aware of it.

As long as healthy HIV carriers are free and have indiscreet sexual practises, HIV/AIDS is here to stay. And more innocent lives will be destroyed.

Drastic mechanisms like compulsory HIV screening and isolation of HIV positives in care centres and even the tattooing of carriers will eliminate HIV & AIDS in Papua New Guinea. It is murder when a healthy HIV carrier intentionally goes around un-leasing the deadly venom on vulnerable and unsuspecting victims under the influence of money, entertainment and cargo.

The certain fear is that as time passes, all the madness, fear and hurly-burly surrounding HIV & AIDS are bound to wane. And Papua New Guinea will soon be heading down the same road that African nations have been through; accepting HIV/AIDS and living with it just like any other common viral infection such as flu or influenza while their populations are still being decimated by the millions.

We don't have the kind of population that the African nations have to play around with. Our 7 million people are nothing compared to the nine digit population of the African nations.

No matter what Australia or the rest of the world may think, culturally we are totally unique from these countries. And as a sovereign nation Papua New Guinea should decide what is best for its people in the war against HIV & AIDS in the context of her own traditions, norms and social behaviour.

Australia and other international donor agencies should refrain from shoving down our throats their ideologies and policy frameworks under the might of their aid money. These ideologies and policy frameworks are not working in Papua New Guinea because they are irrelevant and not conducive to Papua New Guinean society. Why continue to spend millions of dollars pushing for a policy that has been tested over ten years and has proven to be fruitless?

Wake up PNG and get back to the drawing board - the sooner the better.

My Atoll, My Home
Raroteone Tefuarani

My island of Takuu/Mortlock lies about 250km northeast of Kieta in the Autonomous Region of Bougainville, Papua New Guinea.

For some time now it is physically evident that sea levels have risen due to climate change and tectonic plate movement threatening not only food crops but my island homes very existence.

We are not the only atoll affected by the forces of climate change. Also sharing the same fate are our neighbouring atolls Nuguria/Fead, Nukumanu/Tasman and the Catarets.

So far the Papua New Guinean Government has come up with a plan to relocate my people to mainland Bougainville but this is still yet to be fully implemented.

Among the young there is a growing acceptance that maybe it is time to move on but for the majority of the older generation it is hard for them to accept this change.

I am strongly against the relocation of my people and will present to you a few facts as to why I feel we should not move.

Takuu has many exquisitely divine islands that surround it and all of them have something in common and that is their white exotic sandy beaches and crystal clear waters. Amongst these are two main attractions that say so much about our history and should be preserved.

The first attraction is the ruins of Queen Emma Forsayth's house on one of our surrounding islands called *Amotu* and the second attraction is also on one of our other surrounding islands called *Nukerekia*, a pristine island that is our best kept treasure.

Let us start with Queen Emma who came to inhabit Takuu in the latter half of the nineteenth century, not long after a drought and an epidemic had hit the island very badly. It was during this population decimation that 'Queen Emma' who was of American and Samoan parentage bravely set a goal to establish a local cocoa plantation which she successfully did as she had done in New Guinea. To this day her house ruins though weathered still remain untouched on the island of *Amotu*.

Nukerekia, on the other hand is located on the north western side of Takuu and is known to us islanders as *Bird Island* because the island has a reputation for birds laying their eggs on the sand where they are left untouched by all who visit the place. This treasure of ours has been preserved in its natural state by our ancestors for many generations before us meaning custom has taught us never to take anything from this island when we visit, even if it is a tiny shell it is prohibited. On this island strict rules apply for both islanders and outsiders. I believe our traditions must be maintained no matter what the cost. We cannot lose these very important pieces of our history and we must do everything in our power to preserve them just as our ancestors have protected them for years.

I strongly feel that one must take into consideration the importance of education before relocation is carried out. Education is very limited back home due to a number of contributing factors and without the proper knowledge and skills our people will not survive in a modern society apart from the village life they've always known.

The two major contributing factors as to why education is limited are due to the lack of transport to and from the island and the remoteness of the island. The only means of getting to the island is by ship and in cases of emergencies, helicopter.

When there is a delay in the ships schedule it delays the transport of school learning materials which in turn slows down classes for children and most times they never reach the island so the school is forced to withdraw students till they arrive which sometimes takes up to a year.

The remoteness of the island discourages a lot of teachers from taking up their post on the island resulting in a shortage of teachers and when this happens the school is forced to withdraw students temporarily until a teacher shows up or in most cases they repeat the next year when a teacher is available to teach that particular grade.

Villagers who have lived their whole lives on the island are unfamiliar with modern technology. If you look at the life of an average islander and compare it to a person living in modern society you'll notice that there are hardly any similarities between the two. Both girls and boys spend their days learning to tackle the day-to-day chores of an average village in which boys are taught to master the art of fishing, making a canoe, gardening and basic carpentry and girls are taught to garden, weave baskets and mats, cook and wash clothes.

Our people are not prepared to relocate to a modernised society where education is essential for survival. If we relocate our people to mainland Bougainville it will mean culture shock for our people and their lives will change immensely. Their normal day-to-day routine will be ruined and without a proper education most families won't be able to afford the normal necessities in life like food, water, healthcare and school fees just to name a few and this alone can threaten our peoples' existence.

Takuu is the name given to the southernmost and largest of the islands. This island is distinctively broken in half where one half makes up the cemetery and the other half make up our individual family gardens. It is common knowledge that cemetery and gardens hold a very high significance in any cultural society.

We come from the land of Takuu but in actual fact our population inhabits the neighbouring island to Takuu called '*Nukutoa*'.

It is a well-known fact that Takuu islanders have grown 'taro' for nearly as long as the Chinese has grown rice and the land has provided so generously over the years despite the water table rising. We also have banana and coconuts that are well suited to our environment and provides for us all year round just as the taro does. Taro for us has a lot of value and is used a lot in many important traditional gatherings.

Then there is the cemetery where our ancestors and those lost rest. So many generations rest on this island, their graves are decorated with their belongings whether it is a cup, a plate or even their clothes. If we leave we contradict what our very own culture has taught us and that is to respect our dead and families of those buried lose everything of sentimental value.

Our forefathers have fertilised our very gardens with the dust of their bones so how can we just turn our backs on them and leave this island. If we lose this island we lose everything.

People can say that we must move forward with the times but we must move forward in the right way; without our ancestors we wouldn't have made it this far.

If we leave our island and relocate to mainland Bougainville as proposed by the government then we face losing our many attractions, our beautiful surrounding exotic islands, the cemetery that holds the evidence of our past, the gardens our forefathers worked hard to toil and most importantly respect for our heritage.

Another important thing that we risk losing is our traditional etiquette that has always been compulsory for both females and males with most emphasis being placed on the role of a woman. In our society since women are more restricted than men, we are taught from a very young age how custom requires us to dress and behave at all times.

Our main attractions tell the story of our people and how our island came to be. All our exotic islands have meaning and a history of their own and if we move all that will remain is our traditional songs and dances that have been passed down from generation to generation to tell all our children and many generations after of our history and someday that will not be enough

Yes, it is clearly evident that the sea is rising but there has to be a better solution than relocation. I took the time to sit with one of my uncles the other day and I just listened to the way he spoke of this island and of what it meant to him and I realised this is their home, the only life they have ever known. It is because of this island that I have learnt where my roots lay. It has taught me to value the beauty of life itself and to never ever take anything as beautiful for granted ever again.

It breaks my heart to know that my home might one day cease to be but I will never stop fighting and neither will our people. Relocation must be a last resort and not just considered because it is an easy and quick solution. If we leave our identity will be eroded and perhaps even lost forever!

Delusion, Disillusionment and the Devil's advocate: A bedtime story for Papua New Guineans who believe in change
Nou Vada

"I don't dream anymore, I am grounded in the reality. I grapple with the facts as they are. Perhaps there are too many visionaries and dreamers such that no one is there to deal with the reality of life in Papua New Guinea." - Martyn Namorong

Disillusionment can never be a status quo. Disillusionment by its very nature is a reaction that cannot possibly stand alone as an action of its own. Disillusionment is stress, a neo-primal instinct; when the intellectual can't do anything about the state of affairs of things, he shuts himself off; he compartmentalizes himself from his troubles and in the plight of self-preservation, he loses his faith in the power of humanity and the possibility of change. What a terrible thing.

"We thought we could be decent men in indecent times" District Attorney Harvey Dent who becomes the murdering psychopath 'Two-Face' angrily tells Batman in Christopher Nolan's *Dark Knight*.

☐There have been a few moments in my life where I've found myself saying just that.

Disillusionment is one of the scariest forms of ignorance because the ignorance is deliberate and the beholder is someone who is capable of making a change, but has chosen to tie his own hands behind his back.

No good ever comes out of being disillusioned. For the passive, this means looking away. For the active, this means being cynical about what you once believed in. Either way it is a void that consumes one's intellect and humanity. If there is one consolation, a single mark of positivity, it is that emancipation from disillusionment, when it does happen, creates resilience.

In a country like Papua New Guinea, it is easy to get disillusioned. From my own experience I can say that this happens because forerunning the disillusionment is delusion. And there are a great number of delusional people and groups in Papua New Guinea who think change is easy. They have a habit of oversimplifying complex human problems and then romanticizing about the solutions to these problems. I should know. I was one of them.

You go out and work for change, attending workshops and conferences, actively discussing how to eradicate poverty and gender disparity and hunger and Malaria and AIDS and it's all very good. Starry-eyed, you quote Gandhi and Suu Kyi to each other and you sing U2 songs, emphatically tearing up as you sing the bridge in "Crumbs from your table" and or the second verse of "One" or "Where the streets have no name".

You meet diplomats from aid agencies who believe in you and you in them, who believe that you are exactly what Papua New Guinea needs; they even help you sing Coldplay's "In My Place". You have nice little lunches in state-of-the-art air conditioned buildings and do your awareness rounds at a community school, handing out pamphlets on how to correctly wear a condom. You tell yourself PNG will become like Africa if you don't fix the AIDS problem now… and so you listen to more U2.

Then you return home to the corrugated iron shack that is your house in some squatter settlement, to the low income government housing in a pothole and rascal infested street, to the rubbish heap and faeces infested seas of Hanuabada where your sea house built some 70 years ago during World War II still stands and you wait for the dawn to break so you can escape your reality trying to fix the reality of others; saving Papua New Guinea and the world. Delusion.

One day you wake up crying. You've been crying in your dreamless sleep and you refuse to get up off your dusty mattress. You realise that the problem with PNG and the world is too complex and too difficult for you to continue on the same conversations with your friends; conversations about the Millennium Development Goals and the National Goals and Directive Principles. You get sick to your stomach at your own naivety as you stand at the crowded bus-stop, dirty with buai skin and buai sputum, dusty tattered roads and mangled iron protruding out of the ground where the home-brew seller leans and gestures to you that he has in his bilum the finest *steam* in all of Port Moresby. You are waiting for a bus to go to another workshop, another conference. After a week or two of feeling sick and stupid, you curse yourself and vow never again that you be a tree-hugger or a starry-eyed peer-educator. Disillusionment

And it's supposed to be a phase. Some people cling on to it and build the rest of their lives around this disillusionment. Disillusionment is a phase that has to pass so that you come back wiser and more well informed. You come back critical and cautious of everything. You make sure you're not starry-eyed and your reasoning is well grounded in reality and that you appreciate the reality of things in Papua New Guinea.

When you come back, you find your faith in humanity and in the possibility of change is stronger and much more serious. You still listen to U2, but not with God-like reverence as you did before, ignorantly. And you can say things like "Greenpeace is delusional and RH is reckless. What's new?" with a sense of authority and conviction because you know beef stroganoff from bullshit. You are wiser and you are truly objective. You return to doing what you do... working for change. Resilience.

Anyway. That was my story.

A Tribute to My Fathers
Emma Wakpi

At a time when the focus of the world is upon PNG and its attitude toward women, I have been reflecting upon the male influences in my life. I know there are good men in PNG and we need their support and encouragement in order to create a safer more equitable society for both sexes. I want to introduce to you three such men who have impacted my life - my grandfather, uncle and father.

These men influenced me in unique ways and the lessons learned were not from longwinded lectures (although they were prone to those too) but rather from observing how they lived their lives.

What My Grandfather Taught Me
Every individual is unique and must be accorded dignity.

My grandfather had a soft spot for the scorned and oft ignored of our clan and would strive to let them know they mattered. He had a way about him which made it seem that you were the favoured one, that you were special. Most times upon his return from a feast, often the best meat cuts were quietly slipped to the widows, divorcees or the least favoured wife of a clansman. He would cut smaller portions, wrap them in banana leaves and hide them in various locations then give their children riddles to find them – a treasure hunt of his creation. This was something he did regularly with his grandchildren and we thought we were the only ones with whom he played this game. At his funeral however I was overwhelmed by the amount of people (most I did not know well) who told of his generosity and recalled his treasure hunts.

He also made it a habit to every so often, visit the homes of the aforementioned women. He would ask them how they were and if there was something that needed doing. If they required assistance, appointments were made and at the set time he and his family would team up and help; fencing gardens, making new gardens, harvesting kunai to thatch roofs etc. To us children he made such outings an event and would teach various chants and games turning work to play. Firewood distribution was another duty he took upon himself and would ensure that not only his own household was provided for but that of those who did not have a man to look after them. He never made any help seem like charity for he would call on those assisted to reciprocate by helping him in his garden etc.

Words cannot describe the bond I had with him and even though he has left us, his memory and the continuing of this legacy gives life a feeling of completeness.

What My Uncle Taught Me
The most fun you will have in your life is when you take the time to make life fun for others.

My uncle Dau was always looking for ways to make life interesting and fun for the children in his family. He didn't need money or sophisticated gaming devices; his props were long bamboo sticks, an old trap made from a mishmash of chicken wire and wood and his own self. I recall on twilight evenings squealing with glee as he would cut bamboo poles to our size and race around wildly with us hitting at small bats that came out just before dusk, flying low over our huts. If we were successful in catching any he made them seem like the best "snacks" we'd ever had.

Other times we "helped" prepare his trap and he would make a great ceremony out of it. We would take it to a "special" place and stand some feet back whilst he would sneak further with exaggerated caution then dramatically chant a loud rhyme (usually thought up right there) and set it. The fun was in preparing the trap, if he caught something we all rejoiced if he didn't we were disappointed but it was always the affair of the preparation that got us all excited. And oh he could tell stories. His stories engrossed us. Some were fables and rhymes, others he just thought up but it had him singing, crying and gyrating in the dim smoke filled hut grabbing our imaginations and flinging them to far of places where mythical beings and men lived, fought and died. Sometimes his stories were epics and would be told night by night. At such times he could get us to do anything to ensure that the story would be continued in the evenings.

Like my grandfather he too has left us but the simple act of bringing fun and wonder into the lives of others is a legacy which I cherish.

What My Father Taught Me
Love God, Seek Justice, Pursue Peace

There was an incident when I was about 12. We had gone into town and were driving home when we saw two women savagely fighting each other. This was not our area and there were a lot of spectators surrounding the two women - watching, cheering and jeering. All of a sudden Dad stops the car, reverses and shouts at the people to stop them; they give him a weird look and continue watching. He can be fierce when he chooses and he chose to be so at that moment shouting at the crowd, asking them where the fun was in watching two mothers bash themselves to death? People were stunned that a stranger would stop and scream and some of them moved to stop the women. He then told them to take the two women to the nearby hospital, started the car and we drove off. I knew that he would have gone out and physically separated the two himself if people had not listened. He never mentioned the incident and we went about our holiday pursuits but I never forgot what he did. There was a wrong, it was a choice of being passive or responding; he responded.

Another time when we were on holiday our clan got into an argument with another clan and the war cry went up around our area telling us that they were coming to fight. I recall my father racing out of our house to gather those whom he knew were short tempered and would rush out to fight and calling to our clansman to meet at our place. In a short time all the men had assembled and most wanted to fight and I vividly remember my father announcing that he would go face them alone because our tribe knew him to be a Christian and a neutral person.

Trembling and praying fervently for his safety I watched him run unarmed to meet the approaching menace, two younger men flanking him (likewise unarmed). After an eternity he came home weary but triumphant having talked with the other clan and securing an agreement to dialogue for a peaceful solution.

Later when we were alone I accused him of not thinking about us when he rushed of like that and what would we do without him? He replied that it was because of us that he did what he did and that sometimes the greater good of the community would push him to take risks. Peace, he told me, was too precious a commodity to stand by and let it be destroyed. I learned then that life is not always about me and my comfort but that there are some ideals that are worth striving for even if it costs us something.

My father did what he did because of his love for his God and his people. It was the right thing to do and his faith moved him to pursue it.

These life lessons (and others beside) have influenced me greatly. I saw them consult with our mothers on family and clan decisions- saw how they listened and cooperated with them to create harmony in our lives. In doing this they were respected at home and in their community and in this was one more lesson learned; *The character and qualities of each sex can be so much more enhanced when mutual respect and dignity is practiced.*

My fathers are not perfect for we are all human and have our flaws, but I do see in them a sincere desire to pursue good; that is why I honour them.

The Haunting
Emma Wakpi

It was once told to me that oft times beneath the veneer of great beauty and wealth are hidden insatiable debaucheries that destroy. They are manifested in various forms that seem harmless at first but which eventually, if not checked and corrected will overpower and devastate.

Five a.m. and we're landing in Port Moresby. I look out of the plane window and watch the wakening sun tinge the rising mist a soft gold; I am home after two weeks of workshops in Manila. As I get up and collect my gear I remember the chivalrous gestures of strangers there; men who opened doors for me, who got up to offer me seats on public transport, male friends who grabbed shopping bags from my hands carrying them for me - acts that seemed as natural as breathing to them but which made a world of difference to me, giving me a sense of worth and security. Their courteous recognition gratified and prompted me to also want to treat others with respect. The pleasure which this memory evokes makes me smile and it gets broader at the feeling of belonging that is washing over me as I am surrounded by familiar imagery and faces. Going through customs I grin at my wantoks, say a good morning and make my way outside. However once outside I lose the grin and file away the memories, for I must now contend with the dawn of my reality.

The light hearted, carefree feeling is slowly rising up out of me like the mist clearing on the tarmac and wariness sets in. My mind and body move into auto pilot, "careful Emma, smile briefly at those guys, say a quick morning- keep your eyes down, walk steadily, act like you know the place - it's your territory, stride confidently but ooze humbleness- pretend you're taking that lint of your shoulder, steal a covert glance, no one is following, none look too threatening, okay breathe- walk; smile; you're fine, you've reached your destination – you're safe…" Until I have to detach myself from that secure zone and stealthily make my way to another. "Welcome home," I whisper to myself, "This is your life". I love my country, I love my people, but I am haunted; and I am weary oh so weary.

There is a menacing overbearing presence that haunts my being every time I step away from my safe zones (home, family, friends, work); its' clammy tentacles reach out and tunnel deep into my heart and mind and it tries its best to strangle any goodwill I might have toward the faceless populace surrounding my peripheries. Sometimes it's very obscure, other times it screams its presence- it wants to possess me, infiltrate my very core and define me by its standards.

It not only haunts me, the entire nation groans and is slowly suffocating beneath its smothering presence. This haunting seems to be rising from within the core of Papua New Guinea, surreptitiously extending its tentacles into every aspect of society and manifesting itself in various forms; whole mountains are being unceremoniously hacked to pieces, river systems defecated upon in the name of prosperity and local people elbowed aside and ridiculed as uncivilised, then officiously patronized through "programs" and "projects" and other various handouts to placate dissenting voices that might have echoes of truth. It causes the country, pregnant with untapped intelligence and aptitude to prematurely abort its potentials and to term them "failures" haughtily condemning them to the fringes of society. Law and Justice are also slowly being strangled by the grip of these clammy tentacles and the nation is slowly being brought to its knees.

There has to be a way to exorcise this "haunting" before it casts me forever into the abyss of despair and chokes the life out of this nation.

How can I fight an enemy I can't see, can't understand? I know it manifests itself in various forms and has me hacking away at them but from whence lieth its source and how can I clearly identify it in order to exorcise it? The only clue that I have is that it seems to be reverberating from within the core of this country- its' people, including me.

As I step out of my safe zones, I fight the fear within me and rather than rushing past the faceless mass, I now force myself to take the time to look, listen and mingle. As I do this, I notice that amid the war cries, screams and moaning echoing around me a soft hypnotic chant weaves itself in and out of every society and ethnicity within this country. It is so glaringly obvious, it goes unnoticed - the haunting is me-it is you; us...

Imprinted deep within my psyche are a set of beliefs that (should I allow it to) will ply me until I manifest its decrees with detrimental consequences to myself and the society at large. Throughout this vast country there are core beliefs that seem to be common to all, whether educated or not – from highlands to coast to islands, whether male or female, young or old. The haunting chants them out incessantly from within us, "men are of more value than women" true, true, true; "animistic beliefs are real" true, true, true; "might is right - Big Man mentality rules" true, true, true; "Fatalism is a way of life, what can you change?" true, true, true; "promiscuity and lies are a way of life" true, true, true. And I listen, and you listen and we allow it to possess and hypnotise us, becoming slaves who stomp rhythmically to its chants until we are jarred awake by some incident that pricks at our conscience; yet the wave of the chant carries us forward in a death grip marching us toward the precipice to throw us into the abyss of hopelessness that is the manifestation of these chants – AIDS, violence, drug abuse, political upheaval, tribal warfare, police brutality etc., etc.

I realise it is futile to hack away at the manifestations that the haunting produces if I don't address the root beliefs ingrained in me since birth. I must dig deep into the recesses of my heart and mind and pry away the grip of the cursed chant – I must uproot it in order to exorcise it. I cannot let a belief system that is destroying me (and my country) dictate my life. I have to think for myself and question whether what is "pasin", is really right. I must sing a new song of hope and strength – my war cry, "men and women are of equal value" true, true, true; "science and education will enlighten" true, true, true; "humility and integrity will achieve respect" true, true, true; "where there is a will there is a way- life can get better" true, true, true; "family stability and unconditional love can birth a fulfilling life" true, true, true! Until I am sure that I have dealt with all these issues that haunt me, I cannot point fingers and lay the blame on others because how I live and interact within the greater society contributes to its overall wellbeing.

Jarred from my death march I fight to break free; I'm struggling against the masses at times almost trampled underfoot but continue to elbow through, and will do so until I die. I cannot accept this reality and march with the horde - life is short and I don't want to live it out in fear and despair. I must fight.

As I resist and raise my war cry against the chant I hear faint echoes of it rising up from every direction. Struggling to catch a glimpse I find faces amongst the throng and as we sight each other, understanding dawns and strength is garnered anew and we turn back to resume our stance and to struggle on; I will continue to raise my voice against the chant and keep forging my way, I glimpse hope…

Beliefs begat behaviours resulting in the consequences of the society we live in today. I am told that my country is a beautiful and wealthy country, rich in culture and natural resources. What lies beneath its surface?

The Crocodile Prize Anthology 2012

HERITAGE

Barasi – The Manam Way of Celebrating a New Year
Lorraine Basse

Situated twenty five kilometres away from the township of Madang, along the fringes of the North Coast drive and a thirty minute journey by boat from mainland Bogia is Manam Island. Manam, a volcanic island, has fifteen villages and only one language which is Manam Motu. The people of Manam are fun loving, warm-hearted, caring, and hospitable and take pride in their chieftain society. One thing they love to do is to keep their traditions alive and one such tradition is Barasi.

Barasi is a festival about becoming a new person again and is a transitional rebirth from the old self to the new. It falls every year in the months of May, June and July, is a time of plenty and a celebration of a new year and a new beginning. However, this cultural celebration is slowly dying at each passing year as Manam islanders have been displaced after the 2004 volcanic eruption and are now living at Potsdam, Moumba, Daigul, Asuramba and Mangem care centres located at old coconut plantations in Bogia District.

The festival starts when the elders of the village beat the garamut (slit drum) at about four o'clock in the morning as they see a group of stars (Pleiades or Seven Sisters) rise just over the top of the island to announce its commencement. The fifteen villages on the island are then divided into three areas to cater for the months of May, June and July. After celebrating in one area they move on to the next area until the whole three months are over.

Here, there and everywhere hustling and noises of people can be heard as they rush into the central area. Grandparents who can walk, and parents and children all go down to the gathering area as it is custom that everyone should be present in order to be blessed by the spirits of riches, wealth, long life and whatever good the New Year might bring.

A huge fire is then lit for the elders to welcome the people and to drive away evil spirits. After that the people sing, shout and dance with the children towards the slowly advancing elders. As they get closer, some elders quickly grab a child for whipping as it is part of the cleansing ceremony.

The girls and small boys are whipped with the tanget leaves while the bigger boys are whipped with a betel nut trunk. Sometimes some boys fall unconscious when the elders beat them hard enough to knock some sense into them because of misbehaving and disobedience. The elders then put special leaves close to their noses so they inhale and become conscious again. This act helps them to behave and obey the people and the elders.

The girls and smaller children go to another group of dancers to be whipped with the tanget leaves while the boys are normally carried by two elders. While this is going on the people sing and dance to this song;

Goposi, posi be taengru o.
Goposi, posi be taengru o.
Moaede natumanga.
Tanepoa natumanga.
E –e – e – o – o – o kau

When they sing 'kau' that is the time the tanget leaf or betel nut trunk falls on the participants. The song means;

Come and let us fight.
The child of the Queen.
The child of the King

After the whipping ceremony everyone goes down to the beach to wash away the dirt of the past year. Young men and women swim out deep into the sea close to the horizon. They tease each other with songs, while the small children and elders swim closer to the shore.

After swimming for some hours they return to the beach. Sometimes the tired ones are taken back to the shore by canoes.

While the children are still swimming the parents go to their homes to prepare food and traditional items for the main celebration.

The parents then prepare for their hungry and tired children a big feast on the beach. After the feast the children are then decorated with their traditional attire and stay the whole day on the beach enjoying themselves with games, singsings and food.

This time of enjoyment is also a time of socializing as friends visit each other and tell stories or share jokes, eat food and dance traditional dances. It is also a time of betrothal and engagement. Thus, most traditional arranged marriages on Manam Island were formed during this time of the year and have a greater value than today.

This is how the marriages are arranged. The parents of a boy would send some food on a big plate to the girl's parents. If the girl's parents agree then they will accept the food. They in turn will send back the plate of food with a tanget leaf covering the food. From then on the boy's relatives would know that they had accepted their request and will help to look after the girl.

If the girl's parents do not agree then they will not accept the food. The food will be taken back without the tanget leaf. This makes the boy's relatives look for another girl in the next New Year's celebrations.

Meanwhile, among all the excitement and enjoyment, the men in their clan groups go out to get their fish traps which are laid a week earlier. The traps are made from split bamboo and bush rope. Children are not allowed to play near the people who are making the nets as the net makers might not concentrate and will make some mistakes with the weaving. The mistakes they believe will cause the fish to swim out and not be trapped in the net.

When a conch shell is blown from the canoes it means that they have caught plenty of fish. The women then go down to the beach to help the men bring the fish back to the village. The fish are cooked and shared among everyone present.

After a week, the celebrations end.

Traditions of the Bena Bena People of the Eastern Highlands
Anthony Kippel

The Bena Bena speaking people of the Eastern Highlands are found towards the north-eastern side of the provincial capital Goroka, sharing the border with Madang Province to the north, Lufa District to the south and Henganofi District to the East. Today, the number of people who live in this district number about 50,000 and are distinguished by the different dialects of the Bena language that they speak; namely Upper Bena, Lower Bena and Kona Bena. One can easily distinguish the origin of the person by the dialect they are speaking.

The Bena Bena area was one of the first highland areas to be opened and exposed to modern civilization when the Leahy brothers came prospecting for gold up the Bena River. An airstrip was established at Hapatoga with the first mission school opened at Hogisopagu by the Seventh Day Adventists. Some of the later products of this school include Mr Benais Sabumei, a former defence minister and member for Ungaii-Bena and his eminence, Sir AKepa Miakue. The legacy of the Leahy brothers includes the former Collins & Leahy Group of Companies, East-West Transport, the Bena Co-operative Society, the Bena Coffee Factory and the Magitu Tobacco factory.

As in many other societies of Papua New Guinea, the Bena Bena have their own culture, legends, folklore and myths unique to their setting and environment. This environment is comprised of savannah grassland, rolling hills and plains surrounded by guardian-like mountains. Mt Otto, to the north, is called Smanuga Sma, which means 'mountain where snow and mist never fades'. Migipa stands to the East and Ungaii to the South West.

The author was privileged to be able to witness the transition from a traditional culture to a modern western culture brought about by the influences of religion, education and the need to acquire modern wealth. For the Bena Bena, the SDA church had a very profound effect causing the abandonment of their culture & traditions. Today, the Bena Bena people are predominantly SDA's (myself included) and the majority of the SDA's in Eastern Highlands are from the Bena Bena District).

The same has happened in many other PNG societies and include the influence of the Lutheran Church in Morobe, the Catholic Church in East and West New Britain and East and West Sepik and the United Church in Central, Milne Bay and Oro. The latter churches have, however, incorporated and integrated some traditional cultural practices into their teachings and doctrines.

What is happening in all of PNG is that many cultural aspects, such as *singsings*, legends, folklore, dances, stories, practices and even languages are dying 'a natural or cultural death' through a combined effect of outside factors and influences.

My objective in describing the following traditions is that it will serve as an inspiration for modern day Bena Benas to take a moment to reflect back on their cultural and traditional history and, if possible, resurrect some of it in their own way.

Some of the prominent and significant traditions and cultures unique to Bena Bena society and culture that I witnessed and part-took in when growing up as a child in the typical Bena Bena society of Kopafo village in Corner Bena Bena are highlighted and elaborated on in the following descriptions.

I was 4-5 years old when I heard of the Oyafa Hemuki (carrying the old man) tradition. Normally this event takes place during pig-killing ceremonies where one village or tribe will go around giving Osahi (sticks of special significance & meaning) to the neighbouring village or another tribe with the number of sticks given equaling the number of pigs each recipient of the Osahi will get. In most Oyafa Hemuki ceremonies, 40-50 pigs were killed.

Normally, a week or two before the singsing and feasting, the clansmen and tribesmen would go around in the middle of the night (around 1-4 am) distributing the sticks to chosen people from the other tribe or village. During the stick-giving in the night, the clansmen of the host tribe would carry their elderly chief with them. The chief, nestled on a tribesman's back, would have the honour of playing a very rare pan flute, the Folo Mayane made out of a very rare bamboo called Komine. The tune was called the Uho-Uho-Lege-Lege and was played so that the sound resonated throughout the valley and the villages. His clansmen backed this up by playing another tune; Ngoe Lofu Ngoe Lofu Hipa Gume Hipa Gume (the tree that gives in abundance) repeatedly and interchangeably in rhythm with the chief's tune.

What we were told and warned against back then was that when these flutes were playing and coming our way it was taboo for small children and women to go out of their houses and physically see the players and the flutes. My father, who was a village chief, would tell us that a giant from the nearby Migipa Mountain was ferociously hungry and was on the lookout for food. He was armed with a Gutrafa Gui, a very old traditional Bena Bena string bag (bilum) made out of the local lepa tree, and he would grab and eat anything, including mothers and small children. I only came to know the truth and see the Folo Mayane in the 1990s when I was in high school.

The Panii-Zuhuve and the Pai-Nohiti are the equivalent of what we know today as manhood and womanhood. In the Bena Bena society, this is marked by significant events, ceremonies and rituals to mark the transition from boy to a man and girl to woman.

Panaii means "boy" in the Bena Bena language and bo means "man". For the panaii to become a bo he had to go through certain rituals. These were carried out by elderly and reputable men in very remote and secluded locations in makeshift huts made in the bush or in Zahu-Save, or men's houses, well away from the rest of the village and the womenfolk. There was a strong taboo against women seeing the men undergoing initiation because it could invalidate the whole exercise (nagami pipi). It was also forbidden for the boys undergoing the initiation to leave the initiation site for any reason at all.

The boy undergoes what is known as a neheja or zuhuve. Some rituals include the inserting of vines into the mouth and throat so that he vomits out anything that would be of hindrance to his mobility, agility and fitness. He would then go without food or water for several days and stay in front of a huge fire in a crowded hut for a prolonged period of time under intense heat and smoke to test for endurance. Another ritual included piercing the nostrils to enable a special stick called a melemele to be inserted. This stick is often worn by Bena Bena men during singsings. Lessons on how to make fences, dig drains, make hot stones, called efahi kozovo, for mumus and bows and arrows were also given to the boys. Fighting techniques, called luva, were also given by the warriors. The rituals and lessons were often very rigorous and were carried out under the strictest of conditions and only a few would pass the tests. Those who did not pass were not accorded any recognition and were told to stay away from the battle front during tribal fights. The men who passed out successfully from the Zahu-Save and associated rituals were sharp, fit, apt, fearsome and attractive to the young women folk.

Pai Nohoti is the female equivalent of the Panaii Zuhuve. Paii means "girl" and nohiti means "going inside the house". This refers to when the girl experiences her first menstruation; she has to go inside the women's house and eventually come out. When she comes out, she will now no longer be a girl but will be a woman ready for marriage and other motherly chores. Menstruation is obliquely referred to as Ki-Five or Hokave, which literally means "she fell down" in the Bena Bena language. Direct reference is avoided for fear of contaminating the minds of the small children and degrading the womenfolk. Men are not allowed to go into the Paii-Nohiti.

Normally during this period, which takes a week or two, the elderly women will use the occasion to teach the girl all the necessary requirements of womanhood. Normally it is the case that girls will marry far away into distant territories to some unknown man. To prepare her for duties in the man's land skills and knowledge, such as gardening techniques, bearing and bringing up children, looking after and caring for the family etc. are imparted to her. She is also taught taboos, such as not cooking and touching kitchen utensils (smo lape), washing in rivers or going to the garden, walking in front of the houses of elders or through the middle of a village when undergoing menstruation. In Bena Bena society menstrual blood is regarded as dirty and dangerous and these taboos are very strong and are strictly adhered to. When she undergoes menstruation she is secluded and isolated for 3 days in a small women's house called a Sopa Nohi, which usually has a makeshift bed and a cup and plate reserved for usage during the menstrual period. If a woman is caught breaking this taboo she will be publicly ridiculed and forced to kill a pig (zaga hovo). This taboo is waning in today's generations and marriages.

When she comes out of the women's house, she will be clothed in the newest and finest of traditional regalia called tupuna kata signifying her change of status from girl to woman. In the modern context this has become a lap lap and meri blouse. A very big feast called a Nosena will then be held to signify her coming out in public for the first time. The feast is hosted by the person entitled to the bride price (zogo) for the woman and is normally a close relative of her father or mother. Towards the climax of the feasting the would-be bride price receiver will announce the bride price he thinks she is worth to the public. The earmarked bride price is never wavered and the groom's relatives often meet or go above that target.

The traditional form of bride price payment was carried out using shell money (zogo galata*)* and pigs (zaga)*.* With the introduction of modern money, the average bride price amount has gone from about K1500 in the 1980's to about K3000 now. If the girl has some form of education, this might have a value-added effect on her bride price. The highest paid so far that I have heard about is K10,000 paid by Fego Kiniafa of Korofeigu in the lower Bena Bena area.

The Zafa Guna (group courting) ceremony is equivalent to Karim Lek in Simbu and Tanim Het or Vaipa in the Western Highlands. It was a type of traditional dance in which young men and women from different villages invite each other to a group singsing. The dancers go up and down in columns singing and trading affectionate head rubs. So intense was the dance that chins and cheeks often became very sore due to the continuous abrasions received from different persons.

The Zafa Guna was an approved and acceptable form of courtship where someone could safely find a lifelong marital partner. It was difficult in past days to move around freely because of the intense rivalry that existed between the warring clans and villages (*glas*) and courtship would not have been possible without such a dance and mass congregation of young people. What usually happened was that all the girls from the invited village ended up marrying the men from the host village and the vice versa. Often sisters ended up marrying brothers. My village, Kopafo, has such a background with the women from a nearby village called Kemanave in Henganofi District coming to marry the Kopafo men. That entire Kopafo generation is of such origin and make-up.

I am the product of a love affair developed during the Zafa Guna and so are three quarters of the people/children in Kopafo. In fact, the story and pattern of kinship, family relationship and marriage is very similar in many of the other Bena Bena villages, including Kapakamarigi, Korefeigu, Samogo, Katagu , Hofaga, Kapazugu, Kafetugu, Liorofa, Mohuveto, Sigerehi, Mipo-Klopa, Hofagayufa, Safayufa. These days, in the modern equivalent of the Zafa Guna, we are seeing couples meeting on the dance floor, at the bar, at the pool side, at functions, at games, at school and at work.

The Ana- Kata (sending a girl for marriage) is actually part two of the Paii-Nohiti. After the Paii-Nohiti, the girl was available for marriage and interested young men's relatives came to bid for her. They did this by placing special Osahis sticks draped with small clothes and shell money (zogo galata) near her house. As in the Ozafa Hemuki ceremony, the number of sticks was indicative of the number of pigs on offer; normally between 4 and 5 in this case.

Sadly and unlike today's boy-girl relationships and marriages, where one knows the other very well, the groom was largely unknown to the girl and the girl's relatives. This was the accepted traditional norm, however, and the girl had no choice but to follow it and go to where the groom came from, whether far or near. It didn't matter whether he was good looking or even whether he spoke another language.

The actual Ana-Kata took place 2-3 weeks after the bride price had been received. The girl was put into a house called the Logo Nohi (fire house) similar to the Paii-Nohoti but on this occasion several of her female peers of marriageable age would be put in the house with her. Men were also allowed to bring in zafi (sugar cane), nosena (food) and so forth. On the last night before the send-off, after advice from the mothers, there were several acts by both men and women, usually in disguise, depicting, imitating and reciting events fitting to the Logo Nohi.

As early as 4 or 5 am, men heated up mumu stones and slaughtered pigs to take with the bride to the groom's relatives. When dawn came the bride was again dressed up in the finest of traditional attire, this time for the last time. Before the departure to the groom's village, there was much weeping and wailing among the bride's family because their girl was departing their village for the last time and would never be with them again. This time was usually stressful for the biological mother and family because they were losing a sister, daughter and a family member permanently. If the bride was going to a faraway land she could only return if there was a genuine reason, such as the illness or death of her parents; and only then if her husband permitted her. I experienced this sort of loss when Rona, my fourth-born sister, got married to man from Gumine in the Simbu province and personally felt what it means to lose a sister through marriage.

When the bride was finally delivered by her family to her new village there was an exchange of words with the groom's side with them stressing their intention to provide for her care and protection. After the speeches, there was the most dramatic part of the ceremony where the strong men from the groom's side came over to the bride's side looking for her. She would have been well camouflaged amongst the delivery delegation and there would have been some initial resistance put up by the girl's brothers and a struggle would have ensued before she was actually released.

Once she was safely on the groom's side, food was exchanged. In the typical Bena Bena to Bena Bena marriage a separate table was set aside for the biological parents and another for the bride price recipient, who was generally the man who hosted the feast at the time of her Paii-Nohiti. The rest of the delegation was given a combined nosena, which included pork, chicken, banana, sugar cane and kaukau. Some food was also given to someone from the groom's side, usually a distant relative called a Nofo (cousin) to look after her in times of problems, such as during a Luba-Gena or domestic dispute.

The biggest mystery yet remains - the groom is absent in all of these prior proceedings and events. He is normally not seen for about a month or so. Usually a few of the girl's relatives and her mother and father will remain back for about two extra weeks after the delivery delegation departs for home. When the party for the send-off of the girl's remaining relatives happens, the groom eventually shows up and the husband and wife will see each other for the first time over a binding or unification ceremony called the Zafi Gofaha (breaking the sugar cane). This sugarcane was usually a special red juicy one called safa zafi.

During the Zafi Gofaha ceremony, the girl and her parents will stay on one side and the boy and his parents on the other side with a middle man between them. The significance of holding the sugar cane and cutting it is to bring the two married people together. Its modern equivalent is the exchanging of vows and rings. The binding ceremony brought them together to start a new chapter in their lives. After witnessing this ceremony the girl's relatives left her for the last time never to see her again unless circumstances warranted it.

Sometimes, a small girl or boy is left tied to the girl's tupuna kata (traditional skirt) to be her helper and these children grew to become the "first born" of the couple and become citizens of that place. If she is a girl, she marries there as well. I have some people of such background in my village. Unfortunately arguments always arise with people of such background over landownership issues, something which is very rife in the Bena Bena area.

The Logo-Efahi (sending away the dead in smoke) or fire stone ceremony is normally carried out after the death of a person. Usually, when a person dies, a mourning period called Zibi Nohi or Huas Krai is observed for up to week. Usually the deceased are kept inside a house guarded by close relatives who sit beside them. Depending upon the status of the deceased, people from far and near come to the house cry and will be received by crying mothers, sisters and aunties who are usually daubed in mud and ash and wearing broken clothing. The men usually take back stage but also sob and wail.

The Logo Efahi, which literally means "sending away the dead in smoke", is a myth or belief widely held among the Bena Bena. It involves a feast over the deceased to send him or her away through clouds of smoke and fire. Those who visited the deceased during the Zibi Nohi will be called and after the burial the food will be shared and eaten. A very intriguing aspect of this, with a modern twist, is that when someone, especially a man, dies through some unusual circumstances and sorcery is suspected an old radio will be placed in the tomb in the hope that the dead person will broadcast the cause of his death. Usually a brave person who is not normally frightened by gusts of wind or eerie sounds stands guard over the tomb into the night. There have, in fact, been some reported cases of unusual sightings, voices and sounds heard by such persons but I haven't seen any proof myself.

If the death is that of a man, the widow or Keto-A-I will be draped in black clothes at the time of the burial and for a significant amount of time afterwards, usually a year but sometimes permanently. In some cases, after the removal of the black cloth, she may re-marry. This will most likely be to one of the brothers of the husband to allow for the continuity and welfare of the children. There are several cases of this in my village. If the death is that of a woman, the widower, called a Kofuta, *in* most cases will remarry very quickly, usually to another widow.

The Story of Totoga Wai from Babaka Village
Beauty Rupa Loi

The Totoga Wai is the story of my great-grandfathers and their forefathers and the gigantic crocodile and the formation of the precious salt water river at Babaka village, the place I call my home. Totoga is the name and Wai is the river where the Babaka people earn their livelihood and enjoy the environment.

The story is from my father's clan and is true and correct; however I do not wish to highlight the names of people to preserve the identities of the families. Babaka village is situated 200km by road east of Port Moresby, approximately a 3 hour drive by vehicle. It has a population of more than 1,000 people who are subsistence farmers. The educated elites work and reside in the cities and frequently come home and enjoy the flora and fauna of the village environment.

Many years ago there lived a village chief and his family in their bush material house built on high posts. The couple had five beautiful daughters, the first in her mid-twenties and the last in her teens

One morning, the elder daughter noticed the dog barking at something very strange that caught the attention of the family, so the father decided to check beneath the house and to his amazement saw a gigantic male crocodile underneath the house ready and prepared to attack,

The father wondered why the reptile was right under his house and began to ask, with fear gripping the entire family, why he camped there,

The crocodile was motionless and, unmoved, remained calm. The father asked all the questions he could think of from anything that could strike his attention, but the crocodile was never moved.

Finally the father asked the crocodile if he wanted one his five daughters and the huge crocodile wagged its tail and leapt for joy in a very happy mood. The father, with sad face and astonished body language, climbed into the house quietly, no words to utter, because it was not the answer he anticipated,

The mother and the daughters asked the father what actually happened; the father broke the news and everybody kept silent lost in words and thought.

The father asked his four daughters who all refused to accept the reptile enthusiastically but the fifth daughter responded positively: "Because all my sisters refused to accept the reptile, I am giving myself to the reptile to save us from any unexpected circumstances."

The father, after being assured by the daughter climbed down under the house to meet the crocodile, confident that it was not going to attack him

The father stood in front of the huge crocodile and broke the news that his desire to marry one his daughters was granted and the very happy crocodile again leaped in joy and began to dance and move around the house celebrating.

The father called a meeting with the people of the seven houses in the village and the very small population bravely put on a big feast and, with tearful departure, farewelled the daughter from human being to reptile life.

The daughter and the crocodile were decorated with traditional gifts, necklaces, pig tusks and many other items including food.

The daughter sat on the back of the gigantic crocodile which slowly submerged under the creek. A week later the crocodile turned the creek into a big and wide river for the people of Babaka village

After their marriage the daughter was half crocodile and half human (from waist up human figure and waist below crocodile tail).

After the formation of the river the historical sites were named to remember the daughter and the crocodile's family. Wapuli is a local yam. Turage na means 'give'.

At any given time when a person returned from fishing trip and paddled past the site Wapuli turagena and called for food, the daughter would provide them hot cooked yams right from the river.

One day the other sisters decided to see their sister, so they ventured out fishing. Upon their return they called for food and, as the sister lifted the hot dish of yams, the sisters reached down and lifted the sister out of the river and saw her amazing reptile and human figure.

Since then the sister crocodile disappeared and never returned to produce hot yams but the crocodiles never killed any man or dog after the creation of the crocodile human river.

In history and today the Babaka people enjoy the existence of the river and the friendly crocodiles that do not attack any person or animal. We continue to enjoy the river with an abundance of mangroves, seafood and much more.

Whenever people by chance see a crocodile while fishing they are always blessed with plenty of fish or crab to take home and they tell tales of their day's blessings.

The Migration of Wanigela People of Central Province to Tufi in Oro Province
Golova Mari

Long ago my village people of Wanigela lived harmoniously. They shared common bonds by living, co-operating and working together in everyday life. But one day something happened which separated some people from my village.

Altogether there are seventeen clans in my village. One day some people from the Marugai clan went to the bush hunting and gathering food. On their way they came across some dead trunks from some fallen mangrove trees. They stopped to cut up the trunks for firewood and also to extract the edible worms. Worms from dead mangrove tree trunks are good and tasty either cooked or eaten raw when they have been washed and cleaned properly.

They collected plenty of edible worms and firewood from the dead mangrove trunks and returned to the village. They planned to return to their find and get more worms and firewood the next day.

But the news of the discovery reached some other people from the same clan and they went out very early the next day and collected the edible worms and returned to the village before they were discovered.

When the original people who had discovered the dead mangrove trunks returned to the spot later in the morning they discovered to their astonishment that the worms had been stolen and none were left. This really upset them and made them uneasy and they went home after cutting some more firewood and hunting for birds and animals.

Back in the village they found out who the culprits were and a fight arose among the people within the Marugai clan.

After the fight the original victims vowed to leave the clan and the village of Wanigela. They began to build a lakatoi or double hulled canoe. It took them several months to build the lakatoi and upon its completion they loaded it with food, water and their wives and children and sailed eastwards after bidding farewell to the village people. The village people were very sad as they watched their own people sailing away.

They sailed eastward towards Milne Bay Province. When they ran out of food and water supplies they made stopovers at coastal villages to get more. They sailed close to the mainland in case the lakatoi was blown off course and lost in the open ocean.

After sailing for weeks and months they arrived at Samarai Island in Milne Bay Province and after re-stocking with food and water sailed northward to Oro Province and the Collingwood Bay area.

They found that this area was very beautiful with long sandy beaches and swaying palm trees and friendly locals so they decided to settle near Tufi. They started to build a settlement after the locals gave them land to settle on.

The local people were very sad when they told them the whole story of why they left their own village and sailed away in search of a new land.

From that time the settlement grew to become a village and the name given to it was Wanigela at Tufi, now known as Tufi Wanigela.

The Tufi Wanigela people intermarried with the local people and slowly the culture and language of the old Wanigela disappeared completely as the new culture and language was adapted.

Today the Tufi Wanigela people still look similar in appearance to that of Wanigela village in Central Province and wherever both Wanigelas meet in life we call ourselves brothers and sisters.

This is how the second village of Wanigela came into existence in Oro Province in Papua New Guinea.

Modernisation of Tribal War: A Threat to Civilisation
Francis Nii

Tribal warfare has always been an integral part of Papua New Guinean and Simbu traditions. However, modernisation of it poses a serious threat to civilisation.

In Simbu society there used to be two kinds of tribal warfare. In the Yui dialect of Karimui Nomane, they were described as kura magi and kura hamil, meaning internal war and external war.

The internal wars were conducted to injure only and not to kill. Long poles, sticks and stones were used as weapons. Combatants mainly aimed at the heads of the enemies to cause minor lacerations. It was close contact fighting, like sword battles around Europe in the medieval period.

Since the fight was to injure only, dangerous weapons like spears, bows and arrows, axes and bush knives were not allowed.

Although the battle normally lasted for only one or two hours, it used to be fast and intensive. A lot of blood would be spilt but there would be no killings.

Women, children and property were left untouched.

The victor would be the side that had the lesser number of its warriors injured.

An interview with a number of old people revealed that internal fighting occurred between neighbouring clans and tribal allies. That is why it was called an internal war, connotatively meaning friendly fight. Peace and normalcy always prevailed the next day.

In the external war, the fight usually occurred between tribal enemies. Killing, destruction, looting and plundering were the order of the battle. Dangerous weapons such as bows and arrows, spears, axes, bush knives and shields were used.

The battle was normally fought openly at a common ground. The opposing sides, after raising their dander up by hurling provocative words at each other, would then converge on the battle field where all hell broke loose.

The traditional allies of the warring tribes would also take sides and the fight could develop into a civil war.

Sometimes it was one or two tribes against many tribes.

The fight could go on for a week, a month, a year or even more, as long as each side withstood the attack on their own territory and there were less deaths, enough food supply and no police intervention.

Eventually the stronger side would prevail and chase the weak enemy out of their territory and possess their land.

The main causes of tribal wars in the old days were disputes over land, stealing, sorcery, rape and adultery.

The object of starting a war was to end a conflict. Tribal fights were the means to end any conflict in contention. It was the ultimate means of dissolving a contentious conflict that normal peace mediation and compensation processes had failed. When the conflicting parties refused to make peace, they went to war and fought it out and got it over with.

With modern developments, the entire anatomy of tribal war in Simbu and other parts of the country has changed a lot - in weaponry, tactics, causes and objects. Guns of all sorts and even hand grenades have replaced sticks, stones, spears and bows and arrows.

The enemies now attack each other in stealth and use ambush in a guerrilla style of warfare. They open fire at each other from far distances and give chase. When an enemy is caught he will be chopped into pieces and scattered into the bushes.

All property, including schools and aid posts, in the fighting zones are subject to looting and destruction.

The first time guns were used in a tribal fight in Simbu was in 1982. The fight erupted between the Endugla and Nauro tribes of Kundiawa-Gembogl District in a conflict related to the 1982 national election. The fight developed into a civil war affecting many tribes, many lives and much property. It set the precedent for the modern style of tribal war. It also saw the end, or rather, the phasing out and absorption of the old types of war into the modern style.

Since then politics has been the dominant reason for the tribal wars in all the six districts of Simbu and other parts of the highlands. There were and are very few cases of tribal wars related to land matters, stealing, rape, adultery, sorcery etc.

The modernisation of tribal war and politics have paved the way for an aggressive build-up of illegal high powered firearms in Simbu and other highland provinces posing a serious threat to development, progress and freedom.

It is very important that the PNG government seriously deliberate on the Guns Commission's report and enact appropriate gun laws to control and contain guns and the related issues. The sooner this is done the better.

Migration and Mythology: The Way from Shortland to Kieta
Leonard Fong Roka

The oral histories of people in the Kieta area of Bougainville and all of South Bougainville records that the original inhabitants of these places came across the Bougainville Strait from what is now the Western Province of the Solomon Islands.

Geography, traditions, cultures and language support this fact. The most recent immigrants along this route into Bougainville were the Torau'an, who today occupy Rorovana, Tarara and Vito villages in Central Bougainville.

The Torau'ans did not come into Bougainville by chance. The route was well known to them. It was a crossing made by their kinsmen long before. They saw their lost kinsmen's descendants' criss-crossing the Bougainville Strait on peaceful visits or to trade as well as to make war and carry out bride kidnappings. So, they also paddled across and up the East Coast of Bougainville.

All these adventures or interactions, were guided, nurtured or blessed by Bougainvillean gods. Known across Melanesia to dwell in the wilderness, these gods were venerated or paid homage to in order to gain positive results in all endeavours.

Before the Torau'ans, my Basikaang clan ancestors crossed this sea passage into the coastal areas of Buin. In their company was their god and totem, Barama the eel.

Barama was the shepherd of my ancestors. He dictated what to do and what not to do. He was the security and provider. When angered or saddened, he attacked and killed his minders and enemies alike. The duty of my people was to pacify him through food offerings and by living a good life in his presence.

After generations passed, my ancestors reached Haisi in Siwai. Here they dwelled for years and multiplied. Later on they moved into the wilderness of the Banoni area and settled down in the Birosii plains of Bana District. For ages they colonised this area and slowly began to move further northward to the Nagovis area.

In Nagovis, they maintained their presence for a prolonged period in the Takemari area on the Nagovis plains and at O'karu, a mountain area of Nagovis bordering Kieta's Kongara area villages.

It was from Takemari that the idea to conquer the mountainous Panguna area of Kieta was born. Their O'karu relatives would come from the mountains and prompt them to explore the bluish ridges to the north-east. Hunters that reached the Pagara River also reported that yonder on the edges of Nagovis there were wild mountains. Both of these things excited Barama and his human relatives.

So one fine day, a woman told a gathering: 'Ning baru'baru e ono'ai nani' (I will move and settle a bit further). She said this pointing in the direction in which the gatherers and hunters said the great Pagara River flowed.

The woman thus left and settled near the Pagara River and called the place, Baruu'baruu. Whilst, maintaining relations with their Takemari and O'karu relatives, her family line extended and with their shepherd, Barama colonised the whole area as far as what is now Sikoreva Village.

After many decades, a couple of the woman's descendants climbed the Siko'reva ridge. The present day, Darenai and Oune village areas to the north looked beautiful. The Kavarong River below and the Biam'pa tributary attracted them. They moved on and settled on the imposing landscape of the Darenai area called Dato'etu.

They were the first group of people to enter what is now known as the Tumpusiong Valley that comprises the villages of Damara and Enamira on the east bank of the Kavarong River and Oune and Darenai on the west bank.

For years they were based on the top of the Dato'etu "boulder" and explored the area and interacted or went to war with those entering the area from the west into what is now known as the Kosia.

The worst dilemma my ancestors on Dato'etu had was related to marriage and a shortage of wives. They had to get their wives from further afield at Nagovis. There is a reason for this shortage of women.

Legend has it that on Dato'etu, people did not know that labouring women delivered babies through the birth canal. So, when labour pains dawned upon a woman, the men or women, slashed open the woman's belly; freed the infant, and disposed of the woman's corpse over a cliff.

One day, a woman was in labour and the women were at work to execute the delivery process when a visitor from Takemari arrived.

The husband was weeping on the ground with his eyes fixed on his fading sun of love. 'What's all this commotion for?' the visitor, asked. 'Your daughter is about to deliver.'

'We think you do not deliver in a proper manner,' she told them. 'This is why you are not multiplying.' She carried out the delivery and the woman was not killed.

Grief and regret flowed through the settlement. Men wept for their dead wives.

The "boulder" then earned its name, Dato'etu which means, 'they cut' in the Nasioi language. My ancestors also called themselves, the Taing'kuu (now a sub-clan of the Basikaang clan in the Tumpusiong Valley), which means, 'were eaten' because when they disposed of the women's bodies, the cuscus and other animals ate them.

From there, my ancestors moved down to the banks of the Kavarong River, crossed at Dingkuu'mori and made their way up the Damara ridge and settled at a place called Doraro. They interacted with the Damara people for years but then explored and settled on the next 'boulder', today known as, Deumori (Catholic Missionaries built a station there in the colonial era).

At Deumori, my ancestors were vulnerable to regular lightning strikes, so they left and settled at the northern foot of Deumori and called the new place Enamira, which means, 'let me breath'.

The shepherd eel, Bamara, also had its place; a network of waterfalls and caves known as Toro'vau, on the tributary is called Tonau'a. Here it was fed and cared for by my people, the Taing'kuu. The Barama enjoyed its place and socialisation with its human relatives. So, the Enamira people rose in power and prestige across the Panguna, Evo and Kieta areas. Through trade and war they influenced neighbouring clans and people.

One day, at the peak of these glory days, the people received an invitation by some new settlers at Deumori to come to a feast. The villages left a lazy youth, called Paku'musii and his brother, Nuku'eii, to mind the eel for a day. Late in the afternoon, he got some food and visited

Toro'vau.

In disrespect, he called: 'Barama-birama, here is your food'. The eel grabbed him instantly with its tail and knocked him against the rock walls of Toro'vau. Paku'musii died as his brother Nuku'eii wept facing the Deumori 'boulder'.

Barama was also saddened for killing his relative. With guilty tears, it left Toro'vau. Rain, thunder and earth tremors followed as the Barama made its way down the Tonau'a River smashing into rocks as it went.

Reaching the Kavarong River, it turned upstream. It then, followed the scent trail that the Enamira people had left. It left the Kavarong River and travelled up the Oionari tributary. By dawn, it reached the Mai'nokii villages in Evo (near present day Paruparu station). Here it made itself visible to a friendly relative of the Enamira people, a chief called Pirikuu.

Pirikuu and his people, built Barama a grassy compound, fenced entirely with the saplings of a tree known as kempareva. He lived at Mai'nokii silently moaning in guilt.

Then one day, a child hunter who was passing by made fun of him. Barama killed him. The people attempted to kill him in retaliation, but he escaped with a painful bamboo spear (called kabakii) driven into his flesh. He went down the great Kuraro River of Evo, leaving behind a jungle of kempareva in his wake. Sensing humans everywhere Barama by-passed the Siuema villages and headed towards a hillock called Kire.

A plain of silent jungle dotted with wild hills and ridges opened before his pained eyes. He made his way slowly down a stream called, Mo'rong. As he moved in pain he twisted his body around creating a pool in the zigzagging rock wall, called Mero'mero, which means, 'and it turned round and round'.

In agony, Barama reached a river, called Asi'manaa. The current took him downstream. Still feeling insecure, he left the river and went into a stream called Kuru'aa. Slowly he slipped under a tangle of a tree's gigantic roots and the spear was trapped and released and the pain died away. The released spear grew into the largest kabakii field in the marshland of Asi'manaa.

Barama finally, settled on the Kuru'aa marshland at the foot of Banekana Hill inland from Koiare, a place south of Torokina.

The Enamira people slowly followed after Barama and occupied this isolated area of Bougainville.

Today, because of Barama, my family has a long kinship line from Haisi to Birosii to O'karu to Baru'baruu. We also have recognised land ownership in Birosii, O'karu and Baru'baruu stretching across to the Banekana plains. Our sacred sites are dotted all over Banoni, Nagovis, and Kieta and into the Evo areas. From Enamira we maintain the relations set for us by Barama and pay visits regularly.

The Complex Rituals of Death in Kieta Society
Leonard Fong Roka

The Kieta people, who occupy most of central Bougainville and speak Nasioi, maintain their identity and beliefs.

To the Kietas, death brings a weight of responsibility to be executed in accordance with traditional ritual. From the moment of death (*bo*), it takes around three years to declare the death to be over; and is not to be further thought of.

Death brings transformation and new responsibilities to certain people within the immediate extended family. The fundamental basis is to maintain a good relationship with the spirit world. And that communion is always symbolised by feasting.

Once, a person is pronounced dead, the way the body was positioned at the last breath is not disturbed. All persons present withdraw because the death is not yet declared to the spirit world by the immediate family. Mourners may come, but they have to keep to the village edge.

The declaration involves the immediate women relatives who are called together; they encircle the position where the body is lying, eyes fixed to the body, and give out a loud hysterical scream, a process we call wii.

This declaration signals that they have been surprised, and have just lost a family member. As the womenfolk weep, a number of trees, especially, coconut and areca nut palms in the vicinity of the village are felled as part of this declaration.

Declaration over, the death bed is prepared. This involves two tasks: uprooting of taro (aapi) and bathing of the body (duu). The women break into two groups. One leaves for the taro gardens to uproot the taro and pile the taro in an oval arrangement to accommodate the corpse as a bed does. The group that has remained bathes the body with one taboo to follow: if the deceased is a male, the relatives he can relate to as a 'sister' are not allowed there and vice versa.

The body is placed on the taro bed and mourners are permitted to view and touch to show their grief.

From the moment of death, the family is banned from gardening. They are permitted only to harvest. Nearby villages, as a gesture of respect, stop all burning of garden rubbish.

Taro (ba'u) is significant in Kieta society. It is a source of power and prestige. All mythology, legends and folklore can miss out other food crops, but not taro. The placing of the dead on a taro-bed is a request for blessing from the spirit world (mourners bring in their taro) and pay homage to the spirit world for all the good things it has given; hoping in return that the spirits take good care of the community.

After the mourning period is over, the coffin is removed from the house and placed on the grass. Immediate family members assemble near the casket and a village elder bathes them with water and magical herbs (papa'ranang) to remove all negativity so they remain free from conflict with the deceased's other relatives.

As the casket is carried to the grave, an elder equipped with a kind of magical herb called sirivi, which he has purposely removed from the papa'ranang, walks around the village calling on all the spirits (aabo) to follow him to the burial site. As the casket is placed in the grave (daako), the elder places the sirivi in the grave with all the spirits attached to it.

Early the next morning, the day after the daako, all the rubbish created during the funeral is collected and burned (kat'te) by the family. Cleaning up the village shows that the family is free to move on with the other requirements of the death process.

The traditional timing for ending of sorrow (kep'pu-nuu) is always two weeks after the kat'te. The men leave the village for hunting or fishing. The women gather garden food. All these activities are done within two weeks. On an appointed date all those who came for mourning are called together to eat the food.

The sorrow period is partially over with this small one-day feast. Gardening resumes; burning in the gardens is allowed.

This paves the way for two major feasting events: the ntaa-kong-kong that prepares the family for the final feast to officially end the sorrow process, the kat'te turaa.

During the kep'pu-nuu, there are several rites.

In kereng-kereng, people choose to abstain from consuming the various food types the dead person was eating two weeks before death. Certain people will also choose to stop combing their hair and grow dreadlocks (mama'ku) which they cut at the feast of kat'te turaa.

In kabo-kabo-ro the dead person's property is carefully sorted and disposed of. Some things are given to relatives, but a good proportion are put into a traditional bag (tora) and stored for burning during the final feast (kat'te turaa).

For the declaration of ntaa-kong-kong, the people set the date for clearing the bush in preparation for the planting of big public taro garden (kota). Pigs are given to each person of the family.

When all these tasks are completed, the family and relatives get on with their life for a month or so before starting the last two processes of ending the sorrow.

Ntaa-kong-kong is a small feast a month or two after the kep'pu-nuu. It is the ceremony that signals to begin gardening and pig domestication for the kat'te turaa. The women remain in the village and prepare the food and pork as the men clear the bush out for the public taro garden (kota).

Taro grows well in the higher altitudes of Kieta. It usually takes a year to harvest. So, the final feasting to officially declare that the sorrow is over, takes about 18 months, depending on the maturation of the taro.

Kat'te turaa is the final feast to marks the end of the long ritualistic funeral journey. Persons who abstained from combing their hair and, those who abstained from eating certain food bring in their pigs and those they invited as their guests to witness the ceremony come and dance the kovi (flute singsing) until dawn.

At three o'clock in the morning, the deceased person's selected belongings are burned in a fire. As the fire finally consumes the clothing and so on, a singsing group is called to dance over it; indicating that we are now over with this sorrow.

When the sun is up and shining, those who abstained from combing their hair and eating certain food are called and the family of the late person serves them.

When all this is completed the people slaughter the pigs and distribute the meat to various people to take home to their homes.

Death in Kieta society starts a long process of ritual that must be undertaken in accordance with tradition. Non-compliance brings a curse upon the family from the spirit world.

The Last of the Segera Tutubes
Miriam Roko

In the olden days Segera Tutubes, or cannibals used to live on the Island of Tatana here in the nation's capital.

They were violent and aggressive and had no knowledge of the difference between doing good or evil. They were warriors who would kill and eat people. Their home was built in between the Kwila trees growing on the mountain top. This hideout could accommodate fifty to a hundred people or more.

They lived on raw meat, human flesh, pig, fish, seashells or any other meat they could lay their hands on. Sometimes they would go out looking for kaukau, bananas or fruits of any kind.

Children were their main target, so children were forbidden to cry. The parents would warn their little ones not to cry for anything at any one time.

They loved roaming the villages in the night. There was great fear as these Segera Tutubes were hairy, strong, violent and aggressive. They were more like apes than humans.

One night a little baby was heard crying; the mother tried her best to tame the baby boy by breast feeding him and the father also tried his best to sing the baby boy to sleep but without success and the sound of his crying reached the mountain top bringing the chief of the Segeras and his men into the village. The sound of the baby's crying brought them to the very home where the child was and upon the demand of the Segera Tutubes the parents decided to give the child away and it was taken away high up on the mountain with great joy and laughter with their kundu drums beating while feasting on the baby.

Children were claimed many times when the parents were not careful or when the children were heard crying; the parents could not refuse the Segera Tutube's demands for their children to be killed because they feared being killed also.

One day a beautiful young girl was asked by a young man in the village to marry him. Upon her parent's refusal she started crying and lamenting at the top of her voice, going on for two days.

As soon as the Segera Tutubes heard the sound they came down into the village and claimed the young girl.

She was her parent's one and only child and upon realising what was happening they begged the chief of the Segera Tutubes to give them a few days so they could prepare to give her away in a proper traditional manner. The parents and all the village people were very sad and in great sorrow.

That very night the village chief called an urgent meeting to make plans and decide on how they would give the girl away and how they would put an end to the Segera Tutubes demands and terrible abuse and unnecessary killings.

Their plan was that the girl be dressed in her best traditional attire and her parents be encouraged to be strong as this was to be the last demand of the Segera Tutubes.

The second part of the plan was for the men to go out fishing. The men in the village were great fishermen and experienced in catching plenty of fish because they had been giving fish and other seafood to tame the Segera Tutubes.

The women were required to cook food in coconut cream and make sago pudding (dia or bariva) to bring on the canoe when the men would arrive with their catch.

Two days later the sad day arrived for the young girl to be given away; she had her last meal with her parents and relatives and the women decided to dress her up with tattoos, arm shells, bird of paradise feathers, pig's teeth necklaces and grass skirts for when the Segera Tutubes arrived to claim her.

The men started beating their drums and singing and then the girl was given away. That was the saddest day as the parents were in great sorrow and suffering silently.

That very night the men sailed out to go and catch fish. All night long they caught fish while the young boys and old men did the smoking. On the second day they returned to the village, with flags raised as a sign of a good and plentiful catch.

The women started cooking and making preparations. When the men arrived they fed them and continued cooking because they were going to feast with the Segera Tutubes. There were fish of every kind as well as turtles and other seafood. When the food was ready they put the pots onto the canoes, which were big and double rigged.

Then the village chief and leaders invited the chief of the Segera Tutubes to come on to the canoes. When he got on the rest of the Segera Tutubes, young and old, followed and not a single Segera Tutube was left behind.

When the men started sailing out to sea the women and the old men and the young people started singing and celebrating in the village.

When they reached the deep blue ocean the men gave the Segera Tutubes chief permission for them to start feasting.

While the Segera Tutubes were preoccupied with feasting the men started to attack them and threw each and every one of them into the sea. Not knowing how to swim, they all drowned and that was the end of the Segera Tutubes.

When the men returned to the village they started singing:

Segera, Segera Tutube
Amui kau kau amai laiamu
Segera, Segera Tutube
Segera, Segera Tutube
Amui vamu vamu amai laiamu
Segera, Segera Tutube.

Segera, Segera Tutube we bring you your kau kau and meat, Segera, Segera Tutube and that is the end.

How Yari Siwi Got Their Body Decoration
Henry Sape

A long, long time ago, when the earth was young and the animals of the world were friendly, there lived two brothers named Hali and Weki in the deep jungles of Sambo valley in the Southern Highlands of Papua New Guinea. The brothers both being young had never travelled out far from their homestead and did not know what lived beyond those mountain ranges under which they lived.

One evening during dinner, Hali the elder brother told his young brother Weki that he had planned to go on a hunting expedition beyond the mountains and that he was to stay back and collect firewood and gather food supplies from their garden.

As planned, Hali collected his bow and arrows and left the next morning at dawn on the long trip. The thick forest was beginning to come alive with the singing of birds and insects welcoming the beautiful morning.

With eagerness to explore, Hali crossed many fast flowing rivers and travelled over many mountain ranges. By the afternoon, he came across a large beautiful valley that laid stretched out for miles as far as his eyes could see. At the far end of the valley, Hali noticed a spiral of smoke ascending into the clear blue afternoon skies and this made Hali determined to discover who lived in that part of the valley.

He descended the mountain hastily but evening was approaching fast. Hali proceeded further and came across a clearing at the bottom of the mountain where there was a huge breadfruit tree with its branches laden with ripe fruit. He murmured that he would spend the night under the tree and set about building a temporary shelter for himself.

After he had completed the shelter, Hali decided to climb the breadfruit tree to knock down some of the ripe fruit for dinner. Soon after he had knocked down the first fruit, all hell broke loose. There was a sudden fiery flash of lighting that split the valley in half from one end to the other with booming thunder that shook the entire valley. There was heavy rain with fierce winds that snapped off branches and uprooted trees.

In the ensuring minutes, the thunderstorm seemed to encircle the breadfruit tree and Hali was almost torn off the branches by the fierce winds.

Then all of a sudden, Hali could see below him in the dim light a huge ugly giant staring up at him with his big fiery eyes. The ugly giant said in a deep thunderous voice, "Who is up there stealing my fruit?" Then the ugly giant in fury grabbed the trunk of the breadfruit tree and shook it vigorously and tried in vain to uproot it.

In frustration, the evil giant murmured some magical words and slapped the trunk of the tree with all his might with the palms of his huge hands.

Shaken badly, Hali decided to stay the night up in the branches for fear of the giant returning to get him in the dark of night.

Early the next morning, Hali climbed down from the tree to pick up his bow and arrows and head back home to tell his younger brother Weki about his experiences. As soon as he put his foot on the ground, a strange thing happened to him; he was suddenly transformed into a huge black cassowary. Filled with terror and anxiety, Hali the cassowary lifted his foot off the ground to find himself back to normal again. He tried a couple of times more in vain. Every time he put his foot down, he would turn into a cassowary. Hali finally gave up and climbed down from the tree and in the form of a cassowary and made his long trip back home.

Late in the afternoon that day, Weki was astonished to see a huge black cassowary coming towards the house but the cassowary made some advances that made Weki realise that something drastic had gone wrong with his elder brother Hali.

They stayed overnight and early the next morning, they left for the mysterious breadfruit tree, led by Hali the cassowary. As soon as they reached the tree, Hali the cassowary immediately climbed it and to Weki's surprise and joy, Hali the cassowary transformed to Hali himself. The brothers cried bitterly when Hali told the full story of what had happened to him the previous day.

Both Hali and Weki agreed that the area had been cursed by the evil giant and that they should seek help from the mother of cassowaries that lived at the place where the sun sinks.

After Weki had collected a few of their belongings, they travelled for many days towards the west over rivers, mountains and valleys. As they travelled, all the cassowaries (yara siwi) of the world followed them to see and witness the occasion.

Eventually when they reached the mountain cave home, Hali the cassowary was brought before a huge black mother of cassowaries and Hali told her of what had happened to him. After listening carefully, the mother of cassowaries told Hali that he had been cursed by the wicked giant and that to save himself he would have to die first. The mother of cassowaries then signalled to Weki to hold down Hali the cassowary and with all her might, she drove her long sharp third finger into the Hali's heart, killing him instantly. Whilst the dead cassowary was crumbling into dust, the transformed Hali rose from within the crumbling dust to the joy of his brother Weki and the multitude of cassowaries present.

The mother of cassowaries explained to the overjoyed brothers that Hali had been cursed by the wicked giant for stealing his breadfruit.

In appreciation, Hali and Weki gave the mother of cassowaries some colourful paints of blue, red and yellow. The mother of cassowaries then distributed the paints to all the cassowaries that were present to witness occasion.

The multitude of cassowaries immediately painted themselves with the blue, red and yellow colours.

Hali and Weki returned to their homestead and lived there happily thereafter. And to this day the beautiful colours of blue, red and yellow paint given by Hali and Weki can be seen on the necks of yara siwi, the cassowaries.

Malah's Initiation to Womanhood
Hilda Fromai Yerive

This story is from real life scenarios but the character names have been changed

Malah was born to Kenya and Premong. She hails from Sembi village near Wewak on the west coast of East Sepik Province along the highway to the border of Indonesia and PNG.

Unlike other parts of the Province, famous for boy's initiations in the Haus Tambaran, (Spirit house) here girls are initiated instead because of their important role as future mothers.

"Malah! Wake up, your mother has gone to the beach and the sun is up, you never sleep-in," her father Kenya yelled,

Malah hesitated, she was not sleeping; she had been awake before dawn. Kenya knew his daughter was not like the other village girls; she is up before the rest of the household and does her chores for the day. Being a community leader, people come to discuss community issues so he makes sure his house is in order. Premong had taught her only daughter everything expected of a girl in the family.

Malah was unusually quiet; she was in her room in the house she shared with her parents. She had panicked when she woke up in the night and found her bed soiled. Frightened by her situation she was confused and did not know how to tell her father.

Soon after Kenya left, she quickly crept to the rear end of the house and signalled her cousin Wagha. Seeing the fear in Malah's face, Wagah hurried over to her. Nervously she broke the news, whispering to Malah that she was having her first menstruation.

Wagha was older and she comforted Malah and explained what she should do next. At that instant Mala realized that the most memorable and eventful chapter of her life history had begun. Because of her father's status in the community, her mother had prepared her in advance and encouraged her to be brave.

A girl's initiation has always aroused great excitement in the village so news spread fast. Garamut drums were beating continuously, sending messages throughout the communities. Quickly, a cone shaped hut called a popongah (moon haus) was built from coconut fronds for her to stay in for the next two weeks.

Normally, the timeframe would depend on childhood behaviour, if she had been naughty and disobedient; she would remain for a longer period while the elderly womenfolk imposed tough rules and guidelines on her. Malah had been good so she stayed only two weeks. She was allowed only food cooked in charcoal with tea and no protein (she must learn to sacrifice).

Villagers were invited to a night of singing and feasting on the last night before she was let out of the popongah. Kenya was famous so many people had come with contributions of food, money and gifts. That evening the villagers gathered and scattered into groups of their favourite singing partners.

The singing started; Terek-Masisia (poetic songs) were sung with no musical instruments; they are specially composed with rhyming words depicting fond memories of meaningful events or descriptions of someone's behaviour and silly attitudes etc. The songs were sung in segments of time e.g. early hours, midnight and dawn. Food and drinks were served in the same manner during intervals.

Toward morning, Malah prepared herself for her most threatening hour. She had to show confidence and be brave to make her family proud and boast about her. Within her temporary shelter, she could tell from the songs what was happening outside.

Before sunrise a group of men joined hands together singing and swaying while a little boy imitating a cuscus jumped on their hands over the popongah and tore the sides down to frighten Malah out. The crowd quickly made two long lines starting from the entrance of the hut towards the beach. She slowly removed her blouse and wearing only short jeans came out.

Her uncle (mothers' brother), a strong and solid build man, hauled her over his back then started running between the lines. Everyone had sticks and swung them whipping at them from both sides (that was to scare her childhood spirit away).

It was an emotional moment for her brothers and cousins so they ran alongside her to help split the whippings. At the end of the lines she ran into the sea with bruises all over her and washed off before rinsing in fresh water,

Back at the ceremonial grounds, an elderly woman made four deep cuts in Malah's hips then dressed the cuts with herbs and shaved her childhood hair (so that she could carry heavy loads on her head and back in future). Then they dressed her in a colourful grass-skirt and necklaces and she sat on a mat as people came with gifts of all sorts to present to her - cloths, necklaces, money, string bags etc.

Kenya, proud of his daughter and a man of traditional values called out the names of those who had shared the whippings with his daughter and compensated them with money. The uncle who carried her was paid more according to custom.

For the next stage of Malah's rituals, Wagha was appointed Malah's maid for the next five months. Relatives supplied food for them and Wagha did their cooking and washing. Malah was not allowed to do much work; she was to eat plenty of good food and rest while the elderly women would teach her their customs, culture and traditions.

Watchful eyes kept Malah company throughout those days making sure she complied with the rules. Most importantly she must never complain of any mistreatment during the period". It is believed that complaining is a bad habit that will not make a good wife in the future. She should learn to submit to her husband, be hardworking and self-reliant, providing for her future family and taking good care of her husband's parents.

At the end of the fifth month, Kenya compensated Wagha with food and money for taking care of his daughter. Malah's childhood appearance had disappeared; she had changed into a very beautiful model of her native culture; living a legend in her fast changing society as the legacy continues.

Kenya now has the dignity to demand a higher bride-price payment from Malah's future husband.

STUDENTS

Pink and Round
Brenda Anduwan

I go for a walk and wander around,
I stumble across something pink and round,
It's not as pink,
It's not as round
But all I care for is for what I've found

It's soft and tender,
Moist and silk,
It smells like honey,
It smells like milk,
I think its treasure
I think its gold,
'Cause it's a treasure, so untold,
So precious,
So rare,
Would you touch it?
Don't you dare!
Cause all this is,
Is a ripened pear.

Man's Best Friend
Macquin Anduwan

He means so much to me
Who could ever replace him
He's mine, can't you see?

Please don't make him leave,
I've only found him yesterday
Please trust me,
I need you to believe

You've always lent me a helping hand
This time,
It's with man's best friend

I'll do all my responsibilities,
I promise
Just think of the possibilities
I'll call him Thomas,
Maybe even after Hercules

Just listen to me this once
And I'll never ask for anything again
Reduce my money for lunch
To me he's my greatest gain
An opportunity that comes only once
A great dog like him,
Man's Best Friend

Sporty: A Dog's Story
Clara Philomena Are

The first time Sporty ran away, the whole family was spurred to looked everywhere for him. After the second day all hope was gone and everyone was very sad.

'He must have been killed somewhere,' said Michael.

They sorely missed him for two days.

'Listen,' Joan silenced her brother Jim 'I think I hear someone panting outside.'

They opened the windows quietly and peered into the dark starry night but couldn't see anything; only short gasps of panting could be heard.

'Sporty,' Joan whispered into the dark and at once they could hear their beloved dog and friend barking in response and scratching the back door.

'Sporty!' they both cried out.

'Where have you been old man?' said Michael as his four children gathered around Sporty, smothering him with hugs.

Michael and his children had owned a few dogs before but Sporty was just the best.

Year by year Sporty grew into the likeness of his father. He was very well-built with huge mesmerizing brown eyes and sharp ears. Flashing, gleaming white teeth could be seen when he growled. He's a 'king of the road' type. Sporty was indeed a smart dog too, he'd do things like shaking hands, bark furiously when visitors or strangers came at the gate and was a father figure to other domestic animals. Whenever their neighbour's dogs came to kill them he'd always put up a fight.

In the midst of the children playing, Sporty was always seen romping around them and barking, making himself part of their games as well as part of their lives.

One of the most admirable and respectable things he does is that whenever Michael comes home late, Sporty usually waits at the gate till he comes. He's like a guard with his baton ready to strike at the enemies. Sometimes when he gets lonely at night, he'd howl and bark near Michael's bedroom, telling his master to find a partner for him.

'No, Sporty I'm not getting you a partner!' Michael would scream back at him, 'you'll be single like I am.'

Gun shots could be heard on the main road and everyone was running for their lives.

'A fight! A fight!' Donnie screamed and ran to the veranda.

A few minutes later when everything returned to normalcy, they jumped at a loud noise in the kitchen as pots and pans crashed onto the floor.

'What's that?' asked Jim puzzled.

They rushed to the kitchen and were surprised to see Sporty poking his head out of the cupboard wagging his tail in relief.

'Oh, coward dog,' Jim said as he patted and led him out. Sporty's not afraid of anything except gunshots so when he heard the first shot, he pushed open the door and began to look for a space in the kitchen to hide when he noticed the cupboard ajar; he opened it with his nose and hid inside. Unfortunately, the space was too small for him so when he tried to get up he bumped the pots and pans.

He's the first one to greet Michael and his children after returning from work or school. Jumping onto them and licking their faces like an ice-cream.

'Look at what he's doing,' whispered Donnie to Joan.

'I think he's digging the ground to bury something,' replied Joan.

'He's burying his sweet potato,' giggled Joan 'clever, aint he?'

The next day, he went to the same spot, dug it up and ate it. That's his habit whenever he's full. He does the same with solid food or a chunk of meat.

During the final moments of his life, Sporty got very sick. He'd sleep almost every day. His white gleaming teeth would clench tight making it very hard to feed him and so he started to lose weight. Medicines didn't help.

'I think Sporty will leave us soon,' Michael said one night as they were having dinner.

Everyone nodded quietly without saying anything because they knew it was true. They'd spent almost every day with him unlike before.

'We'll really miss you old man,' Jim said whilst caressing him and enjoying his scruffy feel.

'You're the best dog we've ever had,' Joan added sadly.

Sporty just whined. He didn't want to leave them either.

No please, I must not die, thought Sporty whose huge mesmerizing eyes were fixed intently on his master. He tried to move himself to catch his attention though his body was numb and flaccid. He pleaded to his master if he could see him but Michael was busy reading the newspaper and did not notice him. When he was a few meters from his master and in sight, his whole body shook and he fell down hard on the ground, his heartbeat began to slow down and his teeth even clenched tighter, it was now or never before he breathed his last. At his final minutes of agony his beloved master slowly turned around and saw him. Goodbye, Sporty thought, ruefully.

'Theresia come quickly,' screamed her father. 'Sporty is dying.'

They tried forcing a few tablets and water into his mouth but it was too late. He's not going to live. He only waited for his masters' touch and he got it at last. A few minutes later Sporty peacefully passed away.

They were all distressed and cried and gave him a very decent burial.

Rest in Peace Sporty.

Great Man's Tale
Jovie Hriehwazi

I was sad to see him go, it was shocking, heartbreaking and terrifying; for someone I had known so much about and learned so much from, even to the extreme of sharing tears.

He just left without saying goodbye or even letting me say a word of thanks.

The sudden passing of my great uncle, Bill at Port Moresby General Hospital (PMGH) on January 8th 2012, 1.30pm was a remorse and mourning event in my life.

Most people knew him as a man full of laughter and happiness with no grudges against anyone, he always taught to forgive and forget. With a smile on everywhere cheering up depressed people or even greeting an old lady who looked lost in her own world.

He complained of chest pain on the night of January 7th taking in pills, milk and fruits but it did him no good. The pain which he was going through seemed all fine to his family, because he wasn't showing signs of exhaustion or fear of death.

On that night he locked himself in his room for three hours, without his wife's knowledge of what he was going through at that instant.

Three hours passed, about 9pm he came out of the room dashing to the shower with sweat dripping off him as rain, even forgetting his towel which seemed quite odd because he never forgets a requirement.

Coming out of the shower he spoke his last words to his wife and younger brother "I'm ready let's go the hospital".

On their way to PMGH he looked calm and relaxed. With mixed emotions his wife asked "Are you feeling any pain around the chest area?"

With a firm reply he said "Not really," acting all innocent for the true phenomenon in him was just waiting for the right moment to spill.

At PMGH it was very busy with cries of patients in need of help, Uncle Bill, his wife and brother waited till they were attended to at around 12pm.

At that instant when he was told to lie on the bed he began to produce large amounts of sweat, his body was shaking like a trembling child with cold, and his blood pressure began to drop.

All types of reviving techniques were used but nothing could be done. At about 1:30am he was pronounced dead.

As I write this story I dearly miss my great uncle so much, all the good times and bad times but no matter what the family relation was the most important part.

The time for saying a goodbye has come but not goodbyes forever for I know we will still meet up, in the clouds of heaven.

May your soul rest in peace Uncle Bill.

Where Have All the Children Gone?
Hannah Ilave

Where have all the Children gone?
Naught, but their weeping,
Is heard in the night,
Once on the beach, where the sun had shone,
Now, wounded with woe
Tums held on tight.

Where have the Adolescents gone?
Your neighbourhood rebel,
In the barren boulevard,
Once contenders of competition, souls of stone,
Now, hurt with hatred
From life are barred.

Where have all the Mothers gone?
Naught, but the slave,
The nightmare she calls home,
Once filled with love, an unbreakable bond,
Now, pierced with pain
In a cold glass dome.

Where have all the Fathers gone?
Naught, but the drunk,
In his cage of defeat,
Once the hero, got all jobs done,
Now, marred with malice
Swept off his feet.

Where have all the people gone?
Naught, but with sorrow,
On this desolate earth,

Once filled with happiness, every one,
Now, gashed with gloom
Imposed since birth.

Wonderful Sphere
Vanessa Kavanamur

I must have walked into a wonderful sphere
I know there are others out there
But I was meant for this one
They call it family

Love, respect, discipline, and obedience written on it
Colours appear and fade
Every second changing to make it beautiful

There are seasons for everything
For sunshine and smiles
For storm and tears
There are even tests to pass
Yet mostly you learn
To make a prettier you

When I walk out of the sphere
Perhaps a second or two
The colour my sphere gives me shines

That is when I realize
How different I am from the others
I look back into my history book
And find out that it's my sphere
That makes me who I am

Going Through the Unimaginable
Angeline Low

"Life back at home is simple and easy. Not much has changed since you left." Molong said to Jacob in her native dialect.

"But I've been gone for almost 15 years! Surely there should be some development in Boda." Jacob said flabbergasted.

Jacob had grown up alongside Molong on Boda Island located 10km away from Madang. Molong's uncle adopted him and took him to Lae at the mere age of two.

"Yes it seems like a long time but we still have no proper schools, no electricity, no clinics…" Her voice shook at the mention of the word clinic.

Jacob knew that Molong had lost her mother to the deadly disease malaria. If there were clinics on the Island, maybe she could have been saved. He looked down at the slim, dark-skinned girl sympathetically.

"You know there are some things we can't change in life and I know you just lost your mother only a month ago, but don't you think if she were alive she would want you to be happy?" He asked gently. Molong studied the tall, handsome boy for a moment.

Since she arrived in Lae from Boda, he had always been friendly towards her and always knew the right things to say.

"You know what, I'm sorry I said anything. It must be terrible for you. Sorry." Jacob apologized after Molong did not reply to his question.

"No, don't apologize. I was just thinking about how you . . . . "

"Hello children! I see you are up to your usual chit chat again. The lawn isn't going to rake itself, you know." A deep, rusty voice cut in.

Jacob and Molong turned to see a tall, broad muscular man walking towards them from the front gate.

"Uncle Fegsley!" Molong cried out and went to hug him.

"Hi Paps." Jacob said calmly.

"How many times have I told you about using that term son?" Fegsley replied.

"Ha-ha sorry, Papa. How was work?" Fegsley let go of Molong.

"It was all right. Now finish up your cleaning and come up for dinner." He replied sternly.

Fegsley then walked away into the standalone house he called home as the two teenagers stared after him. He had this strong presence that commands people to stop, look and listen to what he has to say. Molong had always admired this about her uncle. Fegsley had brought Molong with him to Lae after Molong's mother had passed away. Molong's father had run away with another woman claiming he could not look after Molong anymore because she reminded him too much of her mother. Fegsley then took the initiative to take Molong in and care for her when the word got out that both her parents were gone.

"You're really fond of him, aren't you?" asked Jacob curiously.

"Well yes, if it weren't for him, I would still be on Boda Island, suffering under my own misery. So yes, uncle Fegsley is like a father I never had. You should be grateful you have him as your father."

Jacob smiled at this. They then cleaned up the yard in silence.

Janet, a short, plump woman who is Fegsley's wife stood at the entrance of the house, one hand on her hips.

"You two, I asked you to rake the lawn two hours ago. What took you so long?" She asked, shaking her head at the same time.

"They were gossiping." said a small girl with a high-pitched voice playing with her Barbie.

"Lynn, you are such a liar. Don't listen to her Mum" Jacob said slightly annoyed.

"Okay, okay. Dinner's on the table." She said while ushering them into the living room.

Lynn is Jacob's little sister and is quite mischievous. Molong started disliking her when she, as she called it, accidentally, put chewing gum inside Molong's cap. When Molong had worn it the gum got stuck in her hair and so they had to cut her shoulder-length hair to remove it. Now Molong has short boyish hair. She had forgiven her already but was not fond of Lynn at all. The whole family as well as other relatives all sat down in the center of the living room and ate dinner, cracking jokes as they ate.

After dinner, Fegsley pulled Molong outside the house where no one was around. She knew she was going to get scolded because this was usually where he took her before lecturing her. It had been two months since

Molong arrived from Boda Island and so she got used to Uncle Fegsley lecturing her on morals and ethics. He was like a father to her. That day however his usual calm lectures turned into loud, terrifying screams of rage. Fegsley took Molong's friendship with Jacob as something else and was very upset about it.

"He is like your brother for goodness sake! Yes, he may not be blood related but that does not mean you can have a relationship with him!"Fegsley screamed at Molong.

"But I never intended on having a . . . ." She was cut off.

"Ah, bullshit! Noken giaman long mi!"He shouted and then took a deep breath. Before Molong realized it, he raised his right hand up and slapped her across the face.

"Get out of my face . . . ." He said. Molong just stood shocked and dumbfounded. He had never laid a hand on her before.

"NOW!" He said.

With that, Molong ran straight into the house, bypassing Lynn, Jacob and Janet who stood staring through the window of the kitchen. She locked herself in the room and cried all night.

The next morning, Molong woke up to the sight of dozens of flowers in her room and a brightly wrapped present. It was a pleasant surprise. She stared at it in complete silence but her curiosity got the better of her and she gently tore the present open. Molong was perplexed. It was a rectangular object with a square reflective mirror in it. She did not know what it was and so she went into Lynn's room to ask her. Lynn explained to her that it was a phone that is used to talk with people. She showed her how to use it before asking her where she got it from. Molong told her that she found it in her room but Lynn did not believe her. Just then, Jacob walked in and when he saw her, he quickly turned around and walked away. From that moment, Molong realized that Uncle Fegsley scolded him too. Lynn realized how tense Molong looked and she quickly remembered what happened last night.

"Ah, Papa mas sore lo yu so em buyim yu fon. Lucki blo yu." Lynn said.

Lynn was only thirteen years of age so she was quite assertive. Molong walked out of her room, showered and went on with her everyday chores, all the while ignoring Jacob.

At around five o'clock in the afternoon, Fegsley came home. He came straight to Molong and hugged her in front of Aunty Janet. Fegsley, then apologized, saying how wrong he was to have concluded something like that about Jacob and her and how terribly sorry he was for slapping her. Molong accepted his apology and said it was alright. He is like a father to me and sometimes fathers and daughters have arguments. It was normal.

The following days, were the same. Molong would wake up to presents and flowers in her room. She knew it was a bit strange but she was too infatuated with all the gifts she had received. Molong felt so loved knowing he cared enough for her to buy her all these gifts.

The next Saturday afternoon, everyone went out for a family gathering and Molong was left behind to look after the house. It was around 6pm when everyone went out. She then went into her room and played with her phone. It was so silent in the house that Molong jumped when she heard a knock on her door.

"Yes, who is it?" She asked wearily in her native tongue.

"It's me, uncle Fegsley, I came back to get something in the house."

"Oh, you scared me." Molong stood up and opened the door.

"Did you find what you were looking for?" She asked.

"Yes..." He replied, strangely calm.

"Oh, I found it. I wanted it so much since the day I saw it but there wasn't enough time for me to find it and get it." He said as he moved closer.

"What?" Molong asked completely dumbfounded. Then before she caught what he meant by that, he grabbed her by the arm. His grip was so tight and strong that she yelped in pain.

"Ssshhh don't scream. It'll be over very soon." He said soothingly then he pushed her down on the bed with him on top of her.

Molong wanted to scream to cry out for help but she was so lost in confusion and shock that she grew completely numb. She thought Fegsley was a nice, genuine man who cared for everyone. He was like a dad to her. She never thought what would happen next would have ever occurred, but it did. He kicked the door shut with his foot and that was when Molong lost her innocence.

After he was done, her whole body had ached and Molong began to sob. Blood covered the whole bed sheet.

"Don't cry… I'm so sorry… I promise I won't ever do that again to you. Please don't tell anyone. Let's keep this between me and you." He said.

Molong continued to cry uncontrollably. She could not dare look at him and she crawled away from him like a scared puppy afraid of thunder.

"I will buy you anything you want. Just promise me you won't tell anyone…" He said almost desperately.

Molong curled up, holding her body tightly; scared he might touch her again. When she didn't reply, he responded by begging her not to tell anyone.

"Okay." She managed to say just to get him away from her.

"Good girl. I'm going to go now, clean up the mess" He commanded before he buckled up, and took off.

Molong stayed in her room for an hour before she gathered up the energy to go wash her aching body. She also washed and hung out her stained clothes and the bed sheet as well, too scared of what uncle Fegsley might do to her if she didn't. Molong was so young and so stupid. She could've gone to the police but she felt too embarrassed to do so. So she spent the whole day in her room crying her eyes out. Molong cleaned up before uncle Fegsley's family and he came back. When they returned from their trip, everyone noticed her sudden change in character.

"Are you okay?" Lynn asked genuinely.

"Yeah mi orait." She lied. Molong knew her eyes were puffy and her posture was terrible but she still tried to appear normal as best she could.

Jacob looked at her concernedly but she just shrugged. Then suddenly Aunty Janet came into the living room extremely angry.

"EM WANEM?" she shouted at Molong while holding up Molong's trousers.

Molong had missed a spot on the back of her trousers and the blood stain could be seen clearly. She grew numb again. Her mind whirled and twisted, Molong couldn't focus. Then someone shook her hard. She regained her consciousness to see Fegsley and Janet arguing. Somehow her mind had blanked for a few seconds. It turned out it was Jacob who shook her. He held her close to him as they watched in silence.

"It was all her fault, she seduced me!" Uncle pointed at her in disgust.

"It's true! She came on to me. She was touching me all over, that little bitch!" He said loudly. Her mouth went dry when she heard this. Aunty

Janet then shot her a look.

"Is this true? She asked harshly.

"I … I … no, it's not true…" she replied.

"Don't lie to me!" she screamed and walked closer to her.

"I swear in the name of Go-"

"Don't say his name in vain. You filthy animal." Fegsley cut in.

"Why is he doing this? How can someone be so cruel?" she thought.

"You came into my house. I feed you, clothed you, did everything for you and this is how you repay me? By sleeping with my husband?" Aunty Janet asked, her tone escalating with each word.

Her fist clenching and unclenching, ready to bash Molong up. She ran back to the kitchen and picked up a knife.

Oh no, this can't be happening. Molong thinks. *I shouldn't be at fault here.* Molong tried to say but words couldn't seem to come out. Her heart rate increased rapidly.

I'm going to die now; she's going to kill me. Molong thinks to herself.

Time seems to freezes and Molong sees everything in slow-motion. Aunty Janet running towards her with the knife. Fegsley trying to stop her. Lynn's jaw dropping. Jacob … What's Jacob doing? Time regains its normal pace and she see Jacob step in front of her just before Aunty Janet launches the knife right into his heart.

"NO!" She cries out. Blood spurts out from his chest, staining his shirt.

One drop of blood lands on her face. Then Jacob drops on his knees, knife stuck in his heart.

"Hes ly...lying... mama..." He managed to say before he collapsed to his death.

Molong staggers towards him holding him in her arms as she cried and sobbed out loud. She couldn't believe she witnessed two deaths so far. There, lying on the floor in a puddle of blood is a young man, full of potential, full of life. He sacrificed his own life for her and for that Molong shall forever remember him. Aunty Janet, Uncle Fegley and Lynn just stood in silence completely shocked and devastated at the same time. Now they knew how it feels to lose a loved one.

"Rest in peace Jacob. I love you." Molong whispered to him while caressing his face gently. Tears soaked up her shirt and she sat there holding him for half an hour in complete silence. Molong's future will never be certain but she will always remember the memories, good or bad.

Sweet Sophie
Angeline Low

She walks into school with a huge grin on her face
Greeting her friends at every turn
Gracious and smart, she strides with no haste
Temporarily ignoring her internal burn
What gives, what takes?
That is her motto
To please is to fake
A smile every day
To please is to make
A 4.0 GPA
To please is to take
Away all that is hers
She is perfect through the eyes of the simple-minded
Beautiful, smart, popular and athletic
What they wouldn't give to be in her position
Little do they know the struggles of her upkeep
Oh Sweet Sophie, Why the need to be perfect?
The makeup may mask the bags under your eye
But will not take away the scars on your wrist
You struggle each day and that is a fact
What gives, what takes?
That is the question
Well to achieve perfection
Is to broaden peoples expectation
To please the expectations
Is to suffocate under your own frustration.
What gives, what takes?
Giving of happiness
Taking away of life
Oh sweet Sophie
You have yet to find the light.

First Day at a New School
Sharina Paliou

Leah looked up at her new school as thoughts of doubt ran through her mind; had she made the right decision to come here, and is this the end of her problems?

Leah is 13 years old with a sweet and caring personality.

In spite of that Leah feels insecure and lacks courage in everything she does. She is someone who is afraid of what people think of her and was not free to be herself. She could not voice her opinions confidently and wasn't sure of how people would perceive her if she did. She finds comfort in her own thoughts. Being around family and friends she tends to remain very quiet and likes to observe and listen. Being quiet is the best remedy for avoiding people and conversations. She was reprimanded by her parents a lot of times and told it was an unfriendly attitude but Leah knew she liked people; it's just that she is lost for words when it comes to talking. How she dreads this and prays that one day, maybe just one day, she will be able to jump over this big hurdle in her life.

Moving to this new school was a decision she bravely took even though she didn't want to. She just wanted to get away from all the pain and teasing from her old school and so her parents agreed saying it was going to be a good break for her and might help to improve her social skills. The school was said to have strict policies on bullying and had a positive environment with lots of support for students who have problems. With her parents support she made the decision to move to this school.

On the first day of school, as Leah walked towards the administration office with her mom and started to climb the stairs thoughts of regret came flashing to her, did she make the right choice but there was no turning back now?

The school was located on a hill near the centre of town. All the buildings were painted pale pink giving a serene feeling to the atmosphere. The school's population was about 300 inclusive of both students & teachers. The school had day students as well as boarding. There was a boarding house at the very back of the school with its mess. The boarding house was the same size as the school buildings. There was a huge hall where assemblies and events are held and a canteen within the hall. There were specialist rooms and all classrooms had their own toilets. It had ample car parking to cater for the school vehicles and those of the parents and visitors. Next to the school buildings is a large swimming pool. It looked really nice and welcoming.

As Leah and her mother were about to enter the office a lady came out, "New student?" she asked. Leah and her mother both nodded. "Then this way please," Leah turned to her mother hoping that she would stay and follow her. But the sinking feeling in her stomach grew bigger when her mother just smiled, hugged her and said, "You'll be okay." Leah didn't even feel okay she wanted to cry because she was all alone and how will she settle in and make friends? She swallowed a sob and hugged her mother back. She quietly offered up a simple prayer to God for courage. Turning slowly, she made her way towards the group noticing that all of them had their heads down and were looking at their shoes but she didn't dwell on that very long because she too did exactly the same thing staring at her feet. She walked with the group not noticing anything but the ground beneath her. It felt embarrassing and humiliating not knowing anyone. To make matters worse no one wore uniforms so that made them stand out as new students. Leah continued walking beside the other students but didn't bother to say hi or tried to be friendly because she was scared and shy. The group came to the first stop: year 7 in room 5, year 8 in room 6. Leah put her head down and leaned next to the post she was standing at. "Okay students you may come in," Leah glanced up, but quickly.

Baia Village
Kayla Reimann

An arcane, silhouetted figure casually approaches us as my sister and I, two young and intrepid adventurers, paddle across the sparkling waters, absorbing the warmth and beauty of this isolated region.

Lost in a tropical paradise riddled with an impenetrable menagerie of natural structures, Baia is truly a captivating spectacle. Concealed between the border of East and West New Britain province, Baia village boasts of its unique and diverse ceremonial practices, beautiful and friendly villagers, linguistic groups (some of which I quickly adopted) and its many paradisiacal qualities and locations.

Papua New Guinea, the land of a thousand journeys always manages to unveil an endless array of cultures and traditions, even after living in the country for a lifetime. As we steered towards another annual season, my sister and I were unaware that we were also steering towards a traditional character known as the "Tugong"... who took pleasure in beating kids!

Identifying the figure, the paddle was quickly snatched out of my hands as we frantically steered back towards the safety of the village. The Tugong was rapidly approaching, sitting on the tip of his canoe and mouthing incantations as an intimidating tactic, whilst his driver determinedly paddled after us. Compared to their years of paddling and healthy structure our so called "bulging" muscles were definitely no match!

To the occasional plane overhead we would have looked out of control as we swerved across the calm South Pacific scavenging for debris to chuck at the enemy. Our creativity won out as the Tugong and his opportunistic one man crew deliberately accelerated towards the beach, which was edged with a crowd of entertained village kids. Instantly they left the scene as the ambitious character approached.

A nearby reef as we eventually noticed harboured two of our friends who alike us had a close call with the Tugong. As we sliced through the water, gently rocking to the rhythm of the waves we could notice every detail and embellishment of the reef as the water magnified and enhanced its beauty. Vibrant fishes darted beneath us, a magnificent display of contrast and colour. Transporting the girls back to land we headed for the nearby waterfall where the villagers sustained its refreshing and pristine water. Boulders carpeted in moss and ferns ascended into a series of pristine water holes, an unrefined ecosystem where prawns dominated and flora and fauna were plentiful and diverse.

Gathering essential garden produce for our next meal, we slipped out of the natural cove steering towards shore. An irregular group of enthusiastic kids populated the shore line screaming, shouting and pointing. Like a synchronized swim team my sister and I dived into the crystal clear waters, abandoning our canoe as the Tugong appeared unexpectedly only metres behind. Motivated by these enthused kids we scrambled ashore in time to watch a resplendent sunset as the sun descended beyond the horizon.

This was definitely one of my many unforgettable experiences; the traditions of Papua New Guinea which are so rich in meaning and history should be preserved for future generations. Unfortunately with the introduction of logging at Baia the eradication of essential natural beauties has also led to the elimination of valued traditions.

Upon my next much anticipated visit to Baia it was hard to recognise the area, secondary roads weaved down the elevated plains that were once disguised by a frontier of lush vegetation. Chainsaws deafened the area replacing tranquil bird calls, whilst soil erosion stained pristine rivers which were dominated by the mighty Black Bass, a prominent game fish species. The waterfall where life was plentiful and abundant was drastically affected as a bridge was erected across a main passage way, an impediment to the water's progress downstream.

Within mere months, complaints were addressed and the loggers moved to areas elsewhere. Garnered evidence proved that no effort at reforestation was made, however in once such a well preserved and healthy environment many species of flora were able to rapidly reproduce, consuming roads and disguising the permanent damage done to the ecosystem. Fauna is gradually populating this captivating paradise whilst game fishing for the challenging Black Bass has become a major drawcard.

Urbanisation has accelerated in the gregarious village where a church, educational facility and clinic have been established. Excluding one of Baia's essential, providing ecosystems and a valued and unique tradition that was lost this remote location has restored its enchanting natural beauty and tranquil atmosphere.

Through impossible conditions this paradisiacal location definitely continues to meet the standards of PNG's national tourism slogan…"Like every place you've never been".

Peace on Earth
Kayla Reimann

I have walked the silent streets,
And witnessed the ghastly deaths,
I saw the torture my family went through,
And am still seeing it yet.

For the screams and cries can still be heard,
And the deaths may still be seen,
The world in its poorest state,
And the grass no longer green.

And as we fight the pride less wars,
The hatred consumes our heart,
It drains our love and forgiveness,
Our soul an empty shaft.

For our kindness is spared by the weakest thread,
And our forgiveness as frail as glass,
Our hope the finest sliver of sunshine,
And our love soon the past.

But within that fine sliver,
Hidden within the golden rays,
Is what we know as hope,
Present through every phase.

We are equal individuals,
And shall stand together as one,
To face the pain that we have caused,
And finish what we have begun.

But to restore freedom and peace,
As we pray each hopeful night,
We must treasure every beauty,
From dusk to the dawn of light.

Fumes and smoke gather no more,
But rays of the purest gold,
For within this new era,
Walks only bright and bold.

The Fight
Joshua Rere

This story is about a fight that happened when we first moved to a new house. It was between two villages in the Eastern Highlands Province.

It was a fine day when my family and I moved to our new home near the Okuk Highway. We were very excited. We had already moved all our stuff from our old house so it was just a matter of sorting things out and putting them in their rightful places. I spent the whole morning fixing my room. When I had completed my task it was already twelve o'clock. I spent my free time playing computer games. I then went outside. That was when I heard the commotion. The noise sounded close so I ran up to the gate. I observed men armed with pieces of hardwood chasing another group of men down the highway. Some of the men being chased jumped over our fence to escape from the fight. After a few minutes the fight cooled down and eventually stopped.

My mum had witnessed this ordeal from the fence so I asked her what had happened. The story she told went like this: There was a fight between the Kafe and the Kamaliki men earlier in town. The Kafes had apparently beaten up a drunken Kamaliki man. Since Kamaliki was one of the places the main highway ran through before going to Kafe, the drunkard and his friends decided to block the road and search the cars for any Kafes.

One wrong thing the Kamalikis did was block the road further up from their territory. Their roadblock was located right in front of our yard and a few metres away from Nalepa village. At one stage they searched a big Hyundai truck that pulled over and found a young man that was involved in the fight. They pulled him out of the vehicle by the hair, wrestled him down to the ground and kicked him with steel capped boots. There was a small sawmill nearby that was located on Nalepa territory. The Kamalikis took the pieces of wood lying around there and beat him with it. A Kamaliki man attempted to throw a rock on the young man's head but fortunately for the Kafe man, he missed.

The Nalepa villagers were having a game of volleyball. They noticed the fight and went to stop it. By this time everyone had gathered around to see what was going on. A teenager who worked at the nearby sawmill suggested in a harsh tone that they carry their fight into their own territory. This angered the Kamalikis so they beat him up. When they did this the Nalepas joined the fight. There were ten to twenty Kamalikis beating one Nalepa and likewise, ten to twenty Nalepas bashing up one Kamaliki. This was the pattern of the fight. The nearby sawmill provided a good supply of wood so there were a number of men using the wood as clubs. The battle raged up and down the highway and after a while the Kamalikis were driven back.

At the moment that I ran up to the gate and witnessed the men jumping over our fence and the fight had cooled down. The Nalepas returned to their village and warned the Kamalikis to apologise with food and money for the fight involving them, which was undoubtedly unnecessary. (They were also angry at the Kamalikis for beating up the Kafe man near their village because the Kafes could mistake Nalepa village for Kamaliki village and bring trouble to the innocent Nalepa men) The young Kafe man that was beaten up was bleeding heavily. He was put onto the truck and was rushed away to the hospital. The war between the Kafes and Kamalikis wasn't over.

After hearing the story I imagined that I was a policeman standing on the branches of a tree showering down rubber bullets from my rifle onto the commotion. I would then handcuff all the men there and bring them to the police station. From there the men could solve their problem while the police supervised. I laughed at my own daydream and went to continue my computer game.

What Have We Come To?
Axel Rice

A World of hunger, a World of hatred, this isn't what it seemed.
Some live lives that are devastated, while others live lives as they please.
Religiously, theologically, culturally divided, a world of many differences.
Countries, groups and many types of people kept apart by ideological fences.
A colour is just a colour, but there is more to blacks and whites,
life is continuously challenging, from dusk till broad daylight.
Father what is happening, this isn't what it seemed
Some live lives that are devastated, while others live lives as they please.

World War one, World War Two, World War Three?
Lives are easily stripped from existence, with bombs and M16s.
Some are luxuriant with mansions in Rome,
when many are left with cardboard boxes, they would happily call their home.
Domesticated, left untreated, mothers are as miserable as could be,
no one turn to, no one to seek to, like an abandoned boat in the middle of the sea.
Child it will be okay, it will be fine, soon we will be free,
but for now close your eyes, as I sooth our misery.
Father what is happening, this isn't what it seemed
Some live lives that are devastated, while others live lives as they please

Wine, bread and the finest meats, the foods they'd dine in a day
While one would crave for just as little as a crumb, I will forever pray.
A million faces, a bustling city, not a 50 toea to spare,
no clothes to wear, no bed for me, no one that even cares.
United as one, divided we stand, what has this planet come to
Racism, poverty, fighting and wars, stormy days and sky blue.
Father what is happening, this isn't what it seemed
Some live lives that are devastated, while others live lives as they please.

We Are Children of God
Pusateryanna Tandak

We have been under the hostage and murderers,
We have been the prisoner's pain, We have been the storms of betrayed,
We've watched our World sinking.

We've seen our stream bloody river, We've heard the screams of agony,
We've seen hardness and stand broken. We've seen with our eyes and never say.

But now we're rising from the ashes. And we are holding out our hands,
And we touch you with our story, See through your eyes and understand.

We know no comfort, we know no shelter. We know no wrong, we know no right.
We've neither glory nor metal, Just the terror of the night.

They felt that in Bougainville, in highland regions of PNG and in Solomon Islands.
We will be bitter the battle. Be friends to us and say no more-wars.
They play the games and he will rule them. They play the rules that never ill.
For them, there's no fidelity. For us the killing is real.

You say it's just the distance thunder, Look into your hearts and you will see.
These are your Sons, and your Daughters .They are you and they are me.

We have all kinds of peace, Inside ourselves,
We have all kinds of love, When the world goes before,
And they know kinds of love.

We can save your lives.
We are -We are the children of God creation.

In the Memory
Jeremiah Toni

This is me
It was me and it will be me
When I am not here, it will be me; gone

This is the rule, it is inevitable
That all follow on
When their bell tolls

This calling beckons
All living things
All things great
All things small
For we are all mortal
Thou shalt live for once
And be gone the next.

This is us
It was us
When we are not here
It will be us; gone
We'll all be here
But
Only, in the memory.

THE CONTRIBUTORS

THE AUTHORS

Brenda Anduwan (12) was born at the Angau Hospital in Lae. Her parents come from Enga Province. She is a Grade 7 student at the Lae Christian Academy. She spent four years in school in the USA when her father went there for post graduate study.

Macquin Anduwan (18) was born at the Angau Hospital in Lae. His parents come from Enga Province. He is a Grade 12 student at the Lae Secondary School. He spent four years in school in the USA when his father went there for post graduate study.

Jimmy Apiu (52) comes from Lae. He lives in Port Moresby and is a technician with Telikom PNG.

Agnes Are (23) was born in Mumeng in Morobe Province. She is in her first year of teaching at Kundiawa Lutheran Day High School. She enjoys writing poems, especially 'love poems'. She started writing poems as therapy after a broken relationship.

Clara Philomena Are (16) was born in Mount Hagen in Western Highlands Province of mixed Simbu (Gumine) and Eastern Highlands Province (Daulo) parentage. She is currently in Grade 9 at Goroka Grammar School. She wants to be a Doctor like her late father when she gets older. She likes reading, going to school, shopping, watching movies and listening to music.

Dominica Are (26) was born and grew up in Mount Hagen in Western Highlands Province of mixed Simbu and Eastern Highlands parentage. She has a degree in Business Accountancy from Divine Word University and works for CARE International. She is single and her hobbies include reading, listening to music, watching movies, go shopping and writing.

Lorraine Evangeline Basse (25) comes from Manam Island in Madang Province. She was born and raised in Goroka, Eastern Highlands Province. She has just completed four years of studies at Divine Word University and will be graduating this year with a Bachelor in Communication Arts (Journalism). She is currently happily working with the Melanesian Institute in Goroka. She is the second eldest and the only girl in a family of eight children. Both of her parents are not working and she is currently taking care of her younger siblings. She likes reading books, writing poems and short stories, sewing and making necklaces and earrings. She also plays basketball, volleyball and soccer.

Kela Kapkora Sil Bolkin (39) was born in the Galkope area in the Simbu Province. He studied to become a Catholic priest but quit soon after completing his philosophical studies and attended the UPNG where he completed a BA majoring in Social Development and Anthropology. He also has a certificate of Leadership in Strategic Health Communication from the Johns Hopkins University (USA). He is now the Senior Policy Analyst at the National AIDS Council Secretariat in Port Moresby. His work appeared in the 2011 Crocodile Prize anthology and he currently has a book about Simbu men's houses with the publisher Crawford House.

Biango Buia (xx) was born at Usakuk on the mainland about 90 kms west of Daru in the Western Province. He is a teacher specialising in the field of teacher education and is currently managing development programmes and activities for his church in partnership with the PNG Government, AusAID, EU, PNGSDP and others. His stories are part of a novel that he is writing.

Werner Cohill (31) was born at Alexishafen in Madang province. He is a parliamentary officer attached to the Parliamentary committee secretariat section of the National Parliament of Papua New Guinea.

Michael Dom was born in Port Moresby. He graduated from the University of Papua New Guinea and now works as an agricultural scientist for a government organisation. He says he writes poetry because he likes to have his say. He also feels that poetry is often underestimated as a powerful means of expression for the collective conscience of people. Some of his work was published in the 2011 Crocodile Competition Anthology.

Regina Dorum (25) comes from Mount Hagen. She is a Chemist with a gold mining company in Port Moresby. She began her interest in reading in Grade 5 when she was eleven years old. She is a fan of fantasy novels and authors like Dean Koonz, Stephen King, David Eddings and Diana Gabaldon. Last year she thought, why not write, anyone can write, and surprised herself by writing 20,000 words of an epic fantasy that she hopes will become a trilogy.

Jimmy Drekore (38) comes from Sinasina in the Simbu Province, which he still calls home. He is an analytical chemist working on Lihir. When he is on leave he does charity work with the Simbu Children Foundation. He styles himself as a "bush poet" who "paints" poems in his quiet moments. He won the 2011 Crocodile Prize for poetry.

Jeffrey Mane Febi (35) comes from Simbu Province. He is a geologist working in the oil and gas industry and lives with his wife and child in Port Moresby. Writing and reading are his favourite hobbies and he has had some success in publishing his work locally. He is an accomplished poet and writer and won the 2011 Crocodile Prize for a short story.

Eric Gabriel (29) was born in Morobe Province but hails from Rigo in Central Province. He is a graduate of the University of Goroka and is a teacher at Magrida High School.

Sophie Garana (55) comes from Siwai in South Bougainville. She is a retired Primary School Teacher who taught in Bougainville and Madang for over 34 years. She has a Certificate in Teaching and a Diploma in Primary Teaching from the PNG Institute of Education.

David Gonol (29) was born at Marapa in the Tambul District of the Western Highlands Province. He is a lawyer by profession and an Assistant Registrar at Waigani in Port Moresby. He likes writing and published his first book, *I've Grown to Love Jesus* in 2011. He is now working on another one. He is not yet married and plans to spend his life serving God and writing books, poems and short stories.

Jovie Hriehwazi (18) was born in Lae and is a student at the Port Moresby International School. He likes playing soccer, reading books and listening to music.

Hannah Ilave (17) was born in Port Moresby. Her father comes from Gulf Province and her mother from Malaysia. She is a Grade 12 student at Port Moresby International School currently doing the International Baccalaureate Diploma program. She believes that inspiration comes from experience and that life is never easy and so must be met head on.

Ian Dabasori Hetri (26) was born in Lae. He is a freelance writer from the Waria valley, sandwiched between Oro and Morobe Provinces, who is passionate about reading and writing. He says that he is a true book worm who writes about anything that fascinates him. He writes about relationships, careers and promotions, environmental issues and Pacific life styles. He also writes poetry and reviews books and movies. He has an honours degree in Agriculture Science and is a candidate for a Master of

Philosophy in Agriculture. But he says "forget about those papers – it is all about writing that I'm passionate about".

Peter Richard Jokise (25) was born in Lae in Morobe Province. He is a biochemist by profession. He is interested in psychology, religion and 'the things that affect humanity'. He likes to read and write; his favourite genres are fantasy, horror and conspiracy theory. In his free time he blogs, watches movies or just daydreams 'new ideas'. His goal is to see PNG 'reach higher levels of civilisation', especially in the way its people socialise.

Ruth Kamasungua comes from the Simbu Province. She is currently completing her Masters Degree in Literature at the University of Papua New Guinea. Her first book of poems, *The Learner*, will be published shortly by The Anuki Country Press and The UPNG Bookshop.

Vanessa Tilber Kavanamur (18) was born in Madang and but has roots in New Britain. She is a Grade Eleven student at Coronation College in Lae. She spent four years in Japan with her parents and while she learnt Japanese her English skills suffered. She is an avid reader and this helped her regain those skills. She first started writing poetry in Grade Nine and it has been a hobby ever since.

Hogande Kiafuli (27) comes from the Lufa District of Eastern Highlands Province. He is a medical officer who currently lives and works in Goroka. He writes occasionally and maintains a blog. He says that writing is more than a hobby. He believes that it's a habit in which the creativities of the mind are inked onto pages. He also thinks that anyone can write, although only the smart ones write well.

Anthony Kippel (32) comes from Kimbe on West New Britain. He currently lives and works on Lihir Island in New Ireland Province.

David Kitchnoge (34) was born in Kainantu in the Eastern Highlands Province. His parents come from the East Sepik and Morobe Provinces. He is a graduate of the Divine Word University in Madang and is a financial manager living in Port Moresby. He regards himself as a rural product and is very passionate about rural development issues.

Mary Avia Koisen (33) lives in Port Moresby and works for Telikom PNG as an account executive for mining, petroleum and gas companies. She enjoys writing whenever she reaches an emotional high. She also loves art and expressions of feelings through paintings and hopes to one day take up art and learn to paint.

Anita Konga (23) was born in Madang with Western Highlands and Madang parentage. She is currently studying Communication Arts at Divine Word University in Madang. Her personal motto in life is 'live simple, aim high'.

Erick Kowa (31) was born in Kaut on New Ireland. His father came from West Sepik and worked for Burns Philp. In 1991, after a stint on Bougainville, his family went to live at Wara Kongkong, outside Vanimo. He went to Green River High School and then St Ignatius Secondary School in Aitape. He studied Chemical Engineering on a scholarship at the University of Queensland and worked for Oilsearch as a Petroleum Engineer until 2009. He completed a Master's Degree in Oil and Gas Engineering at the University of Aberdeen in Scotland while on a British Chevening Scholarship. After that he was employed by IPA, an American consulting house, successively in London, Washington and Singapore, as a Capital Project Analyst for Upstream Oil and Gas Exploration and Production.

Lapieh Landu (23) was born in Port Moresby of mixed Eastern Highlands, Milne Bay and Sanduan parentage. She has completed an Arts degree at the Divine Word University in Madang studying international relations. She is someone who realises the need for culture and traditions to be captured and maintained through writing but also its importance in today's technological society. She was the inaugural winner of the 2011 Crocodile Prize for Women's Literature.

Beauty Rupa Loi (14) was born in Port Moresby. She is a student at St Paul's Primary School. Her father's family comes from Babaka on the Wai River about 200 kilometres east of Port Moresby. She won the school First Prize Award for grade 6A in 2011.

Angela Low (16) was born in Port Moresby and is a science student at the PNG Paradise High School. She is an avid writer, particularly of young adult fiction and essays. She also loves poetry. She hasn't made her mind up about a career yet but finds the idea of journalism appealing.

Peter Maime (44) was born at Kukam Nok near Minj in the South Wahgi District of Jiwaka Province. He trained as a journalist at Divine Word University in Madang and worked with the *Times of PNG*, *Wantok* and *The Independent* newspapers. He is now the Executive Officer at the Office of the National Statistician in Port Moresby.

Golova Mari (59) was born in Wanigela Village in Central Province. He began work with the Finance Department in 1974 and moved to the Postal and Telegraph Department in 1975. In 1999 he was voluntarily retrenched from Telikom PNG.

Grace Maribu (42) comes from Gomlongon village on Siassi Island in Morobe Province. She has been around story-telling people her whole life. Her mother and both grandfathers are gifted story-tellers, imparting to her the love of telling stories. Later, when she started at school, she naturally gravitated towards books and has read almost everything from Charles Dickens to Nancy Drew. She says if the world was equal, she would have first headed down the writer's path, although she has not completely ruled out that option. She still hopes to publish a book one day.

Stanley Mark (27) was born in Mount Hagen in Western Highlands Province. He is a researcher at the Melanesian Institute in Goroka and likes to write about his culture and about social, economic, cultural and political issues affecting grass-roots people in Papua New Guinea.

Patricia Martin (42) was born in Port Moresby and now lives in Lae. She is a teacher and enjoys teaching poetry and story writing. She is hoping to one day have her poems published.

Martyn Namorong (26) was born at Baimuru in the Gulf Province and grew up in a logging camp at Kamusi on the border between Western and Gulf Provinces. His parents come from Madang and Western Province. He was a medical student at UPNG until 2009 but is now a street vendor and 'Papua New Guinea's most controversial blogger'. He won the 2011 Crocodile Prize for an essay.

Francis Nii (49) was born at Yobai, Karimui Nomane in the Simbu Province. He has a degree in economics from UPNG and was a banker with the National Development Bank until an accident left him paraplegic. He is now a patient of the Kundiawa General Hospital. He has had an interest in writing since his UPNG days. He was an entrant in the 2011 Crocodile Prize and his work features in the anthology for that year.

Dilu Daniel Okuk (37) was born in Port Moresby. He has qualifications in creative industry and education and is a high school teacher and a semi-professional visual artist. He is also an elder of the Seventh-Day Adventist Church in Goroka. He is married with four children and lists his hobbies as travelling, reading and 'eating pasta'.

Hinuvi Onafimo (30) was born in Goroka and now lives in Port Moresby. He is a graphic artist who likes writing in his free time.

Sharina Paliou (15) was born in Wewak in East Sepik Province. She is in Grade 9 at Coronation College in Lae. Her ambition is to be a writer. Otherwise, she enjoys life to the fullest.

Gelab Piak (24) was born in Port Moresby and is a student at the Divine Word University in Madang. He began writing poems in 2006. He also writes songs and short stories. He has a collection of poems ready for publication and is seeking a publisher. A number of his works were published in the 2011 Crocodile Competition Anthology.

Kayla Reimann (13) grew up in Kimbe in West New Britain Province. She started boarding at Somerville House in South Brisbane last year. She says that although going to school in Australia is a big change for her she misses all the fishing and swimming. She is having a great time however and loves writing.

Joshua Rere (15) comes from Goroka in the Eastern Highlands. He is a student in Grade 11 at Goroka Secondary School. His hobbies include reading, watching TV and collecting used Digicel Flex cards. His favourite food is fried chicken with potato chips and his favourite sport is rugby league.

Axel Rice (15) was born at Tusa Hospital in Lae of mixed Australian and Papua New Guinean parentage. He is a Year 10 student at Coronation College in Lae. He has lived in Papua New Guinea most of his life. He enjoys writing, especially essays.

Leonard Fong Roka (33) was born in Arawa and grew up in the Panguna District during the years of the Bougainville crisis. He began writing poetry as a student at Arawa High School and has now compiled a collection of short stories and poetry which he hopes to publish. He has returned after a break as a student at Divine Word University and is working on an autobiography of his experiences in the Bougainville war in his spare time. He had some of his earlier work published in the 2011 Crocodile Competition Anthology.

Miriam Roko (50) was born in Tatana Village on Tatana Island near Port Moresby. She is married with three children and one granddaughter. She worked as a clerk, being the sole computer operator at Ela Motors between 1981-3, and then going on to other companies. She also has qualifications in business studies. She is involved in church ministries and is a Youth Parent working with young people.

Henry Sape (60) was born in Pawale Village near Erave in the Southern Highlands Province. He lives in Port Moresby and is a community leader and village court magistrate. He is the Chairman of the 8Mile Block Owner's Association.

Marie-Rose Sau (22) was born in Rabaul in East New Britain Province. She hails from the three provinces of Simbu, East New Britain and Morobe respectively. She is single and currently works at the Bank of Papua New Guinea. Her hobbies include reading and poetry. Along with PNG artist, Jeffrey Feeger, she organized the Poetry Slam reading event in PNG this year.

Peter Sevara (29) was born in Port Moresby. He loves everything Papua New Guinean.

Bernard Sinai (30) comes from Manus Province and now lives in Port Moresby. He started writing fiction while at college and published his first short story in 2006. Most of his work is fiction which draws heavily on his own real life experiences and those around him.

Pusateryanna Tandak (13) was born on Santo in Vanuatu. Her father comes from Pina Village near Wabag in Enga Province in Papua New Guinea and her mother comes from Vanuatu. She is a student in Year Seven at St Michelle Secondary School in Luganville on Santo. When she finishes her Year 10 studies she hopes to go to Papua New Guinea to finish off her education.

Raroteone Tefuarani (29) was born in Port Moresby and comes from Takuu/Mortlock atoll in the Autonomous Region of Bougainville. She works for Australasia Pacific Panel Limited. She enjoys different types of writing and dreams of having one of her stories published one day.

Jeremiah Toni (18) comes from Butibam Village in Morobe Province. He is in Grade Eleven A.

Loujaya Toni (46) was born at in Lae. She was declared Papua New Guinea's youngest poet by the University of Papua New Guinea's Ondo Bondo while still at school in Port Moresby in 1978. Her collection of poems, *A Sense of Interest* was published by the Education Department. In 1985 she launched a string of solo gospel music albums under the name

Loujaya Dunar and has since been recognised as a singer/songwriter. She wrote and performed the song, *Keep the Fire Alive* with *Tambaran Culture*, as a tribute to the 9th South Pacific Games held in Port Moresby in 1991. She is a qualified journalist and teacher who is also a practicing naturopath. She is a part-time tutor at the University of Technology in Lae and a full-time student in the Department of Communication Development Studies. She graduates in April, 2012. She is also an aspiring politician. She contested the National Elections in 2007 and the Local Level Government Elections in 2008, giving her male opposition candidates a close run for their money. She will be contesting the 2012 National Elections as a candidate in the Lae Open Electorate.

Charlotte Vada (30) was born in Port Moresby. She likes to write short stories, flash fiction, radio and stage plays. Charlotte won the Tapa Prize for adult writing in 2011.

Nou Frederick Vada (21) was born in Elevala-Hanuabada near Port Moresby. He spent his early childhood in Wollongong in New South Wales. He is a law student at the University of Papua New Guinea and a great lover of story books. His ambition is to work in a field that marries his legal studies with his interests as a writer.

Emma Tunne Wakpi (32) is from Tombil in the Minj District of Jiwaka Province. She is a business graduate and community development worker with Evangelical Brotherhood Church Health Establishment based in Goroka. Emma says she was discouraged from pursuing a career in writing by her family due to the "lack of opportunities" it afforded. "However, I have always been interested in writing," she says, "especially essays and poetry and in my spare time try to write and have done so since 2006."

Alma Warokra (23) was born in Port Moresby. She says that she has always had a passion for writing but until now has not really had an outlet for it. She enjoyed English in school because it came easy to her and she wrote regularly and enthusiastically, taking part in all the competitions and performances that were held. She is now out of school and doing her residency in dentistry.

Brigette Wase (26) was born in Kiunga in Western Province of mixed Oro and Central Provinces parentage. She completed studies at UPNG and works with Papua New Guinea Immigration and Citizenship Services.

Her hobbies include reading, mostly fiction and history. She occasionally writes poetry.

Elizabeth Wawaga (28) was born in Rabaul and calls Kokopo in East New Britain Province home. She has recently moved to Goroka as a Scientific Officer at the Institute of Medical Research. She likes to write about simple things that people don't immediately appreciate. She also likes to write about the different things she encounters and experiences because she feels that by writing them down future generations can be encouraged and given a sense of direction when they come across similar situations.

Imelda Yabara (36) was born in Port Moresby and lives in Madang. Her partner is a magistrate and she follows him around the country. She is the mother of two girls and, when time permits, loves writing. She has a blog at www.achingforpng@wordpress.com where she publishes her work. She was an entrant in the 2011 competition and two of her poems were published in the anthology.

Hilda Fromai Yerive (48) was born at Boiken, near Wewak, in East Sepik Province. She is a Library Technician by profession and works as a Senior Library Officer at the Michael Somare Library at the University of Papua New Guinea. She hopes to write more stories but feels that she needs a short course to be able to write better.

COVER DESIGNER

Joe Bilbu (45) is a surf wear designer in Fiji who originally comes from Babaka village in Central Province. He completed his primary education at St Peters School in Erima and his secondary school at De la Salle High, Bomana, before moving to Arawa High in Bougainville, and finally Passam National High School in the East Sepik. He has a Diploma of Graphic Design from the National Arts School and a Certificate in Electronic Publishing from RMIT in Melbourne. He is married to a Fijian citizen and has three children. If you are interested in Joe's work contact him at **jbhendrix2000@hotmail.com**.

www.ingramcontent.com/pod-product-compliance
Lightning Source LLC
Chambersburg PA
CBHW071953070426
42453CB00008BA/514